BATTING

Published by The Society for American Baseball Research (SABR)
812 Huron Road, Suite 719, Cleveland, OH 44115
www.sabr.org

Distributed by the University of Nebraska Press
233 North 8th Street, Lincoln, NE 68588-0255
www.nebraskapress.unl.edu

Cover design by Glenn LeDoux

Cover photo courtesy of the University of Louisville
Photographic Archive, Hillerich & Bradsby Collection

Printed and manufactured by EBSCO Media, Birmingham, Alabama

BATTING

by F. C. Lane

Foreword by Frederick Ivor-Campbell and expanded index by Leverett T. Smith, Jr.

F. C. LANE

by Frederick Ivor-Campbell

When he was in his early twenties, biologist Ferdinand Cole Lane, troubled by what he described as "weak lungs," left his part-time job with the Massachusetts Commission of Fisheries and Game and headed for Alberta, Canada, where he "passed the next six months in a log cabin on the remote frontier." Upon his return to Boston he took a job with the young *Baseball Magazine*, where he remained some twenty-seven years, twenty-six of them as editor.

Born on a wheat farm on the western edge of Minnesota on October 25, 1885 (a year before Ty Cobb and nearly ten years before Babe Ruth, both of whom he outlived by decades), Lane "drifted" (his word) eastward with his parents and three older siblings in the wake of his father's successive bankruptcies, first to Minneapolis, then Canton, Ohio, and Lowell, Massachusetts, finally arriving at Truro, Massachusetts, near the tip of Cape Cod, when he was seven. Six years later the family moved to Marion, on the other side of Buzzards Bay from Cape Cod, where Lane attended high school at Tabor Academy. He then worked his way through Boston University, receiving his B.A. in 1907, and continued on to graduate study at B.U. (including courses in the law school) and at the Massachusetts Institute of Technology across the river in Cambridge. It was during his university years that he first indulged his lifelong wanderlust and curiosity about the world with a voyage—in steerage—to Naples. Could even Lane himself have imagined this background as preparation for a career in baseball journalism?

Baseball Magazine, which began publication in the spring of 1908, was founded by Jacob C. Morse, a Boston baseball writer and author of *Sphere and Ash* (1888), the first history of baseball. Morse's new magazine filled a niche. For decades there had been, in addition to baseball coverage in the daily press, baseball annuals and weekly sporting papers, but *Baseball Magazine* was the game's first monthly magazine. Lane was hired in 1910 or 1911. After a period as associate editor and a month as joint editor with Morse, he assumed full editorship with the January 1912 issue as the magazine transferred its office from Boston to New York.

Leverett T. Smith, Jr.—whose biography of Lane for the

Dictionary of Literary Biography, Vol. 241 (2001) contains the fullest and most astute assessment to date of Lane's baseball writing—points out that *Baseball Magazine*, as a monthly publication, "could take a longer view of events than the daily or weekly papers." The magazine, to which Lane himself contributed hundreds of articles and editorials—more than million words in all—featured interviews, reports on the state of the game, biographies, discussion of off-field issues, and innovative efforts to find better ways to measure player effectiveness. Distrusting accepted statistics like batting average, Lane sought (in Smith's words) "to establish an objective, scientific basis for evaluating player performance." His suggestions never caught on with baseball officialdom or the baseball public, but his efforts may have helped inspire the precursors of the current sabermetric revolution.

More important for those interested in the history of the game, Lane (as Smith points out) "became an excellent interviewer and profiler." Researchers have in recent years begun to rediscover the riches in Lane's interviews and biographical essays. The late Jack Kavanagh, for example, found Lane's writings so useful in researching the lives of Walter Johnson and Grover Cleveland Alexander that he wrote a piece for *The National Pastime* (1996), an annual SABR publication, to alert SABR's researchers to this long-neglected writer. Lane would travel throughout the country in the offseason to visit players in their homes. Often he "would be invited to spend several days and would come away with family anecdotes and history," Kavanagh discovered. "As a result, we have far richer knowledge...than what we learn from memoirs and reminiscences written after their starring careers had ended." One important byproduct of Lane's interviews is *Batting*. Quotations garnered from more than 250 baseball figures during Lane's first fifteen years at *Baseball Magazine* form the essence of this book.

Batting, Lane's only book about baseball, was published—on cheap paper, with plain brown paper covers and a price of one dollar—by *Baseball Magazine* in 1925. Legendary SABR bibliophile Frank V. Phelps remembers Batting as "one of the very first baseball books I owned as a youngster," and recalls that it was offered as a premium for subscribing to the magazine. As Phelps observes, *Batting* "stands up well against the many books on hitting which have followed through the years," but its chief interest for readers today may be the insight it gives us on how those who were active in the first quarter of the twentieth century viewed the science and art of hitting.

And how Lane himself viewed baseball offense. Lane claimed to be objective—simply a collector of expert opinion—but Leverett Smith points out that Lane's views show through in his selection and arrangement of the quotations he has gathered on the subject, and in his commentary that binds the quotes together. *Batting*, Smith writes, "is a kind of medley of players' voices, orchestrated by Lane himself."

Lane was ambivalent about the slugging game that Babe Ruth had recently brought to the fore. While he recognized the contribution of heavy hitting to run production, he preferred the "scientific" game of place hitting, bunting, and base stealing. Babe Ruth, Lane wrote in an August 1922 *Baseball*

Magazine article, "assaulted not only the home run record but the long established system of major league batting." In an article a month earlier he had expressed his regret that the recent rise in slugging had been accompanied by a decline in base stealing, "because the stolen base is one of the flashy, brainy plays in baseball and one of the chief elements of a well directed offense." Like writer Henry Chadwick of an earlier era (Chadwick's career ended about three years before Lane's began), Lane preferred the aesthetic excitement of the inside game over the explosive excitement of slugging—brain over brawn. Lane recognized Ruth's greatness, but always regarded Ty Cobb as the game's greatest player. Leverett Smith's novel index to this volume—which distinguishes the authors of quoted passages from references to persons—records Lane's bias, showing that Lane quotes Cobb five times as often as he does Ruth, while otherwise Cobb and Ruth are mentioned about equally.

When Lane left *Baseball Magazine* after the December 1937 issue, he pretty much left baseball behind him. He edited the annual *Little Red Book of Major League Baseball* from 1937 through 1948, but his primary attention lay elsewhere. "While I loved the thrill of the game and prized the many interesting characters I was able to meet," he wrote in his entry for *Twentieth Century Authors, First Supplement* (1955), "sports writing was always a vocation, never an avocation." He wrote that he departed New York "to give the balance of my life to more congenial tasks."

Although Lane felt in 1955 that he was "losing the argument with Father Time," when he left New York in the late

1930s he and his wife Emma—whom he had married in her Brooklyn home in 1914—had nearly a half century of life together yet ahead of them. From their home on Cape Cod—in Wellfleet, adjacent to Truro where Ferdinand had spent his elementary school years—the Lanes traveled the country and the world. For two years—1941-1943—Ferdinand headed the history department at Piedmont College in Demorest, Georgia, where he also taught journalism and geopolitics. In 1941 the college awarded him an honorary doctorate in humanities.

After his brief stint as an academic, Lane turned to writing about what had always most enthralled him: the world of nature. In the six years from 1947 through 1952, Doubleday published five books that Lane wrote for the general reader about the sea and the world's lakes, rivers, mountains and trees. Lane then wrote three volumes over the next four years—on the sea, insects and flowers—for the Random House "allabout" series for young readers. After this flurry of science writing, which included a number of encyclopedia articles, Lane self-published his final book—*On Old Cape Cod*, a collection of his poems—then settled into what turned out to be twenty-six years of quiet retirement, a period equal to his tenure as editor of *Baseball Magazine*. He died on April 20, 1984, at age 98, just two months short of his seventieth wedding anniversary. Emma died ten months later.

F. C. Lane may be the most unjustly overlooked of our baseball writers. Lacking the literary repute of a Ring Lardner, the staying power and self-promotional drive of a Henry Chadwick, the memorable phrasemaking of a Grantland

Rice, or the brisk conciseness of a Red Smith, the value of Lane's baseball writing was taken for granted in his day, then forgotten. Unlike Chadwick, who remained active as a baseball writer until the week he died, Lane left the game at midlife. And unlike Red Smith, he never published a collection of his writings. Lane's legacy as a baseball writer seems never to have interested him, so it is up to us who treasure his work to return it to public accessibility. Jack Kavanagh wrote in 1996: "A graceful writer, an erudite man, F. C. Lane was more than a contributor to the written word of baseball's past. He was an adornment." This republication of *Batting* is a happy first step toward restoring Lane's baseball writing to the prominence it deserves.

Frederick Ivor-Campbell is SABR's Vice President.

BATTING

One Thousand Expert Opinions on Every Conceivable Angle of Batting Science

The Secrets of Major League Batting and Useful Hints for Hitters of All Ranks and Ages Collected Over a Period of Fifteen Years From Nearly Three Hundred Famous Players

By F. C. LANE

BATTING

As a silent coach for the sand lots' ball tosser,—
a ready source of expert advice for the harassed
professional,—a collection of entertaining anecdote and opinion from hundreds of famous
players for the fan, — to the future Ty
Cobbs and Rogers Hornsbys of baseball this book is dedicated.

By F. C. LANE
Editor, THE BASEBALL MAGAZINE

PRICE $1.00

INDEX OF CHAPTERS

THE SCOPE OF THIS BOOK

This book is the essence of thousands of interviews with more than three hundred Major League ball players, collected over a period of fifteen years by the Editor of the Baseball Magazine.

In these extensive investigations he has enjoyed unique privileges. He has been on friendly terms with all the batting stars and other less famous players who are known among their fellows for their mastery of some particular angle of batting. He has talked with these players at their hotels, in the club houses before and after the game, on the player's bench, in the bull pen, everywhere. He has visited many of them in their winter homes and maintained an extensive correspondence.

This book is neither a primer nor a text book. Such books fail and always will fail because they are at best the expression of one man's opinion. The Editor of this book has expressed no opinion. He has merely painstakingly collected and contrasted a vast array of opinions from all the acknowledged experts of batting that baseball has produced in fifteen years. Hans Wagner and Napoleon Lajoie are only memories. But what Wagner said about "batting slumps" and Lajoie's discussion of "batting eye" are as fresh and valuable today as when these marvelous hitters told the Editor all about it years ago.

Ty Cobb said, "Most of the books that have been written about batting are worse than worthless. They express one man's opinion and are inevitably misleading. All that any one can tell another about batting is to give him some possibly helpful hints."

That is precisely the province of this book. Nothing like it has ever been attempted before. It is a book that the sand lot player may read with profit. It is a book that the greatest batting champion might find helpful. For it contains hundreds of valuable hints on batting from literally hundreds of Major League players.

TO THE BEGINNER

Are you in doubt about your bat? Frank Frisch said, "I have never seen a bat that suited me. I change my bat every game or two —experiment, always experiment."

Are you critical of your position at the plate? Edd Roush said, "I change my position at the plate on almost every pitched ball. I generally change after the ball has already left the pitcher's hand."

Are you afraid of getting beaned? Ty Cobb said, "I used to have a horror of Walter Johnson's fast ball."

Your problems are the problems of every batter who has ever scaled the heights of batting greatness. Moreover, they remain a daily problem that always changes and is never solved. Ty Cobb, the wisest batter who ever lived, said, "I learn something every day I play. I have learned something about hitting in twenty years but there's an awful lot for me still to learn."

George Sisler said, "What I have learned about batting nobody taught me. I had to dig it out for myself." Here's a book that will teach you. It will give you the views and opinions of all baseball's favorite batters for fifteen years.

Hugh Critz said, "I used to hold my hands close together and my feet close together. Then one day I saw Speaker bat. He held his hands close but spread his feet. I said, 'he is a great batter. I will follow his lead.' I spread my feet but didn't seem to get results. Later I saw Ty Cobb in an exhibition game. He spread his feet and his hands both—I said 'he is even a greater batter than Speaker. I will follow him.' I did so and immediately found the style that suited me. I have used it ever since." One great star taught him something he needed to learn but not enough. The second great star added the necessary secret. In this book you have the combined wisdom of all the great stars, hundreds of hustling, observing, successful big league hitters.

What Batting Really Is

BATTING is older than recorded history. Doubtless some Egyptian youngster on the Banks of the Nile struck a pebble with a stick before the Pyramids were built. And in its crude essentials, batting remains what it has always been, ability to meet a moving object with a swinging club held in the hands.

In its later day refinement, batting has become the chief item in baseball offense. But it has developed little since the days when baseball itself emerged from the Rounders' stage.

·Keen observers of batting, however, will admit that certain features have improved. The bunt, for example, was an offshoot of legitimate batting, that has now its fixed place in the club offensive. The hit and run play has also developed greatly, and place hitting, the crowning achievement of the batter's skill, has been more evident in later seasons than it was before the dawn of the present century.

Batting in truth, is simple enough until you attempt to analyse it. Many players that I have met have tackled the problem with indifferent success. Here are the opinions of a few of them.

Bib Falk, a mechanical engineer and general mathematical sharp, said, "I've thought a lot about batting, but it's a thing which eludes the investigator. You can't get down to the essence of the thing and put your finger on just what it is. Most batters don't try to grasp the theory of batting. They merely go up to the plate and hit. I'm not certain they haven't the right dope. The batter performs certain acts at the plate, in order to meet the ball, which are complicated enough, if you try to make a diagram of them. But they are no more complicated than digesting your dinner, and most people don't concentrate much on that important job. I don't suppose anybody ever thoroughly understood the secret of batting," continued Falk. "But batting-eye, I suppose, is an important part in the scheme."

Bob Veach, one evening when I caught him after supper in a good natured mood, recounted his experience. "When I was on a good amateur team I knew considerable about batting. I juggled the stick easily, sauntered confidently up to the plate, spat on my hands and dared the pitcher to put one over. Batting was a diversion and consequently easy. But when batting became a business, the source of hats, neck ties and beef stews, I noticed a decided change. It became necessary for me to study my new profession, to discover the real ins and outs of batting. I have been busy with this ever since and I must confess the more I study it the less I know."

Once at the Polo Grounds I overheard a conversation between Frank Baker and a scientific friend of his. This friend was trying to get at the heart of batting and among other things he mentioned the angle of incidence. The Home Run King shook his head and a look of perplexity came into his eyes. "I don't know anything about the angle of incidence," he said, "but I do know that if I swing and meet the ball just right it will sail into that grandstand over there."

Baker's theory of batting was doubtless that of Sam Crawford's, who once said to me, "My idea of batting is a thing that should be done unconsciously. If you get to studying it too much, to see just what fraction of a second you must swing to meet a curved ball, the chances are you will miss it altogether."

I once asked Jake Daubert, in the year he first led his League in batting, how he accomplished this feat. "I honestly don't know," said Jake. "It's the hardest thing in the world for me to explain. When I worked in the coal mines they used to do what they called 'pound the jumper.' That is, one man would hold a heavy iron peg and the rest would swing on it with sledge hammers. If you tried it you probably couldn't hit that peg at all. And yet, men who are used to such work can keep on pounding away with their full strength and never miss, though they hardly have their mind on the job at all. They do the right thing without thinking."

Edd Roush echoed much the same thought in the year when he first won the batting championship. "A ball player," said Edd, "seldom stops to analyse such things. If he's a good hitter, probably nine times out of ten he couldn't tell you why, if he tried. I'm sure I couldn't. Perhaps I had a better eye than most, I don't know. Perhaps I use a better type of swing. All I can say is that I have always considered myself, and been considered by others, as a good hitter."

Hans Wagner also touched upon batting-eye when his failure to hit .300 for the first time in his long career gave him considerable concern. "My batting has fallen off," said Hans, "and I don't understand why. My eyes are as good as they ever were, so far as I know. I guess the breaks went against me. That is the way I would explain it. You know the Frenchman (he meant Lajoie) hit under .300 two years and then came back strong." In his perplexity Wagner fell back on the luck of the game, undoubtedly a potent factor in batting.

Jake Daubert, who discussed this subject more thoroughly than most, maintained that the secret of batting is in the eye. "A good batting eye means more than good eyesight, however," said Jake. "The .200 hitter may see just as far and just as well as the .300 hitter, but he doesn't make use of that eyesight. It's the same in marksmanship. A crack shot can hit a bird on the wing because his eye and his finger on the trigger act together. The amateur hunter can see the bird as well as the expert, but his finger on the trigger is perhaps a fraction of a second too late. The good batter is like the good marksman. His wrists and his shoulders act with his eye. Most batters always keep their eye on the ball. Good batters can generally hit the ball without watching it all the time."

However, George Sisler, admitting the importance of batting eye, emphasized the necessity of finely timed muscular action. "The secret of batting isn't in the eye. The eye is only part of it. I would say that batting skill was fine co-ordination between eye and arms and shoulders. Any slip in this co-ordination anywhere short circuits the whole effect."

Rogers Hornsby in attempting to explain his own surpassing abilities at bat, emphasized batting eye. "No matter how fast the ball may break, your eye is quicker than the ball so is the end of your bat. I won't attempt to follow every step in the process of hitting a ducking curve, but I know it can be done, for I do it my-'self and so do all other good batters who can hit curve pitching."

Tris Speaker drew a clear parallel between the public's idea and the player's idea of what batting really is. Said Speaker, "There are all kinds of theories in the clubhouse and on the bench about the proper manner of standing at the plate, handling the bat and so on. But there is one radical difference between the player's idea of good batting and the public's idea. When the player meets the ball fair and drives it out straight and true, he knows he is stinging that ball, even though he is unfortunate enough to drive it right at a fielder, or is robbed of a hit by a sensational catch. On the contrary when he pops up a little fly and it rolls safe, he knows that he is simply lucky. But the public judge a batter mainly, if not altogether, by the number of balls he drives safe, regardless of how they happened to go safe. And they give him little credit for meeting the ball and hitting it hard, so long as it fails to go safe." In short, in Speaker's opinion the players rate a batter according to the ability he has shown while the public considers nothing except results.

The theory of hitting is, of course, simple. It involves merely meeting the ball with the bat and driving it somewhere so that it can not be retrieved by any fielder and thrown to first base before the batter can reach that goal. In short, batting resolves to that brief but pointed epigram of Willie Keeler's when he said, "Hit 'em where they ain't."

"Where they ain't," is something of a study in geography limited by the playing field and its immediate environs. There are certain zones of safety where the ball may be driven and allow the batter time to negotiate first, but these zones of safety can never be chartered, for they vary with the batter, with the opposing pitcher, with the ball field, even with the stage of the game. There are a number of theories of batting, however, that may be safely laid down and that every batter should comprehend.

First, the speed of the ball when it leaves the bat may be a determining factor. "It was too hot to handle," admits the crowd.

Second, the slowness of the ball may be equally effective. "Too late to get the runner," is the verdict.

Third, place hitting socalled is always effective, but needless to say it is the most difficult art in a batter's entire repertoire.

Fourth, speed of foot is a factor. The fast man is safe where the slow one is caught.

Fifth, pulling the unexpected is always an advantage. "Bunt when they lay back," says Ty Cobb. "Hit through them when they play in."

Sixth, take advantage of shifts in the infield. In the hit and run play the percentage in favor of the batter is often increased from .250 to perhaps .500.

Seventh, sheer distance of the blow is often important. The home run might be caught but the fence was in the way.

The zones of safety are not mere vague patches out there on the diamond or beyond. They are also complicated by the element of time, the speed of the drive, the batter's fleetness of foot, the psychology of the unexpected and numerous other factors. Baseball, as already hinted, has become an effort to limit these zones of safety and to curtail their flexible confines. As Bert Shotton aptly remarked, however, "I often wonder what conditions would be like if they revived the old style game that used to be before baseball evolved from the Rounder's period. If I remember, they once had four outfielders and five infielders. It would look queer now to see such a club on the field, but even if they had all those fielders they couldn't stop some batters from doing their stuff. Take Cy Williams, for example. When he is at bat the first and second basemen shift over near the foul line and the shortstop swings around to the right of second base. Center fielder goes far over into right field, right fielder hugs the foul line. There you have those old time conditions for there are really five fielders massed against Cy. But he still manages to get his share of hits."

To sum up, the secret of batting, the essence of the art, is a difficult if not impossible thing to define. Batting apparently is elemental and has changed little. The players regard batting in a somewhat different light than the public. They believe, apparently, that batting is at least partly an inherited talent, that it comprises batting eye, co-ordination of muscle and confidence. We shall call upon these players, literally hundreds of them, including all the greatest stars of recent years, to explain the various secrets of the batting art in more definite detail.

What the Records Tell Us

THE safe hits of today become the records of tomorrow. The importance of records to baseball was graphically portrayed by John Heydler when he was Secretary of the National League. "President Tener once strolled into the office," said Heydler, "and found me hard at work on batting averages. 'Aren't you making too much of these things, John'? he said. 'Perhaps I am,' I replied, 'I am making just as much out of this job as needs to be made. It's the most important work I know anything about.' 'Yes, it's important', admitted the Governor. 'You're right, it's important', said I. 'When you come to study the situation, what is baseball played for anyway, if it isn't the records? What are the players working for? Records every time. What are the managers struggling for and the owners? The records. You may think they are striving for the Championship, and so they are. But the Championship is only one of the records. Every detail of the game is built upon the records. And while the public may not admit its interest in dry statistics, that same public will wrangle all winter over batting averages. The records are the whole thing in baseball. You can't make them too important and you can't be too careful how you handle them.' I don't know," continued Heydler, "whether I convinced the Governor, but I did state my own opinion. The more I see of records, the more important I think they are."

Mr. Heydler did not exaggerate. Beyond a doubt the records are the framework of baseball. They animate the game while it is being played and perpetuate that game when the last man is out. Baseball owes much of its superiority over other athletic sports to the records.

E. S. Barnard summed up the situation very ably in a single paragraph. "The records are important from the viewpoint of the public. Probably no feature of the game is so popular or so widely discussed among the fans as batting averages. Every magnate recognizes the part the records have played in the advancement of the game and by no means underrates their value. At the same time, they are not so important from his viewpoint as they are from the viewpoint of the public. It is not difficult to see that this is so. The magnate knows his players intimately and does not necessarily value a man for his batting average alone. He realizes how misleading figures can be. For example, one player may beat another one hundred points and at the same time be a less valuable man to the owner. It is these things which complicate the problem."

Mr. Barnard has admirably stated the owner's view of the records. Jacques Fournier, however, in a pessimistic interview, took issue with this claim. "Managers tell you," said Fournier, "that they pay no attention to records. And perhaps they don't. But the owner pays attention to them and has them all by heart when you talk contract with him in the Fall."

Bert Shotton, whose batting average always suffered somewhat from the fact that he was a good waiter, made much the same comment. "The waiter pays heavily in the injury which his batting average suffers. And this is a genuine injury, for in spite of what is said to the contrary, both the general public and the owner rate a ball player pretty much on his batting average."

What the players themselves think of batting averages is interesting. Apparently they give these averages two entirely different values. They are wise enough to recognize the fact that batting averages make a profound impression upon the public. But they do not accept those averages at their face value in rating the ability of a fellow player.

Tris Speaker clearly distinguishes this difference. "A .300 average", said Tris, "means more to the public than it does to the ball player, for the public has set that arbitrary figure as the standard of good hitting. And yet, it has come to be of considerable importance to the player also. For in the long run his salary is determined by his reputation and that reputation is really what the public thinks of him. So you will find players who are hitting somewhere near .300 fighting tooth and nail to boost their average above that mark, knowing that if they succeed their names will be inscribed with honorable mention in the records. That was my experience in the year I hit for .296. Two, or at the most three hits would have boosted my average the necessary four points. Now I am frank to confess that would have made little difference to the Cleveland Club. But I had hit .300 for ten years and being human regretted to see my record marred. Still, my experience was less of a blow than that of Lajoie when he hit .299."

Playing for records evidently is not always good baseball. Not a few players of my acquaintance have commented upon this point. For example, Hugh Jennings once said, "I have little faith in paper averages. A ball player must have talents, and talents, if they are good enough, will win him a place."

George Stallings commented upon records in that great season when he won the World's Championship with the Boston Braves. "Players may stand at the head of the list in the records," said

Stallings, "but what good will that do if the spirit that wins is lacking? No paper records will pull such a team to the top. It was the spirit that couldn't be spelled in black and white that couldn't be figured like batting averages and thus escaped the notice of the critics which won for the Braves."

Dick Rudolph was inclined to view batting averages pessimistically. "To my mind," he said, "there is nothing more deceptive. I would much rather have on my team a player with an average of .270 who was a great hitter when hits were needed than a .350 hitter who wasn't much good in a pinch. It's the hits in the pinch that count. I believe that instead of keeping such close track of the number of times a player makes a hit, a record should be kept of the number of times he drives in a run, particularly a winning run. It is these things which show the value of a batter above everything else."

John Evers had somewhat the same comment to make, in the season which followed his record batting year. Said Evers, "Batting averages are more accurate than fielding averages. But at best they lose half their value. Take my own case, for instance. I batted last season for .341. But at that I do not believe I hit better or more intelligently than I have done in other seasons when my average sunk below .300. A man may be working for his team just as hard when he does not hit at all but is trying to rattle a pitcher, as he does when he lays down a neat single. The records tell only half the story at best."

Ivan Olson stated the same case from a slightly different angle. "Players among themselves", said he, "pay little attention to records. At our skull practice we never get nervous over some champion batter who is going to face us that day. Just as much attention is paid to the man at the tail of the list as to the greatest slugger on the team. And this is only common sense, for the ablest batter who ever lived might go through a game without a hit while even a pitcher might make two or three." Olson's statement reworded might read, "We can ignore a batter's reputation today, for we do not know that he will live up to his reputation."

Ray Schalk, like Rudolph and others, noted the inaccuracy of batting averages as they reveal playing talent. Said he, "I have read with a great deal of interest several attacks on the present system of keeping the records. In my opinion these criticisms are

12

just, though it isn't easy to suggest improvements. Off hand I would say that fielding averages are pretty bad, pitcher's averages punk, batting averages just fair."

Ty Cobb frankly admitted, years ago, that his chief aim in life was to make an unequalled batting record. "I led the American League nine straight years at bat. It was the pet ambition of my life to make it ten straight years. But Tris Speaker beat me out the tenth season and cut short my record."

Sam Crawford also thought much of his records. He once commented upon the season when he hit for .297. "Only three points," said Crawford dubiously, "but .300 sounds a lot better than .297."

Hans Wagner had the same complaint the first year that he dropped under the .300 mark after batting for that exalted figure seventeen straight seasons. Said Wagner, "They don't seem to think I'm hitting if I hit under .300." But Wagner very evidently referred to the public by "they."

Eddie Collins has guarded his records carefully. Said Collins, "The batting and fielding averages assigned to me the first two years I was with the Athletics are not authentic, as I did not take part in games enough to get into the Official columns." Collins, as a matter of fact, took no little pains to discover what those records really were. "Perhaps I may need them," he said, "to complete my all-time average when I am through."

Cactus Cravath admitted the value of the records, at least from the public viewpoint, and at the same time bitterly criticized their inaccuracy. Said Cravath, "The batting averages more than any other one thing determine a player's value as a drawing card, and his ability to secure a good salary. His batting average, then, is the ball player's principal stock in trade and is valuable to him in a personal and business sense. Where the records fail to give him credit due, he has suffered a genuine loss. In 1915, which was not my best year, I made twenty four home runs, a modern record. I also made thirty one doubles. I hit for 117 extra bases. The next best man in the League hit for 76. I scored more runs than anybody else on the circuit and drove in more runs. In all the really effective work of the batter I should have led the League by a wide margin. I really hit for .285. That isn't a bad average, but I was number seventeen on the list. If batting means anything at all, it means smashing offensive work for your club and ability to demolish the defense. Every owner, manager and Big League player will admit as much, but the records wont admit it. There is a certain charm about .300. If a man hits it he is a star, if he doesn't he isn't a star." Cravath's bitter arraignment of the records, however, was directed at their failure to show his own effectiveness as an extra base slugger. He apprciated to the full the importance of the records from the public viewpoint.

Perhaps no more comprehensive glimpse of the whole situation can be obtained than from a statement that Tommy Leach once made to me. "The players," said Leach, "in talking among themselves or in forming an estimate of another player's ability never think about his average. Half the time they don't even know what that average is. They don't think about it because they don't put much faith in it. Averages mean something, but they don't mean anywhere near as much as they are supposed to mean. It is no doubt true that a man can't go on year after year batting .300 without being a good hitter. But it is also true that a player who bats many points less may be a more dangerous and a better hitter. Players realize these things and form their opinions of other players on what they see them do, not on what the records claim they do."

But the public has to be guided by records. They haven't that intimate association with the players and they must depend upon records for their opinions. But the players know and the manager knows and that is the reason often times that a manager keeps one man and lets another go who seems, on paper, to be a better performer.

To sum up, baseball owes a great deal to the records. Batting averages are the most accurate of these records. They serve as the only fair basis for comparing old time batters with modern hitters, or in comparing one present-day hitter with another. The public undoubtedly forms its opinion of a player largely from his batting average. The players themselves appreciate the value of batting averages for their impression on the public. But they discount them, to a considerable degree, in estimating one an other's ability. Moreover some players maintain that the records themselves are inaccurate.

The Batter's Equipment

GEORGE McBRIDE said to me years ago, "It's as natural for the American boy to dream of becoming a Big League player as it used to be for him to dream of becoming a pirate or a bandit chief. The boy must always imagine for himself some active career which has a spice of adventure and, of course, brings it's own degree of prosperity. Where a good, clean sport that also offers a worthy profession, takes the place of the blood curdling and somewhat disreputable occupations which once fired the youthful fancy, a distinct advantage is gained."

When George McBride gave this opinion, he voiced the sentiments of the public. But dreaming about becoming a great hitter will not carry a boy very far, for baseball is a thing of stern realities and the competition grows keener with every step up the ladder of progress.

Before starting on that arduous road which brings failure to many while bestowing renown upon a few, every young man must take stock of his own talents and determine, in so far as he may, just what are his prospects of success.

Dasher Troy, who was a Major Leaguer in the remote first days of the game, once said to me. "My first piece of advice to young fellows who are dreaming of becoming ball players is this: If you have good eyesight, get into the game. If you haven't good eyesight, stay out, for you will never make a good ball player with that handicap."

"Along with excellent eyesight should go a quick brain. Education is desirable, but not essential. But whatever his education, baseball requires a player who is keen witted and intelligent. That type of mind which is not only active but original, always trying something new, is the highest type of baseball mind."

Evidently the batter's equipment is partly mechanical, partly mental. This distinction will grow more apparent as we proceed.

Hans Wagner once said, "As for advice to batters, I can't give any. Just keep your eye on the old ball. It's the only safe way."

All authorities agree that batting eye plays an important role in hitting. Ty Cobb said, "A batter always watches a pitcher's move and tries to figure out what he is going to throw next. The pitcher who can most successfully mask his movements is the one hardest to hit. For me the man who has a side arm delivery or who turns his back when pitching is the toughest problem."

The unfortunate Joe Jackson, one of the greatest hitters who ever lived, elaborated this theme in some detail. "I believe," said Joe, "the best part of batting is in the eye. My eyesight has always been good. But more than that, your hands must work with your eye. When your eye tells you the ball is in a certain place, your hands have got to work at the same time to get the bat to that place to meet the ball. I would advise youngsters trying to make good to watch the pitcher's hands. Watch them all the time. Watch them like a cat, until the ball leaves the pitcher's fingers. Then watch the ball. Never take your eye off that ball. You haven't much time to make up your mind what to do, but in that half second, while the ball is on its way, you have time, if you are quick and can read the signs, to tell you a great deal that you want to know. For instance, by watching a pitcher's hands closely, you can often tell whether he is pitching a curve or a fast ball. Pitchers try to cover, but they can't conceal everything from a sharp eye. Even if you can read nothing from the pitcher's hands, you can tell something from the ball as it comes to meet you. This is particularly true of a new ball. You can tell a curve quite often by seeing the ball rotate in the air."

George Sisler emphasized time when he said, "The secret of batting may be in the eye, but it's also in proper co-ordination. A man's shoulders and arms must work together with his eye. The eye sees; the hands and arms and shoulders must execute and they must work together. The element of time is very essential."

Sam Crawford added a word to the batter's essential equipment, namely, condition. "The whole secret of success in baseball, as I see it, is wrapped up in that one word 'Condition.' The ball player with natural ability who always keeps in good condition is the one who will make good."

Briefly stated, a batter's mechanical equipment is expressed in this four-fold requirement—batting eye, muscular co-ordination, accurate timing, and physical condition. From this brief analysis of mechanical gifts we may pass at once to an equally brief analysis of those less tangible but even more important requirements which we may term, in contrast, mental.

Hugh Jennings said, "A batter must not only have ability, but he must make the most of this ability, otherwise he is merely a mechanical workman. The successful player has energy, perseverance, aggressiveness and ambition. All are important and all enter very largely into his success."

"Silk" O'Loughlin once laid down a few simple rules for beginners. He said, "Let me impress one point upon amateur and semi-professional ball players who aspire to the game. Brains will win. This is the keynote to baseball success. The boys who keep their eyes open and use their heads as much as they do their hands and feet, who think things out for themselves or learn from observation are the boys who will succeed, providing, of course, they possess natural playing ability."

Bill Carrigan who won much fame as a World's Champion manager, once said, "The first great requisite for success in baseball is nerve. I have seen players with speed, hitting strength and grace, but they did not make good. They lacked the prime essential, stoutness of heart. To begin with, of course, a man must have a natural ability to hit, and then comes imagination. Give me the player who can conceive plays, who thinks all the time he is in the game and who doesn't stop thinking when it's over, who goes over every play of the afternoon, recalls how he made this mistake and how he might have avoided that misplay. Nerve and love of the game for the game itself are strong points in a ball player's make-up."

John McGraw offers the somewhat cynical remark, "Never try to make another man think. It can't be done. He is born that way and can't help it. But," added McGraw, "the young fellow who can think is a more valuable player than the old timer who can hit but never acts except under orders."

Lee Fohl discussed much the same problem from a different angle. Said Fohl, "No subject is more talked about or less understood in baseball than brains. The thing that impresses me most forcibly in Big Leaguers is the evident rariety of brains. You have to be with a man day after day to know whether or not he has brains. It is easy to say what a baseball brain is not, but difficult to say what it is. It's the ability to study opposing batters and pitchers, to see the defects in the opposing team and profit by them."

Many experts have claimed that ambition to succeed is the first mental qualification of the batter. That great pitcher with a blackened reputation, Eddie Cicotte, well illustrated this point when he discussed Ty Cobb as a fellow Minor Leaguer. Said Cicotte, "While I was at Augusta we had a hustling outfielder on our team who looked like a comer. He was fast as greased lightning. He wasn't the best fielder in the world, but he was all over the lot after the ball. He wasn't a finished batter, but he was an earnest, slashing sort of slugger who was always dangerous. But the thing about him which impressed me most was his restless ambition. He was always on his toes, always on edge and keen for any suggestion that would tell him anything about playing baseball. In short, he was a live wire; the kind of energetic player a manager likes to have on his team. His name was Ty Cobb."

"Ambition," said Ed Knetchy, "is in a ball player what a main spring is in a watch. It is what makes the thing go."

To ambition must be added another desirable mental quality, namely courage. Hans Lobert once outlined a ball player's start in life rather effectively because he spoke from his own experience. "It is a proud day in the life of any ball player," said Hans, "when he signs his first contract. It makes little difference how small the League, how far down the list of Class "D" Clubs. It is at least a part of Organized Baseball and he is a genuine professional. He does not stop to consider that there are thousands of ball players signed up every year in this way and that only a few of them can hope to rise to the Big Leagues. Usually the young player doesn't make good from the start. He is benched by the manager. This is the real turning point in a Big League player's life. If he has natural ability enough and faith in himself and has spirit and perseverance enough to stand the sarcasm which is heaped upon him he is bound to make good. But if he becomes disheartened, which is more likely to be the case, he loses his nerve and has no prospect but speedy return to the Minors."

The part which courage plays in a batter's progress was once aptly illustrated by Mike Donlin in an anecdote of his early days. "Bobby Wallace," said Mike, "showed me how to win a Big League berth. When I joined Tebeau's St. Louis team in 1899 Jesse Burkett sized me up as a fresh Bush Leaguer and made life miserable for me. One day he bawled me for keeps. I determined to jump the Club that night and go back to California. After the game Wallace called me aside and said, 'Don't let Burkett bluff you any more. Call him the next time he cracks his whip.' One week later in Pittsburgh I ran over into Burkett's field and took a ball away from him. He roared like a bull and threatened to knock my block off. As soon as the game was over, I climbed into the same carriage with Burkett and jostled him as hard as I knew how. 'What's the trouble kid, you ain't looking for trouble with me, are you?' inquired Jesse. 'That's exactly what I'm after, you Big Sour Stiff," said I. 'Cut out the rough stuff,' interrupted Tebeau— 'Jesse was only joshing. Never lose your temper that way again. Shake hands with Burkett and forget all about this affair.' Jesse extended his hand and Wallace nudged me to take it and we buried the hatchet." That affair was the making of Mike Donlin.

Managers appreciate the importance of nerve and some of them are considerate enough to value it above a ball game. Connie Mack once left Danny Hoffman in when he was in a slump and justified his conduct. Said Mack, "I felt certain that Hoffman would strike out and we would lose the game. But if I had taken Danny out and put another batsman in it might have broken his nerve. I preferred to lose the game rather than have Hoffman believe I had lost confidence in him."

Benny Kauff, whose career rose to brilliant heights only to set in gloom, was often criticized for his confidence. Benny took issue with this criticism. "Perhaps I talk too much at times and give a wrong impression," he admitted. "But I don't think I am swell headed. I don't aim to be. I am confident and I wouldn't give much for a ball player who wasn't. I am confident and aggressive on the diamond because I believe I ought to be in order to be a good player."

The aggressive spirit born of courage and confidence was well expounded by Joe Tinker. "John Evers and I," said Joe, didn't use to speak, but we played pretty well together. They make a great deal of such differences among ball players. This is pure exaggeration. You can not expect to be on intimate terms with everybody on your club and there is no reason why you should be, so long as you are playing the game. Baseball is no game for mollycoddles and the man who makes the best player in the long run is the man who has the most spirit and aggressiveness. He must have them if he is to make good."

Ty Cobb rated determination as very high in a batter's mental equipment. Fred Mitchell fully agrees with him. Said Mitchell, "The spirit to win is worth twenty points to any batting average and an additional pitcher to any ball club."

Ivan Olson, always a scrapper, was a stout champion of the same intangible virtue. He said, "There's one thing the records are silent about. They don't tell much of a player's initiative, the amount of encouragement he gives his pitchers or the pep he helps to instill in his club. It is the spirit he shows quite as much as his ability to rap out hits which wins games. In fact, I believe that spirit is more important than mechanical ability. Let a player hit only .200; let him make more mechanical errors than anybody else on the team, but so long as he has the nerve and determination to win, give him to me in preference to some other fellow with twice his natural talent but without his heart."

Big Ed Walsh illustrated how determination to make good is some times the spur of necessity. "I was driven to make good in baseball. The shadow of the mines was on me. It was either make good or back to the mines for me."

Ty Cobb recounted a vivid story in the realm of the purely psychological which well illustrates the importance of a batter's mental gifts. Said Ty, "The champion always has a decided advantage, be it baseball, boxing or anything else. The contender lacks something of the champion's confidence and that is what beats him. I remember, I think it was in 1916, that Joe Jackson started out at a tremendous pace. He was going to get me that year sure. He came into the club house and told me that he was going to get me. I laughed at him, whereupon he grew earnest and offered to bet. 'All right, Joe,' said I. 'I will bet you five hundred dollars that I beat you out this season.' He thought it over for a minute but he didn't bet. That game I believe I made two or three hits and he made but one. Next day I walked over to the bench where he was sitting. He spoke to me, but I did not answer him. I knew he would be puzzled. A little later I walked over again. I thought he might have imagined I didn't hear him speak, so I looked at him, straight in the eye, until I got very close. He spoke to me again, but I made no reply. I knew what was in his mind. He was wondering, 'What's he sore about now.' And he didn't make any hits at all that game. The final game, I walked over with a broad smile, clapped him on the back and said, in the most friendly way, 'Joe, Old Boy, how are you?' This seemed to astonish him more than anything else. All the rest of that season I had his goat, and I beat him out by forty points." This illustrates one of the infinite tricks with which Ty built up the most amazing batting average on record.

The familiar proverb, "Practice makes perfect" has its place in baseball. To the mechanical gifts and mental talents which are essential in the successful hitter, must be added experience.

Dode Paskert, once remarked, "They say baseball is a game for young men. But the most important thing a batter can have is experience. It stands to reason that the older he is the more experience he can gain. If a fellow could only stick in the game until he was fifty or sixty, he would be some player."

Zack Wheat echoed this thought when he said, "The man who can hit ought to grow better until his eyes go bad. Why shouldn't he? He doesn't lose the power to hold the bat or to take his swing. He may lose some speed of foot, but he ought to hit just as hard until his eye sight fails. Besides, experience counts. He knows the pitchers better. He knows how to handle himself better. All the tricks at batting that it took him years to learn he now uses unconsciously." Zack even applied the same theory to the work of a single season when he said. "The test of a good batter is this, does he improve as the season advances? If he does, he's a good batter."

Jake Daubert said, "Work is the keynote of all baseball success. No player ever yet achieved prominence without the hardest kind of hard work. Baseball is no place for a lazy man. A player must first of all have ability. But ability is not enough. He must have ambition, for unless he strives to succeed he will not succeed. Ambition means hard work."

"Nothing can take the place of experience", said George Whitted. "When I broke into the Big Leagues, I was nearly driven out again by curved balls. The pitchers pestered the life out of me with curves. I couldn't hit one of those things with a canoe paddle. But fortunately I realized how rotten I was and made up my mind, to master curve pitching if it cost a leg. So

I used to go out to the ball park at nine o'clock in the morning and persuade some rookie pitcher who needed exercise and was willing to undergo the ordeal, to pitch curves to me. I spent hours swinging at curves from every direction and every elevation. There had been a time when my knees would sag under me when I saw a pitcher cut loose with a curve. But before I was through, I got so that I could hit curves as well as I could fast balls."

Even Minor League experience is worth while, according to Billy Kelly who won a momentary fame as the battery made of "Twenty-two thousand five hundred dollar" Marty O'Toole. Kelly, while recounting his experience in the Sticks said, "I received enough to eat while I was down there and that is about all. Still the time we are playing in the Bushes for a ham sandwich is not lost for it all goes as good experience."

Even the game itself improves with experience, according to Chief Meyers, the famous old Indian catcher. The Chief was one day reminiscing about the Big Game before he made his final ado to the Big League fans. He said, "The character of the game and of the players themselves has changed mightily in the past few years. The general standard of ball players has improved and is higher today than ever before. By standard I mean not only the playing ability of the men but their morals and general behavior. It is a clean sport and the tendency today is to make it even cleaner."

From this sweeping bird's eye view of a batter's requirements, let us pass on to a closer, more intimate study of those numberless details which the experience of many Champion hitters has proven worth while.

Taking Advice

EVERY ball player from Ty Cobb to the humblest sand lot's performer is willing, yes eager, to take advice. The sole requirements are that the advice be worth while and readily followed.

For example, Max Carey, one of the stars of the National League, said, "I have often wished that I might have gone to Detroit instead of Pittsburgh. At Detroit I would have enjoyed the supreme advantage of Ty Cobb's coaching. Old as I am, I believe that even now he could improve my batting perhaps twenty points." And yet, Carey has five times hit for .300 and has been considered one of baseball's top notchers for years.

If such a man craves coaching, how much more the ambitious rookie who is struggling to improve himself. But advice to such a player is difficult. As Jack Coombs said, "It's disappointing for a conscientious veteran to hand out advice. For he realizes that at best he can only state the chances of the game."

Ty Cobb who doubtless knows batting better than any one player who ever lived, said, "Volumes have been written about the science or plain inherited talent of batting. Much that has been written is worse than worthless. But there are hints now and then which prove valuable to the individual. You can lay down no general rules in batting which will apply to all cases. The most you can do is to throw out here and there some possible helpful hints. I have made a close study of batting for twenty years. I think I understand how to hit myself and also how to teach others how to hit, provided they are willing to learn. When I took charge of Detroit, the club was hitting .265. The next season they hit .316. Their former average was bettered by fifty points. I think I could take any young player, with ambition and without much experience, and better his average that many points. So long as a man is hitting well I say nothing to him. Consciously or unconsciously he is doing the right thing. Nor do I care in the least what awkwardness he may show or what errors he may seem to commit. So long as he is driving out safe bingles, he can stand on one ear, if he wants to. Where I could improve a young batter is by correcting his stance at the plate, adjusting the weight of his bat and so on. After all there is a limit to what you can teach a man. Nobody ever taught me how to hit. What I have learned I have learned myself. The best knowledge is that which a man digs out for himself."

In a few paragraphs Ty Cobb covers the entire field. Most players, however, are continually striving to improve themselves. They not only seek advice, but they watch other players at bat, hoping to learn something which may be useful. Said Charles Grimm, "I realized a long time ago what my weak point at bat was and I have tried hard to overcome it. Ever since I can remember, I have watched other players and learned things for myself. I am still learning. You can get many a useful point by looking over

23

the leading batters of an opposing team during batting practice, the way they handle the bat, the swing, the position of the feet, all these things are important. Batting is difficult to learn, but I believe it can be learned. I do not say that anybody can become a second Hornsby, but I do believe that anyone with ordinary strength, a clear eye and a love for the game, who is willing to work and work hard year after year, can become at least a satisfactory hitter. This was so in my own case. Fielding came natural to me. Batting I had to learn."

Willingness to learn is always essential. As Pat Moran said about Grover Alexander. "With all his ability there is nothing overconfident about him. He's willing to learn every day and he never gets offended when you make suggestions to him."

Ball players learn batting in three ways, by observing others, by practice and by depending upon the advice of a competent teacher. The teacher is important, as Hugo Bezdek said. "A man may have vast knowledge of baseball, but if he cannot impart that knowledge or persuade his man to act upon that knowledge, he might as well be ignorant of the most obvious detail."

There are players who doggedly turn their backs on most advice and insist on fighting out their own salvation. Some of them even scoff at the value of advice. Zack Wheat is one of these. He said, "How do I explain the fact that while I was never much of a hitter in the Minors, I became a .300 hitter in the Majors? The explanation is simple. When I was with Mobile I was young, inexperienced and fast on my feet. The fellows that I played with encouraged me to bunt and beat the ball out. I was anxious to make good and did as I was told. When I came to Brooklyn I adopted an altogether different style of hitting. I stood flat footed at the plate and slugged. That was my natural style. Nobody advised me to do this. People simply didn't give me any advice at all, so I had a chance to follow my natural bent. That's the secret of every batter's success. Every batter has a natural style of hitting. Let him follow that style regardless of what others tell him. Then, whatever talent he has, will come to the surface. Advice is all right when it tends to overcome some technical fault, but advice should never go so far as to change a batter's style."

Even a technical fault is defended by some players, so long as it is natural. Jack Bentley, with one of the oddest and most faulty apparent stances on record, proved a sensational hitter through most of his career. And he was consistent even in his advice to others. He said, "A ball player should always be original. Copying other ball players never gets you anywhere."

Sturdy old Nap Rucker echoed this fundamental thought when he said, "The main thing that I have learned from ten years of playing experience in the Big Leagues, is this. Let every man stick to his own last."

These seemingly contradictory opinions, however, are not so inconsistent after all. What the Bentleys and the Zack Wheats say, is the fundamental truth that a batter should follow his natural bent. Doubtless Ty Cobb, with all his brilliant success, as a batting coach, would grant as much.

Advice, like all other good things, may be overdone. Some batters doubtless pay too great respect to the theories of hitting. For example, Branch Rickey said, "Johnny Lavan knows too much to be a good hitter." His meaning in this statement was obvious.

George Sisler expressed much the same idea in explaining why certain batters are not very successful. He said, "In my opinion catchers do not ordinarily hit well because they know too much about pitching. They've exhausted their own ingenuity in trying to circumvent opposing batters. When they become batters themselves, they picture the opposing catcher as having worked all the regulation tricks and invented a few new ones. Their minds are not free and centered on the task in hand. They are thinking about curves, batter's weaknesses and a lot of things. Hence they magnify the difficulties which confront them and usually they don't shine at the bat."

A bit of advice that rings 100% true is this. Learn all you can about hitting and never stop learning, if you have as long and brilliant a record as that of Ty Cobb. But when facing the pitcher, concentrate on Rogers Hornsby's simple statement, that the only thing a batter is called upon to do is to meet the ball.

Choosing a Bat.

A WELL-TESTED bat is the batter's best friend. For after all, mechanical ability and mental talents and experience must all express themselves by means of this inanimate bludgeon.

Ball players recognize the importance of securing a bat that is suited to their peculiar requirements, and they experiment almost continually in search of a bat that is "just right." A player rates a favorite bat among his most intimate treasures and his vexation borders upon actual grief when such a bat is broken or mislaid.

I recall a conversation I once had with Ty Cobb. He was seated in the sheltering calm of the players' bench driving thin wire nails into a battered bat with an ancient and rust-encrusted hatchet. "It's against the law to do this," muttered Ty, with his mouth full of nails. "But in my opinion that's a fool law. Of course, I understand that you ought not to put lead in a bat or to shave one side of it flat or otherwise alter the shape or weight. But why a few nails will help or hurt a batting average is beyond me. You see," continued Ty, "as one of the nails bent in a beautiful loop at a misdirected drive, "I hold some of Ed Plank's views. He used to claim there were just so many strikes in his old soup bone, and he was very cautious how he used up those strikes. This is a good bat, a first-rate bat. It got slightly cracked when I leaned a little too hard on a fast one. But in my opinion there are a few more hits left in it somewhere from the handle to the blunt nose."

Ty's care of this much misused war club was characteristic of the attitude of most players. Not a few of them spend many hours in scraping and polishing some particular bat. Nor is this care time wasted. A bat that is "just right" means many more points on the batting average and well the player knows it.

In general bats are of two kinds, light and heavy. Both divisions are somewhat shadowy. There is no clear cut dividing line. Moreover, the weight of the bat does not vary as the weight of the ball player, though there is in some cases a rough connection between the two.

Babe Ruth, for example, used a very heavy bat. He once discussed this bat with me. Said Babe, "They tell me I swing the heaviest club in baseball. It's not only heavy, but long, about as long as the law allows. And it weighs 52 ounces. Most bats weigh under 40. My theory is the bigger the bat the faster the ball will travel. It's really the weight of the bat that drives the ball and I like a heavy bat. I have strength enough to swing it and when I meet the ball, I want to feel that I have something in my hands that will make it travel."

Babe did not, as a matter of fact, use the heaviest bat in the game. Hack Miller, the ponderous strong man, had that distinction. Hack's every day club weighed 47 ounces. But he had in his possession a curious bludgeon of oak or hickory or some such heavy wood which, so he claimed, weighed 65 ounces. Hack said he liked to use this bat because it didn't sting his fingers. "I get the old bat out now sometimes," said Hack. "When I was on the Pacific Coast I had a bat that weighed 67 ounces: It was a good bat too and I liked it."

Hank Severeid, the strong man of the Browns, also liked a heavy bat. "I agree with Ruth in one respect," he admited. "The bat I use weighs 50 ounces. It is very long and the weight is distributed all the way down. It is one of the heaviest bats in the League, but it seems to suit my style. I don't think it's as awkward to handle as much lighter bats that I would term top-heavy. But a bat for a ball player is like a neck tie, a matter of individual taste."

Edd Roush was no Hercules in strength, but he also favored a heavy bat. "My pet war club," said Roush, "weighs 48 ounces. This is heavy, much heavier than the average. In fact, it's one of the heaviest bats in the National League. But I find that it gives me the best results. I swing almost entirely with my arms, but the bat I use is so heavy and solid that when it meets the ball it will go for a hard drive anywhere."

Ken Williams, who beat out Ruth one year for home run honors, also favored a heavy bat. "Ruth uses a little bigger club than mine," said Ken, "though not much. Late in the season, when hot weather comes, I cut down on the weight of my bat. But I always like a heavy one because when you connect with the ball with every ounce of strength in your frame, the weight of the bat is going to cut a big figure. That's my theory, anyway, and it seems to work."

Zack Wheat, a formidable slugger, takes issue with this reasoning. Said Zack, "The weight of the bat is of no particular consequence in my style of hitting. It's the snap that you get into your wrists that drives the ball and naturally you will get more snap with a lighter bat. I once used a bat that weighed 46 ounces. I now prefer a bat that doesn't weigh over 40."

Harry Heilmann, a huge man and a ponderous hitter, was even more critical in his remarks about heavy bats. "I weigh over 200 pounds," said Heilmann, "and have height and strength enough to use a very heavy bat, if there were any sense in doing so. But I don't believe there is. Years ago I had an old club that weighed 40 ounces. My present bat weighs 36 ounces, but has plenty of wood. It is my belief that the weight of the bat has nothing to do with driving the ball hard."

Bill Jacobson, the brawny Swede who is husky enough to use the biggest bat ever turned, also favored Heilmann's philosophy. "I use a bat that I can handle," said Jacobson. "Perhaps with a heavier bat and a follow through motion, I could hit the ball harder, but I wouldn't hit anywhere near so often. I might make more home runs, but my batting average would suffer."

Rogers Hornsby is very fussy about his bat. He said, "Every batter probably has a type of bat that is just suited to him. I have experimented a good deal with bats and now have a special model which averages between 38 and 40 ounces in weight. Some sluggers prefer a heavy bat. Chief Myers was a big man and strong and used a very heavy bat. I understand Babe Ruth does also. Of course, if a man has the strength to handle a heavy bat as easily as a smaller man would handle a lighter bat, he can drive the ball that much farther. But most batters will discover that an extra heavy bat cuts down the speed of their swing more than enough to offset what the weight of the bat can accomplish. Sometimes, in batting practice, when I am feeling exceptionally good, I will try out a heavier bat. You can usually tell from such experiences whether you are in good batting form. I like to swing a fairly heavy bat against a pitcher with a lot of speed. But for all around work, I prefer a lighter bat."

Ed Konetchy once said, "I plan always to have a bat that is just suited to my weight and strength so that I can feel the ball when I hit it." Many batters have expressed the same notion. But at the same time they try to avoid the opposite extreme, a bat that will "sting their fingers when they meet the ball."

Cy Williams, the home run slugger of the Phillies, said, "It is no part of my philosophy to use a bat too heavy for ordinary work. You can hit plenty hard enough with a lighter bat. My usual war club weighs about 39 ounces. In the very hot weather

I have a bat somewhat lighter. You've got to be able to swing a bat easily and get it around in time. There's a limit to the weight of the bat that you can use to the best advantage."

Bats vary not only with the weight and strength of the batter, but with his batting style. Arm hitters that depend on a quick snappy meeting of the ball usually prefer a light bat. Ponderous sluggers with the Babe Ruth follow through motion are inclined to favor a heavy bat. Edd Roush, a typical place hitter, preferred a heavy bat because in his peculiar batting style he needed a heavy bat to time his swing properly, a point that we will take up later. Players change from a heavier to a lighter bat very frequently as the season advances. Even Harry Heilmann favored using a heavier bat in the spring, but he said, "I want a bat at least six ounces lighter when the hot weather comes. Hot weather usually means faster pitching and a lighter bat is easier to swing and therefore better adapted to pitching of that type. Besides, changing to a lighter bat sometimes helps a batter to get out of a slump."

Players like Zack Wheat and Rogers Hornsby often have two or three different weights to their bats, using the heavier bat on a cold day and changing to the lighter club on a hot day. Such batters also shift against certain pitching. In general they favor a lighter bat against curve pitching. Against a pitcher who generally depends upon speed, they are inclined to use a heavier bat.

Players vary greatly in the care which they take of their bats. Dan Comerford, for many years property man of the Brooklyn Ball Club, cited two well known examples. "Jacques Fournier," said Comerford, "the heaviest slugger of the club, is the easiest man on bats I ever saw. He had but two all one season. He's very fussy about his bat. He calls it "his baby" and won't let anyone else touch it. Zack Wheat, the other slugger of the club, is exactly opposite. He's very hard on bats and generally makes way with a couple of dozen during the season. Besides, he doesn't object to other batters using his bats, but rather encourages them to do this."

Bats sometimes have a queer history, reminiscent of a period in the batter's own life. Joe Jackson of melancholy memory, one of the greatest hitters who ever lived, always used a black bat. He once explained the origin of this bat to me. "When I was about fourteen years old," said Joe, "before I joined the Greenville

Grangers, I had some reputation as a ball player in my home town. One day a well known fan of the city, Captain Martin by name, called me into his place and presented me with the original of the black bats I have always used. The bat he gave me was much the same as the one I use today and it was black. I have that original bat now and although it is broken with hard usage, I would not take Five Hundred Dollars for it. I do not know that I am specially superstitious, but these black bats have led for me in the batting percentage of four different Leagues and they have hit for me over .400 in the American League. I have all my bats made after this one pattern and they are all black."

No doubt the most curious of all bats was that of Heinie Groh. His bats were the extreme limit in diameter, were cut away sharply with a narrow handle and looked much like a bottle. Moreover, his bats were shorter by at least two inches than other bats. But they were heavy, weighing 45 ounces. Heinie designed this peculiar shape for his own special requirements and he spent a lot of time in getting just the bat that he believed best suited to his needs. "The bat," said Heinie, "is almost like a paddle with the weight on the hitting end. I don't swing it very much but punch with it, and I can place hits pretty accurately. The handle of this bat is wound with tape. Ordinarily I choke up on the bat, but some times I will slide one hand down to the end of the handle and swing more like a slugger. It's designed specially for a chop hitter and I am convinced that many other chop hitters would find this peculiar bat much better for them than the ordinary club. I am rather easy on my bats, seldom use more than two or three a year. They are more apt to get chipped than broken." Furthermore, Heinie confessed that in batting practice he used a similar bottle shaped club made of oak which weighed 54 ounces. This was merely so that he might become accustomed to a heavy bat. When he entered the game with his normal club it seemed light and easy to handle in comparison. It's precisely the theory of the sixteen pound shot putter who uses a seventeen pound shot in warming up practice.

Bats are as variable as the characteristics of the batters who use them. They vary not only with individuals but with the same individuals. And all batters, save possible Heinie Groh who seems to have hit upon the style which suits him, are forever experimenting in search, it may be, of such a bat as Hans Wagner once pictured—from an old table leg of some mysterious Oriental wood—some bat that will enable them to give perfect expression to their batting powers.

Position at the Plate

TRIS SPEAKER once discoursed upon a batter's position at plate. He said, "The batter's stance looks easy, but I know players who have spent sleepless nights wondering if their position at the plate could be improved. I confess I have done this myself. For example, the batter in a slump often finds himself backing away from the ball unconsciously, or perhaps, if he is over eager, stepping into the ball too soon. Be sure of one thing, his position at the plate has much to do with his trouble. And yet there is no set rule that you can lay down for a player on this point. For every batter has his own style."

George Moriarty, when he was a player, was sometimes worried about his batting. "In the latter part of June, one year," he said, "I found myself hitting for the impressive average of .190. Jean Dubuc came to me and asked, 'George, why don't you take a different position at the plate? I have watched you and you always crouch.' 'I know,' I admitted, 'but I am afraid they will feed me low balls. I don't like them and I want to bend over so that I can be sure to hit them.' 'That's all wrong,' said Dubuc. 'Most of the balls you hit you pop up. You are hitting under the ball all the time. Stand up straight at the plate and lam them out.' 'I know, Dubuc,' I said, 'but I have batted this way so long I am afraid that if I change my position at the plate I will look still worse.' 'George,' said he and he laid his hand on my shoulder, while his voice trembled with emotion, 'George, you couldn't look any worse.' So I took his advice. I took some lessons in batting and I have been hitting .400 ever since."

Moriarty's surprising reversal in form was merely one of an infinite number of illustrations that might be cited to show the importance of a proper position at the plate.

Naturally the question arises, what is the proper position? Mike Mowrey answered that question years ago when he said, "There is no rule for standing at the plate. Every good batter has his own style."

Jimmy Archer echoed this thought when he said, "The managers never try to teach a man how to hit. They know he must hit in his own way, if at all."

Jimmy Callahan once told me, "One thing I learned early in life. The system that works for one ball player will not necessarily work for another. Every man is his own best judge of what is fitted to his peculiar needs."

Roughly speaking there are two general methods of standing at the plate. One is the erect position, the other is the crouch, more or less pronounced. Ty Cobb, Joe Jackson, George Sisler used to be shining examples of the erect position. Most players have a certain amount of crouch.

Jacques Fournier has the crouch in its most aggravated form. He bends nearly double at bat. "The more I crouch," said Jacques, "the better I can hit. I can see the ball better by getting my head down and am not apt to be fooled so much on a curve. What is fully as important, I can hit harder. I can get the full strength of my body into my blow when I slug the bat around the ball."

Probably Napoleon Lajoie was as graceful a batter as ever lived. But Larry never thought much about this in the days when he was baseball's batting champion. "It comes natural to me. That's all," was his brief comment.

Few batters approximate Lajoie even in appearance. But for their comfort, be it said, this isn't necessary. Big Bill Jacobson was uncommonly awkward at bat, but he got results. "They criticize my stance a good deal," said he, "and I don't know that I blame them. It probably isn't pretty to look at. I can't say that I like it myself. But when I am at bat all I am thinking about is stinging the old ball. If I were posing for a statue or trying to originate some harmonic dance steps it might be different and I would be a failure. But hitting is my business and I can hit."

Hy Myers used to stand erect at the plate, but he would often bend his knees when he swung to meet the ball. "That's because I'm a little weak on the low ones," he explained.

With few exceptions batters of the present stand "side on" to the pitcher. This position was not always so popular. Dasher Troy, whose experiences embrace the early days, once said to me, "When Pop Anson went to bat, he grasped the bludgeon firmly, faced the pitcher, with his feet squarely on the ground, and as the ball whirled from the pitcher's hand he stepped forward to meet it. Why is it that as baseball progressed the batter turned more and more from his headon position until he finally stood with his side toward the pitcher and had to crane his neck if he would see the pitcher?"

Jake Daubert said, "When I was in the Minor Leagues I used to face the pitcher. I always thought there were good arguments in favor of that style. But I was a weak hitter and experimented to improve my hitting. No doubt if I had been able to hit at first as I have learned to do since, I would have stuck to my natural style of facing the pitcher."

Heinie Groh is the only batter of recent days who won any prominence by following this once approved old style method of facing the pitcher. Heinie justified his system with some plausible arguments. He said, "By standing with your face toward the pitcher you can see both foul lines, watch the pitcher's windup motion better and follow the ball better. Besides, from such a position the batter unconsciously steps forward to meet the ball when he swings. The force if the swing itself carries him toward first and really gets him into his stride."

Carson Bigbee emphasized one important element in a batter's stance. He said, "Position at the plate is important for it is really the batter's takeoff position when he starts to sprint. If he hits the ball he must swing instantly into a rapid dash for first base. The fraction of a second lost at the start would spoil what might otherwise be a safe hit." In other words, position at the plate has a two-fold importance. It is at once the position of the batter who is to hit and of the base runner who is to sprint.

Not a few players have called attention to the fact that the batter must mask his intentions by his position at bat. Urban Shocker, speaking from the pitcher's viewpoint, said, "You can often tell what is in the batter's mind by the way he shifts his feet, hitches his belt or wiggles his bat. Keep him guessing. That's the point."

Tris Speaker, discussing this phase of the situation, mentioned some interesting details when he said, "The pitcher recognizes the importance of the batter's stance at the plate and often tries to break up the batter's system. If he is standing close, the pitcher will hook one over on the inside to drive him away. The pitcher calls this 'Dusting off the platter.' It is legitimate in baseball, for he is entitled to the corners of the plate. He also uses various other tricks to disconcert the batter."

George Sisler, who was an apostle of place hitting, emphasized the importance of a proper stance. He said, "The first essential of place hitting is a correct position at plate. Have your feet right and your arms will be inclined to take care of themselves."

Experts frequently size up a batter by his position at plate. Otto Miller said, "In my years of catching I have learned something about good batters. A competent catcher can tell a good batter by his form, notwithstanding form varies as widely as the players. Batting eye is important, of course. But what is fully as important is a thing that I would call rythm of motion. There is a general harmony in the movement of the shoulders, the wrists, the grip of the bat, the step forward and all the other complicated motions which enter into a swing to meet the ball. By rythm of motion I certainly don't mean grace, but a sort of definite coordination which is difficult to describe but rather easy for the skilled observer to detect."

Tris Speaker, however, reminds us that it is easy to be misled by surface indications. He said, "I can detect in a young fellow all the points which would appeal to me. But they may not be points in his favor. In the same way, I can pick flaws that would seem defects to me, but he might prove in his own case that they were strong points. Every batter unconsciously judges another batter by himself. But all the time he knows that no two batters are alike and that what is good for one fellow is poor dope for another. So how can you lay down any general rules? Little men use heavy bats; big men use light bats. Some step into the ball; others step away from it. Some swing from the handle; others choke up. Some stand in the front of the box; others away in the rear. Combinations are infinite. Nothing else, whether batting form or defects, or strong points cuts much ice when contrasted with safe hits."

Not only do batters differ widely among themselves, but the individual batter not infrequently changes his own style, always experimenting, seeking some new idea which will help his work. Ty Cobb said, "One thing a batter must learn early in life and never forget. He must learn to shift at bat to conform to circumstances beyond his control. He will shift day by day against certain pitchers, but he will also make fundamental changes in his style with the mere passage of time. I used to stand erect at the plate and pull the ball to either field almost at will. Often I would crowd up in the front of the box so that in case I bunted I could get a quicker start with a shorter run to first base. Now I stand away from the plate and crouch. My eye is not so keen as it was. I must get a closer view of the ball. In other words, I have had to change my batting style."

George Moriarty, after years of umpiring experience, said "A weak batsman should try different stances at the plate until he discovers which one brings the best result. Your first position and the one you have clung to without change is not necessarily the most natural or the best suited to your particular case. If you can not cope successfully with a low-pitched ball, try a medium crouching attitude at plate. Many professionals have found a crouch more effective than an upright position. If you stand too close and do not hit well, move away. Some of the most powerful batsmen stand in the extreme rear of the box. Give each new stance a thorough trial, but do not make the mistake of adopting the stance employed by your favorite Big Leaguer as it may not be suited to you."

Zack Wheat said, "I shift my position at the plate more often than people think. I'll shift my shoulders more than my feet so as to meet the ball at a different angle. You must vary your position with the different pitchers or they'll soon get your number."

In general, a batter tries to develop a style which will fit all emergencies. Tris Speaker said, "I hold my shoulders high when I swing at the ball. The batter is more likely to hit true if the bat moves parallel with the ground. If the pitcher throws a high ball it is impossible for the batter to swing parallel with the ground without elevating his shoulders. I try to elevate my shoulders from habit so that I am always in a position to hit a high ball."

However he stands at plate, the batter must never forget the supreme importance of balance. Max Carey said, "Balance is the first lesson I should teach a beginner. To be sure, no one taught me, but I consider it the basis of successful work in any one of the three departments, batting, fielding and base running. Many a batter is robbed of a hit simply because he was off balance. That's why pitchers throw inside to a batter. They not only wish to drive him back from the plate, but to get him off balance. Then he is much less likely to meet the ball. And even if he does hit it, he can't hit it hard. That's one reason for Hornsby's phenomenal hitting; his perfect balance. In all the times I have watched him at bat, I have never seen him off balance. The free position he takes at the plate makes it practically impossible for him to get off balance. That is one reason he hits so often and so hard. Hitting hard isn't a matter of brute strength. It's a matter of balance and hitting the ball just right."

Some batters develop so much originality that they are guilty of what would seem fundamental defects. Take Jack Bentley, for instance. Though he was known as the greatest hitter in the Minor Leagues and hit over .400 on rejoining the Majors, his batting pose was anything but impressive. As the pitcher released the ball, Bentley would step back, raise himself slowly on one foot, much the same as a shot putter would do, and lunge forward. When he met the ball he was literally standing on one leg. Obviously a batter standing on one foot, his whole body in motion describing an arc through the air, could not shift readily to meet a sudden break in the ball. Nevertheless, Bentley was successful. He defended his system quite logically by saying, "I can hit the ball harder that way. That is my main object, to hit hard. The ball will go safe often enough if you put the strength behind it. I wouldn't recommend my style for others, but it works for me. I would recommend one thing, however, and that is to let everyone find out for himself what is natural for him and then do it, regardless of what people tell him."

The manner in which batters grip the bat also runs through infinite gradations. The quiet confidence, the easy grace which made Lajoie worthy of the name Napoleon, were all disclosed in his position at the plate, and the manner in which he gripped the bat. The massive strength and iron endurance which kept Hans Wagner in a Major League berth at forty-four were equally apparent. Very often the characteristics which distinguish the baseball star find eloquent and adequate expression in his position and the way he handles the bat. Lajoie's pose, for example, was graceful, confident, not a particle of waste motion anywhere. The one word which might best express that pose was "ease." Wagner was an opposite type. He sprawled all over the plate. He swung from a crouched position, griping the bat in iron hands, while the muscles stood out on his forearms like steel cables. The one word which would best describe the famous Dutchman at bat was "strength."

Whether the batter chokes up or swings from the handle; whether he holds his hands far apart or close together, all authorities agree that he should follow his natural bent. And they further agree that he should experiment, avoid a fixed system and shift his style to conform with changing conditions.

With so many varieties of stance at the plate, some of them grotesque and yet effective, the beginner might well inquire in puzzled tones, "Is there a perfect stance?" Ty Cobb, who knew more about batting than any man who ever lived, said, "Yes," even though he himself did not employ it. Rogers Hornsby, according to Ty Cobb, had the perfect stance at plate. "I would call it bombproof," said Ty. "He stands well back from the plate and steps into the ball. He can meet the ball with equal ease either on the inside or the outside, high or low. His position at the plate is perfect. And with it all he has an easy, forceful swing, without an atom of waste motion, that makes a powerful drive. "Yes," continued Ty, "Hornsby is the greatest natural batter I ever saw."

So far so good. But lest we be inclined to over-rate the importance of position and the grasp of the bat, admitting that these things are important, we might quote the words of Donie Bush, "This is only the beginning. A batter's position may be just right, but it won't amount to much without a lot of other things to go with it."

How They Stand In The Box

THE batter's box gives the player a certain freedom of motion. Within that limited area he may stand where he will. In general batters may be divided into four divisions, depending upon their mannerisms in the batter's box; namely, those who hug the front of the box, those who stand well to the rear, those who crowd the plate and those who stand well away from the plate. Technically we might make a fifth division for those who stand in the center, if there are any such. Usually a batter combines two of the above types in his own peculiar style of standing in the box.

Whitey Witt was one batter who stood in the front of the box. In fact, he stepped across the dividing line as he swung to meet the ball. Witt said, "The batter who stands in the front of the box is really a foot nearer to first base than the man who stands back. Besides, there are other advantages. Some pitchers don't curve a ball until just before it reaches the plate. By standing well up you can thus avoid the curve. Certainly this is the proper position to take if you are going to bunt, and I bunt a good deal."

Comparatively few Major Leaguers follow Witt's style. Most of them stand well back in the box. Hazen Cuyler said, "I stand back in the box, far from the plate and step into the ball. I can watch a curve better from that position. When a spit ball pitcher is on the slab, I am inclined to move up a little in the box and try to connect with the spitter before it takes its downward break."

Babe Ruth said, "When batting, I stand a few inches behind the plate. As the ball approaches, I step forward sharply and swing my bat with the full power of my shoulders and back."

Hans Wagner had a very awkward position. As Barney Drefuss said, "He stands so far back from the plate that it would seem difficult for him to reach a ball going directly over the rubber. But notwithstanding this, he hits balls that are on the outside with apparent ease."

Eddie Collins used to crowd the plate. This made him a difficult batter to pitch to. You couldn't sneak one by him. And yet, he wouldn't offer at a ball unless it was over the plate.

On the other hand, most batters stand further away, some of them at the other side of the box. Rogers Hornsby, who, so Ty Cobb said, had the perfect stance, stood far back with one foot on the rear line of the box and away from the plate. He stepped forward, however, and toward the plate when he swung to meet the ball. Theoretically the disadvantage of this stance, if any, is the fact that the batter might not detect so clearly a ball that was just on the line. In other words, the pitcher might occasionally fool him with a ball. On the other hand, the batter who hugs the plate may be obliged to hit the ball while stepping away. Ty Cobb, Eddie Collins, many other great batters, often hit while stepping away from the ball. In fact, Ty Cobb explained that this was necessary in his particular style of place hitting. In stepping away from the ball, however, the batter is not so likely to meet it fairly or to hit it hard. In general batters who depend upon their speed of foot for beating out slow hits, favor standing in front of the box. Such men as Archdeacon, John Tobin, Sam Rice and others stand either in the front half of the box or roughly in the center and take a decided stride forward when they lunge to meet the ball. From that position they are ready for a shorter sprint to first.

Sluggers, on the contrary, are inclined to stand further toward the rear of the box.

Frank Frisch, a noted speed artist, when batting right handed stood well back, but with one foot thrust far forward. His position would seem unnatural to many, but it worked for Frisch. As he swung he took off on his forward foot from a position in the front of the box. In other words, his position gave him the two-fold advantage of shifting instantly from the rear to the front of the box, depending upon the way he shifted the weight of his body from one foot to the other.

Occasionally a slugger will run up in the box. Babe Ruth used to do this, even running entirely out of the box in his furious rush to meet the ball.

There are obvious advantages and disadvantages in any one of the four positions outlined. The batter must choose the particular position which is best fitted to his individual style.

Edd Roush invariably changed his position in the box after the pitcher had delivered the ball. No pitcher could tell his intentions by watching his position for he always changed that position at the very last moment. As Burleigh Grimes said, "I have been watching that fellow for years and I never found out yet whether he was going or coming, trying to slug or bunt," needless to say such antics in the box are most disconcerting to the pitcher and fielders.

Most batters however, find this quick shift difficult to master. They are the batters who like to "get set" by digging their spikes into the dust and gaining what they call a "toe hold" even such batters however, while they hit from a set position, change that position at times to meet pitching conditions or in the attempt to improve their batting style.

How They Grip the Bat

BY the manner in which he grips the bat, the batter shows his intentions. Just what has he in mind?

In general batters are divided into two classes, chop hitters and sluggers. Their preference for one or the other of these types of batting is usually revealed by the manner in which they grip the bat. Jake Daubert said, "You can tell by looking at a batter whether he is a natural chop hitter or a slugger. Sam Crawford is a typical broad shouldered slugger. Joe Jackson looks slender but he is of that deceiving wiry type and he has a lot of strength in his arms and shoulders. Frank Baker doesn't look so big, but he has big wrists."

Not a few chop hitters have become sluggers. They have entirely altered their manner of gripping the bat. Fred Nicholson said, "I played with Hornsby in the Minors. He was a light, rangy lad like myself and thoroughly in love with his profession. But I cannot claim that he gave any great indication at that time of the success which has come to him since. He was known as a good hitter, but not particularly as a slugger. He was inclined to choke up on the bat. After he became a regular Big Leaguer, Hornsby changed his style and began to hit as hard as anybody in the National League."

Bob Veach said, "Years ago I choked up on the bat. Choking up has the effect of shortening the bat and it seemed reasonable to suppose that the shorter the bat the more quickly you could swing to meet the ball. In theory this was sound, but in practice I found it wouldn't work. Most of the really good hitters swing from the handle of the bat."

Sometimes even an old veteran shifts his grip on the bat with advantageous results. Dode Paskert, when he was already the oldest player in the National League, said, "I wouldn't have supposed I could have changed my system of batting at my time of life. Yet that is precisely what I did do this spring. I am not naturally a .300 hitter, though I have reached that altitude occasionally, but this year I started at a gait far above any I ever had before and I am still going strong. How do I explain this? I changed my style of batting. Heretofore I have generally choked up on the bat and usually I have hit into left field. This season

I determined to try another style. So I practiced holding the bat by the handle and taking a much longer swing. I not only hit the ball harder, but I frequently hit into right field so the fielders are not able to play my hits so well as they used to do. In fact, I believe my hitting has been better than it ever was before."

These are examples of batters who profited by shifting from a chop hitting stroke to real slugging. Other batters have had a precisely opposite experience. Pie Traynor said, "I always thought I was a good natural hitter. Perhaps that's one reason why I haven't done so well as I expected. I took too much for granted. Last year I slugged a lot. Three baggers looked good to me. This year I have changed my style. I have choked up on my bat and am going after singles more and am hitting much better than I did."

Andy High said, "I have been slugging the ball considerably, but I believe I would do better if I would develop as a chop hitter. I haven't the strength or the weight to tear the cover off the ball. But I can give it a smart belt."

Generally speaking natural hitters swing from the handle. Joe Jackson said, "Chop hitting is good for those who like it. I am a slugger or nothing. I like to get hold of the handle and swing with the full length of the bat. I can hit better that way and I don't believe a batter can change his style to suit somebody else. Every man has his natural style and should follow it. I have my style and I can't hit if I tried to copy somebody else."

There are natural chop hitters just as there are natural sluggers. Some of them are bad men to face. Burleigh Grimes said, "Heinie Groh is a batter that I never like to see in the box. In my opinion, he has really a better batting eye than Rogers Hornsby. It is almost impossible to fool him. He stands at the plate and pats the air with that little club footed bat of his and he taps the ball through just about where he wants it to go, just over the infield where it hurts. Hornsby, of course, is a great hitter. Swinging from the handle is his natural style and yet he hits the ball square on the nose. If he choked up on the bat like Heinie, he would theoretically hit better but in actual practice he wouldn't hit half so well. Every batter has his natural style so he is wise to stick to it. The pitcher has to match his strength and wits against all styles."

There are several types of sluggers. The ideal slugger of the Babe Ruth model gets a toe hold and swings from his feet. There are not a few sluggers, however, who are known as arm hitters. Hans Wagner defended this type. He said, "Most youngsters who can hit at all, like to slug. That's all right too. I believe in hitting the ball hard myself. But in trying to slug, these players are apt to get into a bad habit of swinging with the whole body. This is the wrong dope, as I have observed it. I have never seen a player who swung with his body who was a good hitter. Not one. Arm and wrist hitters are those who make good. I have always hit with my arms and so has Lajoie. So have all the other good hitters I have known. Cactus Cravath is a good hitter and gets much of the snap into the hit with his wrists. That's right. A good grip on the bat is what drives the ball. You can't meet the ball so well when you swing with the body. I have tried it and found it a failure. When you swing with your arms or your wrists, however, you have no such trouble."

Hans Wagner, needless to say, gave this decisive opinion before Babe Ruth appeared on the scene. And yet, his words ring true for most sluggers, even in Babe Ruth's era. Zack Wheat, for example, stoutly maintained that he was an arm hitter and condemed the other system. Rogers Hornsby also asserted that he was an arm hitter and he commended that system of slugging in his advice to all would-be sand lot's Hornsbys.

Even batters who are true body hitters do not always defend that system. For example, Bob Veach said, "The more a batter is in this game, the more he learns that the things he supposed were important about hitting are not really important at all. I generally get my shoulders into the swing, but if it wasn't natural for me I wouldn't do it. There are players who don't, who bat with their arms and wrists and who drive the ball just as far as I do. You sometimes see a bunt sail clear out to the infield when the batter was actually trying to coax it to roll only a few feet. You don't have to put so much strength behind the bat to get it to do its work. A sharp crack will often make the ball travel just as hard as a long, swishing wallop."

When does a batter start his swing to meet the ball? Heinie Groh said, "I aim to start my swing the instant the pitcher lets go the ball. I follow the ball every instant with my eye and try to be in a position to paste it when it crosses the rubber. Sometimes, however, when I am over-anxious, I find myself starting a bit too soon and then I know I am off my stride."

Eddie Cicotte said, "If you watch the batters carefully as I do all the time, you will notice that most of them start their swing when the ball is at least fifteen feet away. Some of them start sooner."

John Evers said, "Frank Schulte would stand with his bat over his shoulder until the ball was almost on top of him. Then he would make a lightning cut at it."

Obviously opinions even among experts differ on this important subject. Doubtless what really happens depends entirely on the batter. I once conducted a series of experiments to determine the rapidity of the end of the bat as it lunged to meet the ball. Big League players that I interviewed on the subject estimated the speed of the bat anywhere from four feet to one hundred and fifty feet per second. All of these estimates were much too low. There is good evidence to believe that the end of the bat when it is traveling at full velocity to meet the ball, moves at times with the astonishing speed of seven hundred feet per second. Camera exposures of a batter's swing one eight hundredth of a second in duration, sometimes revealed a seeming bending of the bat of nearly a foot. In other words, the bat had traveled nearly a foot during the time of exposure, one eight hundredth of a second.

Obviously what happens is this. The batter begins a forward lunge of the bat while the ball is still some distance away. But his final quick cut, the decisive cut is made when the ball is close at hand.

Doubtless the slugger, swinging from the handle, overcomes at least some part of the apparent handicap against his particular style of hitting by virtue of the fact that the end of the bat, sweeping through a long arc, travels at the moment of impact with almost incredible velocity. The chop hitter, on the other hand, swinging through a much shorter arc with a shorter bat because he has choked up on it, has less distance to cover in swinging to meet the ball. But his bat travels with proportionately less velocity.

Most great hitters are sluggers. It follows, therefore, that most systems are doubtless a combination of the two. Hans Wagner, surely one of the greatest hitters who ever lived, said, "You hear about batters who swing from the handle and there are others who choke up on the bat. I do both. Often I swing from the handle, but a good deal of the time I choke up. Lajoie always did the same thing. Fred Clarke, who was one of the wisest baseball players I ever saw and a great hitter, taught me the foot shift as an aid to batting. I have always depended upon the foot shift ever since. I always stand on my right foot when I am batting. The weight of my body comes on that foot. But I stand in such a manner that I can shift my left foot around. You can cover a good deal of ground by shifting that foot. You can step away from the plate to hit a ball close up or you can lunge right into the plate to hit a ball that is on the outside.

Ty Cobb, undoubtedly the greatest of hitters, echoed Wagner's theories. He said, "My idea of a real batter is a man who can choke up on the bat when he feels like it or slug from the handle when it is necessary. And he can accommodate himself to almost any kind of ball the pitcher gives him by stepping away, if it's too close, and wading into it if it's on the other side of the plate. A combination of proper handling the bat and good foot work will go a long way to offset any system of pitching that has ever been devised."

Hitting at Bad Balls

ROGERS HORNSBY said, "The secret of good batting, in my opinion, is to hit only good balls. That is what I would tell any young batter. Let the bad ones alone. The pitcher must put the ball over the plate or pass you. You can afford to wait. Don't be led by impatience to go after bad balls. That's exactly what the pitcher is trying to make you do. The batter should never do what the pitcher wants him to do. When the pitcher gives you a ball to your liking, then is the time to hit it and hit it hard."

Hans Wagner said, "A natural hitter will not swing at bad balls. Besides, he is a better judge of when to hit and when not to hit than the manager can possible be for he is facing the pitcher and can see the balls as they cross the plate and he can generally tell which balls he would be able to pickle, if given a chance."

Pitchers dislike a batter who wont bite at a bad ball. Walter Johnson said, "Eddie Collins is always a dangerous batter, for he is a good waiter. You can not bribe him to hit at a bad ball."

Grover Alexander said, "These wise batters with gimlet eyes that can tell the course of a baseball to a hair's breadth make pitchers grow old before their time. I particularly have in mind John Titus who used to play on the Phillies when I was with that Club. He had one of the best batting eyes I ever saw. He would take his position at the plate with the easiest and most confident air in the world. Generally he had a tooth pick in his mouth. If the ball was an inch outside of the plate, he would watch it go by and never bat an eye lash. If it was an inch inside, he wouldn't move. He would just draw in his stomach and let the ball pass. But if you put the ball over the plate, he would whale the cover off. It used to exasperate me merely to watch him. Many a time I have said to myself, 'If I were pitching, Old Man, I'd knock that tooth pick out of your mouth and maybe then you'd move.'"

Sherrod Smith said, "The first ball game I pitched against the Yankees, I passed Babe Ruth four times. It raised an awful howl from the stands, but I intentionally passed him just once. The other three times I was trying to work him, but he wouldn't work. He took his base instead. If Babe got balls somewhere near where he liked to hit them, he would bat .450. He seldom gets a good ball. A pitcher is foolish to give him a good ball, especially with men on bases."

Hitting at bad balls is a tendency of batters who chafe under managerial restrictions. For example, Bert Shotton said, "Some good batters never seem to learn to wait a pitcher out. They have an irresistible desire to hit at a ball when it is to their liking. If they are forbidden to do this, they fret and fume and are apt to hit at a bad ball. It requires not only a keen eye, but the proper mental poise to enable a batter to restrain his natural inclinations and to follow a set formula in his work."

Whatever the advantages of waiting out the pitcher and refusing to hit at bad balls, most batters fail to live up to this requirement. As Grover Alexander said, "Don't think for a minute that the batter never hits at balls unless they are over the plate. Most batters haven't a good enough eye to tell whether or not the ball is going over the plate. If it is anywhere near the line, they simply take a chance and whale away."

Babe Adams said, "There's many a safe hit made off a bad ball.

If your great slugger is so anxious to hit, let him stretch his arms a little and hit. There's no law against it."

George Dauss said, "Most batters are apt to hit the ball if it is a little outside. And most hits are made off fast balls. Curves bother the great majority of batters, although few of them will admit it."

Zack Wheat while admitting that batters often hit at bad balls, said, "They are harder to meet than the good ones. You can hit them safe, but it's more of a job."

Cy Williams said, "Of course a grooved ball is easier to hit for the circuit than any other kind. But the batter with any reputation is not going to get many grooved balls. Even a bad ball will go for a homer if you meet it right. For example, on the last day of the season of 1922, I hit a ball that was only a few inches off the ground, over the right field fence at Brooklyn."

Not all experts criticize a tendency to hit bad balls. For example, Ty Cobb while discussing Harry Heilmann said, "Perhaps he has a tendancy to hit at a bad ball. I don't know and I don't care. One thing I do know, I am not going to try to tell a fellow who is hitting for .400 how to bat."

Perhaps as Cy Williams explained, "When a batter is going good, luck seems to break for him. I remember," continued Williams, "Heinie Zimmerman in his best year. He was as good a hitter that season as I ever saw. And what was he doing? He was swinging at balls a foot over his head and driving them safe. You can get away with murder when the luck is with you."

Even good batters who seldom hit at bad balls will do so under certain conditions. For example, Ed Reulbach said, "Hans Wagner with two strikes on him was always nervously eager not to miss the next one. And he was so eager that he was likely to strike out. Willie Keeler, on the other hand, always insisted that the ball cross the plate before he would even offer at it. He would never bite at a bad ball. Wagner sometimes would."

Fear of striking out impels many batters to bite at a bad ball. Claude Williams said, "I seldom try to work the batter unless he is in a hole. There you have him at a disadvantage and he is very likely to hit at a bad ball simply because he realizes he is in a tight place and likely to be called out on strikes."

Not all batters object to bad balls, that is, at balls which are not over the plate. For example, Joe Jackson said, "I don't care whether the ball is over the plate or not, so long as it looks good. You can hit a ball just as far as a strike, if you meet it right. Batters can't be choosers. They have to take what the pitcher gives them. And pitchers are not very accommodating."

Even a very bad ball can be dangerous. For example, Walter Johnson said, "I once gave Babe Ruth a ball at least eighteen inches outside the plate. If he hit it at all I would have sworn it would go to left field. But he stepped into it, reached out with that long bat of his and actually pulled the ball around to right field for a home run."

One of the tragedies of Grover Alexander's career was woven about a certain bad ball. He said, "I hadn't allowed a hit for eight and two thirds innings. There were two men out in the ninth. And then the next fellow had to spoil a no-hit game for me by rapping out a safe bingle. I wouldn't have minded so much, but the ball he hit was so much of a ball that it was almost a wild pitch. But he swung wildly at it and managed to connect."

A bad ball isn't necessarily bad simply because it isn't over the plate. It may even be pretty good, if it's about where the batter likes to have it. For example, speaking of a certain game, Bert Niehoff said, "There was a man on third and two out. The pitcher decided to pass me to take a chance on Killifer. The count was three and nothing. He then cut loose with the fourth ball which would have given me my base, but he edged it a little closer to the plate, about the elevation I like to have the ball and about the kind of a ball I like to hit. I couldn't resist the temptation, and though it looked like bad baseball, I met the ball and drove it out for a solid two-bagger. Incidently, that hit won the game."

Sometimes the umpire's reputation has a direct bearing on hitting at bad balls. Said Rogers Hornsby, "I have sometimes swung at a bad ball that was not a true strike because I didn't dare take a chance on the umpire's calling it a ball. A good many safe hits are lost on this account. Very likely the umpire isn't to blame. He does his best, but when you have to swing at a really bad ball, you kiss good-bye to most of your chance of hitting safely."

"Hitting at bad balls,' said Urban Shocker, "is the greatest favor the batter can do the pitcher. For consider this. Above all

47

things the pitcher dislikes a waiter. The waiter makes him extend himself, pitch more balls and keep putting them over the plate. There's a common saying in baseball, 'If you have the batter swinging you have him beat.' Naturally if you have him swinging you can feed him on bad balls a good deal of the time."

Nevertheless hitting at bad balls, though a failure in theory, does not work out so poorly in actual practice. For from his experience of thirty years in baseball, John McGraw said, "There are as many safe hits made off balls as off strikes."

Hitting the Next Ball

"THERE comes a tide in the affairs of men," says Shakespeare, most famous of baseball scribes "which taken at the flood leads on to fortune." That particular time in the experience of the batter at the plate occurs when it becomes his duty to hit the next ball.

In a sense, the batter is on the defensive. As Ernest Shore said, "There is little he can do except stand at the plate and hit what the pitcher may give him. His only choice is a choice of the ball. And you will see a batter trying to shift his system within the narrow limits at his command, either by stinging the first ball pitched or by adopting the opposite extreme and waiting the pitcher out."

Whatever he elects to do, however, assuming that the pitcher doesn't give him four balls, the batter is sooner or later confronted with the imperative necessity of "hitting it out." Bert Shotton said "No rule in baseball is a hard and fast proposition which must always be followed. Someone has said that rules were made to be broken. That is certainly true of the waiting rule. While I do not usually try to hit at the first strike and commonly let even two strikes cross the rubber before offering at the ball, there are times when I hit at the first ball pitched."

Having spent several innings in sizing up the pitcher, the manager will frequently order his batters to hit the first ball. John McGraw said, "After you have played the waiting game for a time, it is frequently good policy to order a sudden change. With a break in the luck, for games like battles are often decided by breaks, you may shell the pitcher off the mound before he wakes up to his own danger."

This system is advisable under certain conditions. Ty Cobb said, "With men on bases, I generally lay for the first ball over the plate. It's dollars to dimes if the pitcher can put that first one over he will do it. The majority of batters will pass it up no matter if it cuts the plate. I favor going after that ball. Nine times out of ten I go to the plate prepared to kill the first one if it's over."

"In general," continued Ty, "it's good policy to go after a ball that the pitcher doesn't expect you to hit. You can read his mind to some extent. Take the extreme case where the count is three balls and no strikes. The batter will get bawled out from the bench for going after the next one and generally he will deserve it. But I have hit the next one under those circumstances on the logical theory that the pitcher was bound to get it over, that he wouldn't expect me to hit and that he wouldn't have so much stuff on the ball. And I have made hits by pulling just that unexpected play."

There is one period in the game where the batter is called upon to hit the next ball no matter how unlikely he is to come through. That is when he has signalled the runner for the hit and run play.

Sometimes with a runner on bases, Max Carey takes issue with Ty Cobb on hitting the first ball pitched. But he had in mind the welfare of the runner rather than the batter. He said, "If there is a fast man on first the batter should refrain from hitting the first ball pitched. Hans Wagner was a great player and smart. He used to follow me in the batting order and he might have been very helpful to me in stealing bases. But he wasn't. He liked to hit too well. If the first ball looked good to him, he would pickle it. Naturally I got little chance to steal."

Hitting at unexpected times is doubtless good policy. George Sisler said, "There is a tendency in baseball to hit cripples. With the count three and one, batters will figure the pitcher has to get it over and will swing at the ball. The pitcher occasionally crosses them by divining what they have in mind and giving them a bad one. I have never yet hit with the count three and one. Batters occasionally do this, but I question if it is good dope."

That rare exception, however, does work at times. William Killifer said, "It is best to ignore the established rules of baseball now and then. For example, in a game at Brooklyn I had Hollocher hit with the count three and one. Most people would call this foolish. But there were two men on and he came through with a hit. I had a reason for calling the play and it worked. But the fans razzed me unmercifully. Some of them asked me if I didn't know anything about baseball."

The oft repeated slogan of the fans is true, "It only takes one to hit it."

Pulling the Ball

ROGERS HORNSBY said, "Very few batters are true straight away hitters. That is, most batters have a preference for one field or the other. I am a right handed batter and would ordinarily be supposed to hit better into left field. Such is not the case. I actually hit harder into right field. I believe this is because I step into the ball and try to hit straight away. I seldom pull the ball."

Ed Reulbach, one of the cagiest pitchers who ever lived, listed a tendency to pull the ball as a batting weakness. He said, "A batting weakness so-called, is not the sole worry of the batter. He may have a dangerous tendency to hit in a certain direction most of the time. Perhaps he is a left field hitter who is known to be such. If so, unless he is a slugger, he is often at the mercy of the opposing pitcher and fielders. Roy Thomas was an example of such a hitter. He not only hit almost all the time to left field, but he was a short field hitter as well. This tendency handicapped him tremendously. When Thomas was at bat, the left fielder moved close to the foul line and came well in. The center fielder shifted away over toward left and at the same time advanced close up behind short and second. Third baseman moved over nearly to the foul line, and the shortstop followed him to a point at least fifteen feet beyond his natural position. At the same time he fell back and played a rather deep field. With this combination against him, Thomas was like clay in the hands of the pitcher. Mordecai Brown was a pitcher with excellent control and he doted on just such a situation. He would shoot over a fast ball on the outside of the plate and away from Thomas, who was a left handed hitter. In nine cases out of ten Thomas was literally forced to hit the ball to left field. There were four fielders waiting for him instead of one, or at the most two. Thomas naturally realized the force of the conspiracy against him. But if he tried to pull the ball to the other field, the nearest he could come to that aim would be perhaps to loop it over the pitcher's box. But the second baseman was also in the conspiracy. When shortstop moved over, second baseman followed, so that instead of being considerably to the right of second base, he was literally in line with the bag, so he was waiting ready for the ball if Thomas "pulled" it. The sole defence against such a conspiracy is ability to hit hard. Thomas, however, unfortunately for him, did not possess this ability."

Donie Bush outlined much the same situation and its sole cure. He said, "Almost all batters have a tendency to hit to one field or the other and the opposing pitchers and fielders make capital of that tendency all the time. Usually the pitcher would encourage the batter to hit to his natural field, arranging his fielders to cut off any possible base hit. It's a pretty combination and very difficult to overcome. Sometimes, however, where the batter is a slugger, the pitcher knows it will be dangerous to let him hit the ball where hitting is easy for him, so the pitcher will try to compel him to pull the ball into another field, having his fielders stationed there to take care of the ball when it comes their way. For example, Frank Baker is a dead right field hitter. But in a pinch it certainly isn't safe to let him hit to right, for he hits too hard. No matter how many fielders you put there, he is likely to drive the ball through them or over their heads."

The fielders are well aware of the batter's natural tendencies. Dave Bancroft said, "There are some hitters that you can bank on to hit a certain kind of a ball in a certain direction. I always aim to take up my position in short field where the opposing batter is likely to drive the ball, if he connects."

A natural tendency to hit the ball in a certain direction is generally regarded as a defect. For example, John McGraw said of Davis Robertson, "He will be a better hitter when he has corrected a tendency to drive the ball into right field." However, not a few batters accept this tendency of theirs and make the most of it. In fact, it often becomes a strong point in their batting repertoire. Roger Peckinpaugh was a dead left field hitter. He knew it and at one time tried to overcome this tendency. Later he decided rather to make the best of it. He said, "I admit I did not succeed in overcoming my natural preference for hitting to left field. On the other hand, I practiced hitting to that field, getting my full strength behind the ball. As a result I hit hard and I don't believe my batting average suffered."

Some batters have tried to develop a tendency to hit to a certain field. For example, Jacques Fournier said, "I had generally been a left field hitter. But one winter I got to thinking the situation over. I figured that if I could pull the ball a little more, being a left hand hitter, I could get my strength behind it and drive it a good deal harder toward right field. Slugging seemed to be the order of the day and a right field hitter, if he hits hard enough, can sometimes drive the ball over the fence. To be sure, the fielders would lay for me in right, but I wouldn't object to that so long as I could get enough force behind the ball."

Ty Cobb, though he regarded place hitting as the secret of his success, developed a tendency to pull the ball to left field. This was entirely contrary to his natural bent. He said, "As a left handed batter, I could reasonably be expected to hit more easily into right field. I admit I can hit harder toward right than anywhere else. But I have schooled myself to hit toward left. Usually it is better to hit to left than to right. If you happen to make an infield hit, there is a much longer throw from the shortstop than there is from the second baseman. It follows that more often it is advisable for me to hit to left field and that is where I do hit more than half the time."

With the exception of Ty Cobb, Babe Ruth doubtless pulls the ball more effectively than any other batter. But his tendency is all toward right field. Still Babe, in his early years, objected to this tendency. He said, "When hitting to right field, a left hand batter takes a half swing and calls into play all the strength of his shoulders and his arms. When he hits to left field, he pushes the bat more. To gain success as a batter, however, a man must be able to hit to both fields."

Fearsome stories of Babe's ability to pull the ball are current. George Dauss said, "I have pitched a ball to Babe that was at least a foot and a half off the plate, on the outside. But Babe reached out with those long arms of his and pulled the ball into the right field stands."

Pulling the ball is natural or acquired. When natural it is a mere tendency to hit in a certain direction. This tendency is bad for weak hitters, but may even be a source of strength to sluggers. The acquired art of pulling the ball is most frequently seen in the batter's determination to cross the pitcher by hitting toward his natural field or by those select few known as place hitters. Some batters, including conspicuous examples like Rogers Hornsby and Tris Speaker, are straight away hitters and seldom make any effort to pull the ball. Pulling the ball from the batter's viewpoint is like the famous proverb: "One man's meat is another man's poison."

The Pros and Cons of Left Hand Batting

THE advantages of batting left handed is generally recognized. Said George Sisler, "Most of the great hitters have schooled themselves to hit from the near side of the plate, though they may be left-handed in no other respect. From this side the runner has a shorter sprint to first base. This difference, three to four feet, in many cases decides whether or not a batted ball is safe. Again, the left-handed batter normally swings into his stride and should be in a position to make a quicker get-away to first than the right-hander."

Max Carey develops this idea. He said, "Naturally I was a right-handed hitter. But I forced myself to learn left-handed batting. Even now I can hit a ball harder right-handed, but the percentage in favor of the left-handed batter is too great to be ignored, especially where the batter wishes to capitalize his speed as I have done. I am very sure, for example, that if Rogers Hornsby batted left-handed, he would better his present average by at least thirty points."

Natural left-handers in baseball have always been the butt of much good natured criticism. Said Nick Altrock, "I am a left-hander, and in baseball a left-hander is always a 'nut.' He is guilty and it is up to him to prove himself innocent, if he wants to try. I never tried myself. So long as they insisted on calling me a 'nut' anyway, it seemed easier to be a 'nut' than to prove that I wasn't one."

Eppa Rixey defended left-handers in a humorous paragraph which has a strong under current of sound sense. "There are," admitted Rixey, " 'some nuts' among us left-handers. But look at all the right-handers who have their wires crossed. I tell you we are not properly appreciated, we left-handers. We are really a small and select circle. I believe something like two out of one hundred people are born left-handed. If that percentage is correct, then perhaps 2 percent. of the ball players should be left-handers. But there is really a larger percentage. And not only that, but among the limited number of left-handers, see how many are genuine stars. There are Babe Ruth and George Sisler and Tris Speaker and Jake Daubert and Edd Roush, to say nothing of the left-handed pitchers. What would baseball be without left-handers?"

Walter Pipp reminds us that in one position at least left-handers are at a premium. "They are something of a joke in baseball," admitted Pipp, "but every manager would like to have a left-hander on first base. The left-hander can make a quicker throw to second than the right-hander. And the nature of his work requires him to throw to second base much more often than to any other."

Harry Heilmann admitted the heavy handicap under which a right-hander must hit, but he, nevertheless, defended the style "which comes natural to a man." "A lot of good hitters," said Heilmann, were born right-handers, but have made themselves over into left-hand hitters. The man who does that may better his average, but he suffers at least one defect. He can't hit so hard. No doubt I lose a few hits because I am further from first base and can't get a quick start. But in my opinion I make up for that loss by hitting the ball harder. If you hit the ball hard enough, it will go through the infield like a sieve, unless it happens to be aimed directly at a fielder. In other words, one type of hitting capitalizes speed, the short sprint and the quick start; the other capitalizes ability to hammer the ball hard."

Left-handed batters suffer greatly from left-handed pitching. This, however, according to some batting experts, is a difficulty that can be overcome. Said Ty Cobb, "I have been bothered by left-handed pitchers all my life and even now I can't say that I like to see one of those fellows on the mound. I believe, however, that in the case of a good hitter, the handicap against port side hurling is greatly exaggerated. I will go on record with a statement that any good hitter can conquer left-handed pitchers if he is given the opportunity to go in there and learn how."

Right-handers also object to right-handed pitching, though not so strenuously. Harry Heilmann said, "I find it harder to hit against right-handers than I do against left-handers. This is specially true of a curve ball. Many players are not curve ball hitters. They prefer to face almost anything rather than a curve thrown from the side of the plate they bat on. Left-handed batters usually like right-handed pitchers. Now there are probably four right-handed pitchers in baseball to one left-hander. Hence, it follows that the left-handers enjoy a much greater opportunity to hit the type of pitching they thrive on than the righ-handers do."

On the other hand, George Sisler, a natural left-handed hitter, finds one curious item against left-handed batting. He said, "I admit the difficulties in hitting from that side of the platter. But like all other things, there are compensations. It is much more difficult for a left-hander to bunt toward third than it is for a right-hander, because the infielders are looking for just that kind of play. Usually they play well in at any stage of the game when the batter would be likely to bunt. Against right-handers they are not so cautious. Hence, I have often thought that it would pay a right-hander to bunt toward third."

Admitting that both types of batting have their advantages and defects, a few batters, such as Max Carey and Frank Frisch, shift from one side of the plate to the other, depending upon the type of pitching. Frank Frisch explained his system. "Though I usually bat left-handed, I switch to the other side of the plate when a port side pitcher is in the box. That gets rid of all possible risk of being bothered by a left-hander. Personally, I haven't found it difficult to shift. I took up the system because I used to be uncommonly weak against left-handed pitchers. I remember once in spring training I got hit twice in the chest because I couldn't see the ball at all, when a left-hander was pitching. Bancroft coached me to switch to the other side of the plate with very good results. I would think that more managers would recommend this shift to left-handed batters who find it difficult to hit port side pitching."

When a right-handed batter changes to a left-hander, he develops a tendency to pull the ball to right field. This is because he can hit harder to that particular field. Cy Williams said, "Theoretically it is better to be able to hit to either field. But most good batters are either right or left-field hitters. That is because they can naturally hit hardest in that particular direction. As I am a left-field hitter, I have developed a tendency to hit into right field. This was not always the case. When I was at college, I hit as often to one field as the other. When I entered the National League, however, and tried to capitalize my ability to hit hard, I naturally developed into a right-field hitter. This tendency is likely to prove costly. I don't doubt that my own proclivity at hitting right field smashes has cut down my average perhaps forty points. But it hasn't robbed me of many extra base hits. For if I can really get behind the ball the way I want to, with my full strength and the full force of my swing, I can hit it beyond the point where the fielders bother me."

Rogers Hornsby, greatest of right-hand hitters, is inclined to ignore the batter's pitching preference. "One of the greatest fallacies in baseball, said he, "is the theory that a left-handed batter can not hit left-handed pitching. This is a theory that has been advanced by most managers and has become prevalent in the past few years. I believe it is growing There are plausible reasons for it. Players who accept the theory at its face value believe they can not hit certain types of pitching. By working the groove of this idea in a player's mind, his confidence is shaken and he fails to hit, largely because he has been taught to believe that he can't hit. Besides, the manager will not give him the chance to practice against left-handers and this in itself adds to his batting weakness. Theories are all right in their place, but in my opinion a lot of good batters have been spoiled simply because they have been taught to believe they cannot do certain things."

Batting With the Feet

SPEED of foot is a talent in itself wholly unrelated to batting ability. And yet speed is of such importance in batting that it has proved the explanation of more than one championship.

Cactus Cravath said, "The present system of batting averages is all in favor of the man who is fast on his feet, who can beat out bunts and scratch singles." This is true, but speed of foot is a help in batting to a far greater degree than appears from the averages.

Frank Frisch said, "Speed is mixed up with batting more than some people imagine. Many a bunt or an infield hit is safe if you can run fast enough. Many a single can be stretched to a double if your feet can negotiate the distance."

Jake Daubert in the best season he ever knew, when he won the batting championship of the National League, admitted that his success was due to the fact that he had beat out an unusual number of infield hits. In explanation Jake said, "Speed is a big part of batting success. It is thirty yards from home plate to first base. I figure that a fast runner will cover this distance at least one stride sooner than the slow runner. That means that the fast man would have beaten out the throw on the same play that retired the slow man. Now both, we will say, hit the ball equally well, equally hard and true. It wasn't batting that decided whether the blow would be a hit or an out. It was speed. You see many a play of this kind," continued Jake. "A fast man may drive the ball to shortstop and beat out the throw by a foot. The slow runner would be an easy out on the same play. Not a few batters hit perhaps .250 with their hands and add a good fifty points with their feet. That's one way of hitting .300."

Fritz Maisel, one of the fastest of runners and a great base stealer said, "I was always fast on my feet, I guess the fastest in my neck of the woods. I use speed in base running mostly, but of course it plays a big part in batting.

In reality speed is merely a method whereby the player makes the most of his hitting ability. Speed transforms outs to scratch singles and mere singles to doubles. As John McGraw said, "Fast base running and good sliding are great helps to hitting. This is the only way to make hits count for their full value."

Clifton Heathcote, a fast man and good base stealer, said, "I am not the best batter in the world, but I make my legs pay for their passage. Speed of foot, after all, is as much a part of batting as meeting the ball fair and true. The fast man beats out many a crippled grounder that would be an easy out for the ice wagon. Speed of foot, just like speed of the batted ball, works to the advantage of the batter."

William Killifer said, "Speed is the most encouraging talent a young player can have. When he knows he is fast, this naturally helps him not only in fielding but also in batting. Frank Frisch has been the most scintillating player on the diamond. Take away his speed, however, and where would he class. Speed makes even a mediocre ball player look brilliant. The fast ball club scores runs on a minimum of hits. Speed makes baseball ability show up for a little more than it is really worth."

Speed plays a prominent part in extra base hits. At first blush long hits would seem to be the special province of the slugger. They are really the province of the speed artist as well. For example, Ty Cobb said, "Taking an extra base on a momentary fumble may seem like an act of quick thinking. It is, I suppose. And yet the one unvarying rule of my career has been always to go as far as possible on a hit. I have taken many desperate chances and have lost out a lot of times. That was inevitable. But taking chances is only another way of 'playing the game.'"

How a temporary loss of speed can cripple a hitter was well illustrated by Jake Daubert when he was suffering from a strained tendon in one leg. He said, "My bad leg in itself is enough to account for most of my batting slump. I have always been successful in beating out bunts and infield hits. Naturally in doing so I use a good degree of speed. If your speed is cut down even a little, you will be thrown out at first on the close ones. My bad leg has cut my batting average at least thirty points."

Frank Snyder bewailed his slowness of foot. He said, "I have always been handicapped in my batting by a lack of speed. I don't believe I have made half a dozen infield hits a year. The ball has to go some for me to reach first base. Apply that rule to a lot of fast young batters and see how their averages would shrink if you cut out the close hits."

Even the Official Scorers make a bad matter worse by unconsciously favoring speed. Lew McCarty said, "I am one of those slow boys on the bases. The Official Scorers never give me the better of a decision on a close one. The speeders get those breaks and it fattens their batting averages all the more."

Speed alone, however, is not sufficient. It requires good judgment also. Hugh Jennings said, "One of the fastest men I ever knew, a real speed marvel, was out of place on the bases. Whenever he got to first he clogged the base paths. Much slower men than he greatly excelled him, for he did not know how to use his speed."

Elaborating this idea, Max Carey said, "I have always made speed of foot the basis of my work in the Majors. Whatever reputation I have earned is due mainly to the ability I possess of getting over the ground rapidly. To my mind, however, natural speed while important, and in fact necessary in any brilliant showing on the base paths, is of no great consequence unless improved to the limit. Here I believe many ball players make a serious mistake. Because they are naturally fast they assume that speed will tell in their work with no particular study or exertion on their part. Whereas speed must be developed and used with as good judgment as batting or fielding."

Davis Robertson was very fast and capitalized his speed of foot. In fact he preferred making an infield hit to a long single. He said, "It is foolish to predict a batting average, but I am quite certain I could have developed into a .350 hitter if I had been left alone. I developed a quick get-away which carried me to first base as fast as any of them. In fact, I grew so sure of myself in making this quick start that I preferred to rap out an infield hit rather than to drive the ball to the outfield. This may sound absurd, but it isn't, for an infield hit gets the infield up in the air and unsteadies them more quickly than anything else I can think of. I practiced infield hitting until I had it down pretty fine. I discovered that the instantaneous start after you hit the ball was very essential, but by no means the only thing to be considered. Above all things, I study the pitcher, and what I did any fast man could do. Many pitchers have little peculiarities which aid the infield hitter. For example, if the pitcher is accustomed to take a long stride forward just as he is in the act of delivering the ball, he can not recover himself quickly enough to beat me in the race to first base, if he is called upon to cover that bag while the first baseman is chasing the ball. So if you can contrive to dump a neat little infield hit just out of his reach, so that the first baseman must chase it, you have a fine opportunity of making first."

George Sisler said, "I believe I do not exaggerate when I say I was naturally as fast as Cobb. But unlike him, I have never made a close study of infield hitting. Ordinarily an infield hit is a mistake except in the case of a bunt. The batter didn't intend to make an infield hit. Cobb has his system and with that system he is unconquerable. But, while I admit he has been my model, I have not followed him in every respect. Still I fully appreciate the importance of speed. I doubt if any hitter who is a slow runner could continue to hit for .350, let alone a higher average."

Sluggers miss speed of foot the least. For example, Cactus Cravath said, "They call me wooden shoes and piano legs and a few other pet names. I do not claim to be the fastest man in the world, but I can get around the bases with a fair wind and all sails set. And so long as I am busting the old apple on the seam, I am not worrying a great deal about my legs."

Not a few fast men lose much of the value of their speed by foolish mannerisms. Ed Reulbach once conducted some experiments on this interesting phase of the question. He said, "It is a curious sight to see so many batters lose valuable time in watching the ball. Perhaps every batter is guilty of this fault to some extent, but the masters of the craft generally avoid this particular mistake. It takes the average batter from three and three-fifths to three and four-fifths seconds to go from home plate to first base. If this same average batter would make the best possible use of his speed, his efforts would meet with success much more often than they do. Now one of the things which handicaps him is the well-nigh fatal tendency to watch the ball. I once sat through a World's Series with a man who had been an expert timer at athletic events, who brought his stop watch. I had often wondered just how much effect watching the ball had on batting. But I had never before enjoyed the opportunity of finding out. Here are a few interesting things that happened.

"Harry Hooper, a fast man, beat out a single to first on a very close play in three and two-fifths seconds. Later in the game he made a solid smash, slowed up a little on his way to first to watch the ball and reached the bag in four seconds flat. On that particular play he could not have made second base, but he lost three-fifths of a second by watching the ball none the less. On another occasion he just beat the throw to second on a hit that went as a double. Again he slowed up on his way to first and reached the bag in four seconds flat. He then sprinted desperately for second base and just made it, without an atom of time to spare. He would have made it easily had he not loafed on his way to first. As it was, he might well have been thrown out instead of being safe at second. That one play might have changed the score of the game, might conceivably have altered the winning of the Championship. Such important results often come in baseball from a misspent fraction of a second.

"Watching the ball on his progress to first base costs the runner often at least three-fifths of a second. A fast man will go fifteen feet in that length of time. That shows how a man can cut down his speed by the unnecessary habit of watching the ball."

Grover Alexander once contrasted Brooklyn with the Giants. He said, "A Giant player gets to first. Almost any kind of a single advances him to third. Then the least little slip will score him. A Brooklyn player gets to first. A single will send him to second base, but no further. It takes a lot to score him from second. As a result the Giants make a much stronger offensive, not because they are better hitters or better players, but because they make the most of their hits by sheer speed of foot. Speed on the base paths very often spells the difference between a pennant winner and an also-ran."

Bert Shotton said, "Speed of foot is natural and perhaps cannot be acquired. But there is one element of speed, fast or slow men can learn. That is a quick getaway. And a quick getaway is half the battle."

Maurice Archdeacon, called by Ty Cobb "the fastest thing in a spiked shoe," said, "I believe I can get to first base as quickly as anyone I ever saw. That is not because I am naturally fast of foot, but because I make a quick getaway."

Pep Young said, "A good deal of getting down to first is due to the start. Some men have already taken a full stride and are going full speed before other batters have even started. A quick start is just as important as speed, after you get started, perhaps it is even more important, considering the shortness of the sprint. I am often on my way to first before I have even met the ball with my bat."

Cy Williams said, "One reason for Ty Cobb's amazing success was his quick start. He was the only batter I ever heard of who could take one jump and be going full speed ahead."

Davis Robertson, while admitting the value of the quick start, points out an element of danger. He said, "Like all other good things, this quick getaway has its drawbacks. It gives the batter a tendency to pull the ball. In my own case it has led to my becoming known as a right-field hitter, for when a left-hander hits to right field it often means that he has hit a fraction of a second sooner than he would have done had he hit to center or left. In trying to speed up his start, he hits that fraction of a second sooner and thus pulls the ball to right field."

Fred Clarke gives a melancholy reminder of the veteran players' inevitable end. He said, "I believe my batting eye was just as good when I quit baseball as it ever was, but my legs were beginning to slow up. I could detect the difference with almost mathematical certainty. When I was a young fellow I could rap out a hit and beat the throw to first base by two feet. Years passed. I could then beat the throw by a single foot. Later it became a nip and tuck race. Then finally the inevitable happened. They began to get me at first by a foot or two. For me it was the danger signal. I knew it was time to say good-bye to baseball."

The Secret of Heavy Hitting

"THE public," said Rogers Hornsby, "likes to have a batter slug almost as well as he likes to slug himself. There is more war whooping and general hullabaloo in the stands when someone knocks a homer than from almost any other cause. Dinky little hits are all right enough and no doubt scientific, but ball players and spectators alike want to hear the bat meet the ball with a resounding crack and sizzle through the air as it skyrockets across the field."

Hornsby's expressed opinion is doubtless correct. Slugging has fairly dominated baseball in recent years. And there was a time when it played an even more commanding role. As John McGraw said, "When I broke into the game thirty odd years ago, I was considered something of a freak. Ball players at that time were selected much as football players are now—for their size. Unless a player were a six-footer and husky to boot, he wouldn't command much attention as a player. Size and weight were supposed to be necessary because a ball player in those days was, first of all, a batter and a slugger. And the bigger a man was, the harder he could hit. This was rather primitive reasoning, but the records of those days will show that most well known players were big men who put a lot of beef behind their wallops and frequently drove the ball for a homer."

Governor Tener, reminiscening of still earlier days, remarked, "My recollection of famous sluggers goes back to Pop Anson.

Anson was a terrific hitter. And there were others. Ed Delehanty could hit the ball an awful wallop. And Nap Lajoie was a heavy hitter."

The advantages of slugging are obvious. As Cactus Cravath remarked, "With men on bases, it is not scratch singles or bunts that clear those bases. It is the long, extra base clout. The big man in the pinch is the batter who can drive out a crashing double, knock the opposing pitcher out of the box with a well placed home run; who, even when he does not connect safely, can be depended on for a long fly to the outfield that will score a runner from third."

Slugging has not received the credit it deserves in the playing records. For example, Victor Saier said, "One player may outhit another fifty points in the averages and yet be a less valuable batter. There are many chapters to batting that have never been written. The only one the experts take the trouble to write is the exact ratio between the number of times at bat and the number of safe hits. That's only one of a good many things to consider. Chief of these is extra base hitting."

Harry Heilmann illustrated the value of slugging from his own experience. He said, "Since I am not a place hitter like Ty Cobb, I have to follow a much different system, if I can call it a system. The place hitter is successful because he can drop the ball more or less at will where the fielders can't get it. For batters who can do that sort of thing, all right. But there are not so many of them that they are crowding the Big League circuits. My system is much simpler. I try to hit the ball as hard and as often as I can. I know that if I hit the ball often I will get a fair percentage of safe hits. I know that if I hit hard that percentage will greatly increase, for a hard batted ball will drive through the infield where an easy tap would be fielded. Hitting a ball hard really reduces the ability of the infielders and the outfielders to cover ground. The slugger makes fielding ineffective in two ways. He gives the fielder less time to cover ground. He also gives him a more difficult chance to handle. Besides, the hard hit ball will net more bases and drive in more runs than the ordinary placed hit."

Chet Thomas commented upon driving the ball through by sheer force. He said, "Babe Ruth hits the ball so hard that it does things that no other batter can make it do. A line drive from his bat over the infielders' heads will take a quick drop to the ground and carrom off at all sorts of freak angles. If he hits the ball on the ground it seldom bounds true, for there is so much English on it."

Carl Mays said, "I have seen Babe top a ball so badly that he almost missed it. But he put so much force behind it, it bounded through the infield for a single."

William Killifer said, "Of late years baseball has fallen into a rut. The game has become a slugging match. The fine points of pitching and aggressive base running have gone into the discard. The most careful pitching in the world is no proof against an occasional long fly and a long fly hit hard enough, and perhaps the sport of the wind, may sail into the stands for a home run. Such long flies are the curse of good pitching and break up many an otherwise interesting ball game. Besides, the lure of the home run has completely distorted batting values."

Red Faber said, "The sluggers have wrecked baseball. They are a thorn in the side of every pitcher. You never know when you have the game won. A home run dumped into the stands may rob you of a victory any time until the last man is out."

Bob Veach said, "I have watched a good many players who try to murder the ball, and in my opinion they are all guilty of the same fundamental fault. Their chief thought is to drive the pellet a mile. But distance is only the second thing to consider. The first and most important is to hit the ball square. In fixing their attention on distance, these would-be sluggers are apt to fail when it comes to meeting the ball."

Trying to murder the ball, as Veach said, has doubtless damaged many a batting record. Most batters admit this. But home run hitting, according to Cy Williams, has never cut into his batting record.

"My whole object," said Cy, "is to hit safe. Homers are merely incidental. Never in my life have I deliberately tried to hit a homer."

Rogers Hornsby defended slugging without any qualification. He said, "Common advice on the diamond is, 'Don't try to kill the ball.' To me this sounds exactly like, 'Don't try to be a good batter,' for surely all the leading batters in both leagues are sluggers. Roush and Wheat and Cravath all swing from the handle. Ty Cobb pickles the ball and so does Tris Speaker. Joe Jackson is a true slugger and Babe Ruth is the best of the lot. Hans Wagner and Lajoie were sluggers. Most, if not all, the great hitters, past or present, were sluggers. There's a reason for this. The natural way of doing a thing is the correct way. Watch a bunch of kids playing ball on the sand lots and see how many of them slug, easily 100%. Only when the batter has faced a clever pitcher and his own shortcomings are revealed, does he fall back on chop hitting. And he does so simply because he isn't a good hitter." To Hornsby, slugging and good hitting are one and the same.

So much for slugging pro and con. What is the secret of heavy hitting? Babe Ruth, admittedly the prince of sluggers, might pose as the leading authority on the subject. Babe once attempted to explain to me the theory of his terrific hitting. "Well," said Babe, thoughtfully, "I am not a little guy. Hitting hard is strength and weight as much as anything else. I am tall and heavy and strong in the arms and the shoulders. And it isn't just strength and weight. Height and long arms are an advantage. A tall man, especially if his arms are long, can get a better swipe at a baseball than a shorter man of the same strength and weight. The stronger a man is and the heavier he is, the harder he can lean on a baseball. It is like boxing. In the ring they say a good big man can always beat a good little man. But, of course," continued Babe, "I wouldn't say beef was everything. My theory is that the bigger the bat, the faster the ball will travel. It's really the weight of the bat that drives the ball. My bat weighs 52 ounces. Most bats weigh 36 to 40 ounces. Do you see those mud hooks?" continued Babe, extending his enormous hands. I pleaded guilty to the accusation. No microscope is required to see Babe's hands. "There's a lot of strength in those hands," said Babe, as he gripped the handle of the bat until the muscles stood bunched and knobbed on the backs of those hands and his sinewy fingers seemed embedded in the solid wood. "And do you notice anything about those hands?" continued Babe, as he unclasped them and extended them, palm up. I looked and saw that there were callous spots on the hands and fingers. "I got those from gripping this old war club," said Babe. "The harder you grip the bat, the faster the ball will travel. When I am out after a homer, I try to make mush of this solid ash handle and I carry through with the bat. When I swing to meet the baseball, I follow it all the way around. You know, in boxing, when you hit a man your first generally stops

65

right there, but it is possible to hit a man so hard that your fist doesn't stop. When I carry through with the bat, it is for the same reason.

"And footwork is important. You often hear of a batter being 'set to swing.' That means he has a toe hold so that he can hit the ball hard.

"And the eye is always important. The main thing in hitting is to hit the ball fair. You may rap out a fluke single off the handle of your bat. But you wont knock it into the stands unless you meet it with the heavy part of your bat, just right. That means a good eye."

Babe Ruth is, and doubtless will remain, the grand model of baseball sluggers. Walter Johnson said, "I have often been asked what I consider the secret of Babe's heavy hitting. To me this is simple. He has a good batting eye. He is tall, heavy and strong. His weight is in his shoulders, where it will do him the most good. He is a tremendously powerful man. He uses an enormous bat, so heavy that most players would find it an impossible burden. To him, however, it is just right. He grasps the bat with an iron grip and when he meets the ball he follows it through with his full strength and weight. For his size, Joe Jackson is as hard a hitter as Ruth, but that margin of thirty pounds in weight and enormous reserve strength enables Ruth to give the ball that extra punch which drives it further than anybody else on the diamond."

Slugging, however, is not necessarily a matter of build. Bob Veach once brought out this point. He said, "Sam Crawford always claimed that the stronger and heavier a man was the harder he could hit a baseball. Other things being equal this is doubtless true. But other things are not always equal. I am rather below average baseball size and tip the scales at 160 pounds. But I could always give the old baseball a jolt when I met it right. One thing I discovered early. There are all kinds of sluggers. Some are big, burly brutes. But others who are slender can pulverize the old horsehide. I have found that the best system for slugging is to develop a style which will insure your hitting the ball hard and then forget about it. Put all your attention into hitting the ball. If you do, it will travel. Learn to hit hard unconsciously. If you try to slug with a conscious effert, aiming to drive the ball a mile, the chances are you will miss it altogether."

Rogers Hornsby, a fearsome slugger, was also of the slender type. He explained slugging as follows: "I have a considerable amount of strength in my shoulders and arms, but I do not lay my long hitting to any unusual strength. I believe it is due rather to meeting the ball fair, with a quick snap motion that sends it straight and true out over the diamond. The popular idea of a slugger," continued Hornsby, "is a huge man with beefy shoulders who swings a bat too heavy for the ordinary hitter. Most, if not all great sluggers, were strong in their wrists and shoulders. Even if they were not big, heavy men, most of them were tall men, for a tall man can get a better swing at the ball than a short man. It doesn't follow, however, that a heavy bat is necessary. Some sluggers use heavy bats. Chief Meyers did and so does Babe Ruth. Most batters will find that an extra heavy bat cuts down the speed of their swing more than enough to offset what the extra weight of the bat can accomplish. I prefer a rather light bat. I find I can handle it to better purpose. There are two things which drive a baseball hard; the weight of the bat and the speed with which it moves. The two are direct opposites. No matter how much strength a batter has, he cannot handle a heavy bat with as much speed as he would a light bat. You can swing a light bat with a quick snap of your wrists that will drive the ball with great force. In fact, if I were giving advice on the subject, I would say that in general the chop hitter would best use a heavy bat and the slugger a light one. The chop hitter pokes at the ball and the weight of the bat is important in getting force behind the blow. The slugger, however, swings his bat through a big arc. He can meet a sharp curve much better with a light bat than he could possibly do with a heavy one."

Harry Heilmann also took issue with Babe Ruth on the subject of bats. "It isn't so much the weight of the bat," said Harry, "which drives the ball. It's the quick snap you get in your wrists. It's the same principle as cracking a whip. It isn't so much the weight of the whip. It's the quick snap of the lash which cuts. I discount weight in a bat almost entirely. In fact, I use a light bat and I think Babe Ruth, with all his success as a slugger, would be a greater hitter if he discarded that wagon tongue of his. There is only one type of ball that a heavy bat can drive farther than a light bat. That is a straight, fast one, over the plate. Such a ball

Babe could hit a mile. But how many such balls do the pitchers give him? Curves and slow balls and bad balls in general he could hit harder even than he does if he used a lighter bat with a quick snap of his wrists."

Grover Alexander emphasized this point when he referred to Hack Miller, the Cubs' strong man. "Even slugging at its worst," said Grover, "is something of a science. It is surely not a mere matter of strength and weight. If it were, Hack Miller would be the greatest slugger in either league, for he is by all odds the strongest man on the major circuits. But Rogers Hornsby can hit the ball harder than Hack. Miller is short, thick-set, ponderous. Hornsby is tall, loose-jointed, of slender build. Hack could take him in his two hands and double him over his knees. In strength there is simply no comparison. Besides, Hack probably outweighs Hornsby by forty pounds. Still, Hornsby is the harder hitter of the two."

Some sluggers, according to Hornsby, are not consistently good hitters. "Big, burly batters," he says, "who swing from their shoe tops look impressive and when they do connect the ball travels. But they strike out often and are at the mercy of a clever pitcher with a slow curve. They are specialists in long hitting. I want to hit all kinds of pitching hard. Weight isn't everything in slugging any more than it is in boxing. Fitzimmons was lighter than I am, but he was an awful slugger."

Harry Heilmann said: "Ruth is a fly ball hitter. He hits not only hard, but high. He is a specialist at home run hitting. Generally I hit more on a line. The ball will often go for extra bases but it isn't so likely to go over the fence."

Rogers Hornsby brought out much the same point in his own way. "There is a difference," said Rogers, "between hitting hard and hitting far. My main explanation of slugging," continued Hornsby, "is in the eye. If you meet a ball exactly right, it will go like a bullet. You often see a weak hitter meet the ball just right and drive it with surprising speed. There's a place on your bat, not too near the handle, not too near the end of the bat, I should say about four inches from the end, where you can get greater force behind the ball than meeting it at any other point. If you miss hitting the ball right by even a quarter of an inch it won't go nearly so hard."

Harry Heilmann emphasized this point. He said, "Hitting the baseball hard is a good deal like golf. I took my thirteen-year-old cousin golfing the other day and he outdrove me on nearly every stroke. His superior stroke more than offset my superior weight and strength. No doubt the same principle applies in baseball. If you hit the ball just right it will travel no matter who is behind the bat."

Zack Wheat discounted Babe's follow-up motion. "There are all kinds of sluggers," said Zack. "Those that swing from their feet; those that get their shoulders into it, and what I call arm hitters. I am an arm hitter. My wrists are strong and my forearm is bigger than my biceps. The strength to hit as I do is in my wrists and forearms. It isn't so much the swing you give a bat as the quick snap just as you meet the ball. That's what drives the ball. It's the same as in boxing. A long, roundhouse swing that comes halfway across the ring and then bumps into a man will shove him out of the way, but it won't hurt half so much as a quick, short jolt from a boxer who knows how to hit. When you snap the bat with your wrists just as you meet the ball, you give the bat tremendous speed for a few inches of its course. The speed with which the bat meets the ball is the thing that counts. You can tell when the ball is going to travel by the quick, sharp crack when the bat meets it."

Jacques Fournier said: "My secret of hard hitting is to hit the ball out in front of me. I can then get the full leverage of my body pulling it into right field. I use a fairly heavy bat—42 ounces—and I always put all the strength I have behind the blow. Something has to give when the ball meets the bat."

Ken Williams followed Babe Ruth's system. "I use a heavy bat," he said. "A bat that weighs 48 ounces. I swing from the handle and grip the handle with as much strength as I have in my fingers. And I swing from my toes. I think the man who slugs should swing not only from his shoulders but from his feet. If he doesn't stand right and get the utmost leverage with his legs his hit will lack power. "Sluggers," continued Ken, "have two opinions about hitting home runs. Some of them use a light bat on the theory that they can swing it faster and get better results. Others, myself included, prefer a heavy bat. It's all a matter of taste and batting style. Babe Ruth is the model of all home run sluggers, so I guess I don't have to apologize for my own preference."

Cactus Cravath emphasized gripping the bat. "I cannot tell anyone how to make home runs," said Cactus. "I can tell what I do, and if there is any information in that which is of value to anybody else, he is welcome. In the first place, it does not take unusual strength to hit home runs. The smallest and weakest men in the league hit an occasional homer. At the same time, it is true that strength is an advantage, if a man knows how to use it. I never try to hit the ball as hard as I can. Here many young players make a mistake. The first aim of every good batter is to meet the ball fair. When he learns how to do that it is time enough to put force behind his blow. By learning to meet the ball fair, I gradually acquired the knack of getting my weight behind the blow. But I seldom try to kill the ball, for if I do I am likely to pop up or miss it altogether. Much more important than hitting the ball hard is to hit it right. Many batters make a big mistake here. They wallop with all their might, but the ball doesn't travel half so far as you would think it would. That is because they don't get the final snap at it with the bat. For it is the way you hit the ball which drives it more than any strength which you put behind the blow. The true slugger always grips the bat as hard as he can. He holds the handle in a vise. When the ball comes in contact with the bat there is absolutely no give to that bat. It is a firmly resisting surface. In bunting you hold the bat loosely so the ball won't travel very far. In slugging you grip it as tightly as you can because you want it to travel. Many players throw the bat when they swing. No one in the Major Leagues ever saw me throw my bat. I do not try to sqeeze the handle off when I am merely waiting at the plate, but the moment I swing to meet the ball I grip that handle with my full strength."

Certain types of pitching are conducive to hard hitting. For example, Rogers Hornsby once remarked: "I would like to bat against Walter Johnson, not because he isn't a great pitcher, but rather because he is. If you meet a fast ball just right the sheer velocity of the ball will make it rebound from your bat with even greater force. Speed pitching and slugging go hand in hand."

Ty Cobb explained Ruth's greatness as a slugger with a word of criticism of slugging in general, which he considered "one-sided batting." "Ruth is the greatest slugger in the game," admitted Ty. "He is undoubtedly the greatest slugger who ever lived. He has the build. He has the eye. He has everything. But he enjoyed a peculiar advantage which gave him his start. Ruth is more than a slugger, he is a home run hitter. Fortunately for him, he began as a pitcher. A pitcher is not expected to hit. Therefore, he can follow his own system without managerial interference. Ruth made the most of this opportunity. As a pitcher he took a tremendous cut at the ball. At first he was rather awkward. Left-handers bothered him. But he persevered. He kept on trying to murder the ball. Gradually he gained confidence, experience and knowledge of pitchers. When he ceased to be a pitcher himself he had become a home run specialist. Ruth is a slugger; the greatest the game has ever known. I have tried to make myself a batter, which is something quite different. A batter is a man who can bunt, place his hits, beat out infield drives and slug when the occasion demands it, but he doesn't slug all the time."

Whatever may be said of slugging as "one-sided hitting" deficiency in slugging marks weak batting. As Herbert Hunter, the famous coach of Japanese ball players, remarked: "The Japanese are most deficient in hitting. They are of slight build and there are no Babe Ruths among them. But slugging aside, they can chop at the ball as well as anybody."

William Killifer no doubt summed up the situation in a brief paragraph when he said: "If a man is a true slugger I believe in letting him follow his natural bent. But if he isn't, and most batters are not, then he must make up in technical skill for what he lacks in sheer slugging ability. I never could slug myself, and most players can't. But it's not necessary that they should. Bunting and poking out sharp singles have their place in baseball no less than circuit drives."

The Theory of Place Hitting

PLACE hitting is a veritable bone of contention among batting kings. It has been, and is, a vexed question causing more differences of opinion among .350 hitters than any other detail of their difficult profession.

Willie Keeler defined place hitting in the ungrammatical but meaty phrase, "Hit 'em where they ain't." Theoretically place hitting is the ability to direct the course of the batted ball at will to some point on the playing field where it will fall out of reach of the waiting fielder.

Some star batters openly ridicule this ability as a myth. Others claim that even were it possible, it is poor dope to "pull" the ball. Most batters, while admitting that place hitting is possible to the select few, do not attempt to place hits themselves. But some of the greatest batters who ever lived, practice place hitting almost continuously and maintain that their ability at this most difficult of batting arts is the real secret of their success.

Rogers Hornsby said, "I have heard a great deal about place hitting, the knack by which some players claim that they can dump the ball about where they want it to go. I never took much stock in such stories myself. In my opinion, batters who make such claims are talking purely for effect. But even if I believed all they say, I wouldn't recommend their system to any one else. I surely don't follow it myself.

"I am a right-handed batter. Suppose the pitcher put one on the outside of the plate. I can drive that ball with great force into right field. I could hardly pull that ball around into left field, if I tried. But suppose I did try and were successful. I surely couldn't get as much force behind my blow. In other words, I could not make the ball travel any where nearly so hard or fast even though I could govern its general direction. And the speed with which the ball travels is, nine times out of ten, more important than its direction.

"Fancy hitting and all kinds of scientific frills are nice to read about. But the plain, old fashioned knack of meeting the ball hard and square is the best rule I know for making a successful hitter."

Lee Fohl said, "I believe place hitting is a mistake. If you try to pull a ball to a certain field when its natural direction is toward another field, you inevitably cut down on the speed of your drive. And what is more, you can't be certain about the direction more than a fraction of the time. In my opinion it's more important to hit a ball hard than it is to hit it in some certain direction. For a feeble tap or a little looping fly can often be scooped in by the fielder even though it didn't fall where he expected it would. But many a hard drive right into the fielder's hands has been too hot to handle and gone for a hit."

The foregoing are samples of baseball experts who openly criticize place hitting. Many other experts have found place hitting of little use in their own experiences. Sam Crawford said, "Once a year, perhaps, I may place a hit, in the common acceptance of that term. At all other times I merely meet the ball hard and square."

Harry Heilmann said, "I never try to place my hits except in bunting or on the hit and run play. Then it is an advantage to hit through short or through second and hit on the ground to advance the runner. Inasmuch as about one hit and run play in five is successful, and even then not wholly because of place hitting, the percentage is pretty slim. Place hitting to the outfield is still rarer and more unsatisfactory."

Tommy Leach said, "So far as batting is concerned, Willie Keeler was the best I ever saw. They talk about place hitting, and I admit it is impossible to the average man, but Keeler could place the ball within twenty feet of where he wanted it to go almost every time. He was the only one of his kind."

Hal Chase discussing this same Willie Keeler, once said, "Keeler would sit on the bench and talk over the situation with himself. 'Let's see,' he would say, 'there is one runner on the bags and we are one run behind. About the only way we can catch up is with a home run. Where can I hit a home run? The best place is near second base. It may get between the fielders.' Then he would saunter up to bat and four times out of five he would drive the ball to the field where he said it was going. Of course, the ball didn't always go safe and it didn't often go for a home run. But it did show how close he could come to doing what he set out to do."

Hans Wagner said, "Ty claims he can place a hit pretty well on a fast ball, and do it more than half the time on a curve. I think he is right. I watched him when we played against him in the World's Series of 1909. He wasn't having such good luck, but I could tell pretty well what he had in mind. He was pulling that old ball around about where he wanted it to go."

Tris Speaker once attempted to determine the prevalence of place hitting in the Major Leagues. He said, "Perhaps 10 per cent. of the batters in this league can hit either to right or left field more or less according to their will to do so. The remaining 90 per cent. have a decided tendency to hit into one field or the other. And even the 10 per cent. that you can call the batting elect, with all their ability, can never quite avoid the natural tendency to hit to a certain field."

George Sisler said, "I not only believe that Ty Cobb can place his hits, but I consider that this ability is the secret of his wonderful success. There is more than one batter in baseball who is as good a straighaway hitter as Cobb ever was, if not his superior. Where Ty distances them all is in his unmatched ability to drive the ball where he wants it to go."

I well recall an argument I once had with Ty Cobb on the Detroit playing bench. I had ventured the remark that place hitting must be pretty nearly impossible. "I used to think so myself," said Ty, half shutting his eyes and squinting reminiscently out over the diamond. "Do you see that long legged heaver putting them over for the boys?" he queried. "That's Ehmke, a hard guy to pull a ball on. He is cutting loose with considerable stuff too, you will notice. Now I will tell you what I will do. I will go up there and hit a couple to right field." As he said this, Ty hitched up his belt, grabbed his favorite war club and sauntered to the plate. Ehmke was putting a good deal of steam behind the ball, but Ty methodically, and quite as a matter of course, drove five batted balls in succession into right field.

"I gave you a little extra for good measure," he said, as he ambled back to the bench. "Next time up, what would you like to have me do?" he queried.

"There's generally a gap around second base, if you can get one by the pitcher."

"All right," said Ty. The first ball he fouled. The next went like a rifle bullet through the pitcher's box. The next he sent in an easy loop over the pitcher's head. The latter lunged for it with his gloved hand but it eluded his stab and rolled into centerfield.

"You see," continued Ty, as he resumed his position on the bench, "there really is a good deal in this place hitting. I observed long ago, that many good batters have a fundamental weakness at bat, a tendency to hit either into right or left field. That is bad, for it gives the fielders too much of an edge. I naturally had a tendency to hit into right field myself. I overcame that tendency and now hit more often into left field, but if I want to hit to right, I can do it. I will not claim that any batter alive can drop the ball on some particular square yard of turf. But I will claim that when I am going right, I can drive four out of five balls within fifteen feet of where I want them to cross the infield. I can't be sure that I will hit the ball square. I may loft the ball or ground it, but four out of five times it will go in the general direction that I want it to go. Naturally I depend mostly on fast balls. I couldn't be so sure of a curve. But I believe I can control the direction of a curve ball, when I meet it, more than half the time. Naturally it's easier to pull the ball in batting practice, but I'm going into the game today with my eye on that right field wall over there. If you hit the ball just right, it will clear that wall and go for a homer. I may strike out two or three times, who knows? But some time during the game, I shall try to cut one loose in the general direction of that wall."

Ty had a bad day. Three times his offerings were smothered by fielders. The fourth time he faced the pitcher with a coolness and decisiveness in his batting pose that was conspicuous. The pitcher's first offering was a ball. Ty didn't bite. The next he fouled viciously. He hadn't quite got the range. The next was also a ball. The next—there was a ringing crash and the ball shot on a line to right field. It collided with the wall some distance from the top and the racing right fielder held Ty at first on the play. But it is safe to say that it was one of the longest singles Ty ever made and it crossed the infield almost exactly where Ty wanted it to cross. The direction was perfect.

George Sisler early took Ty Cobb as his batting model. He said, "My main effort in batting is to develop place hitting. I am making good progress, but I need to practice more before I can approach Ty's absolute mastery of the bat. But I am convinced my own improvement as a batter has been entirely due to place hitting, for I doubt if I am any better straightaway hitter than I was when I first joined the League."

Edd Roush said, "I am committed to the proposition of place hitting. With the single exception of the hit and run, few batters try to place their hits. In fact, some batters, and good ones too, scoff at the whole theory of place hitting. I have heard them call place hitting a myth. They were wrong, however. Place hitting is a reality. But it's the possession of the few rather than the many. And it's an expression of the very highest type of good batting."

On another occasion Ty Cobb unfolded an additional chapter in the mysteries of place hitting and the prominent role it had played in his own unparalleled career. It was in the late spring and Ty had not yet struck his customary stride. But this did not worry him in the least. He said, "Perhaps the main reason why I usually make a slow start is because of the system of batting I have worked out for myself and always follow. That system is the painstaking and persevering development of place hitting which I begin with the first game of the year and follow religiously until the last game.

"Take this afternoon's game for instance. If I want to bat every time it was my turn, and put my whole attention into meeting the ball, and hit it hard, I might very well make a couple of healthy hits. But I shan't even try to do that. Instead, I shall try to place my hits, and because I am none too sure of myself, I shall be lucky to make even one hit. So far as today's game is concerned, I would be better off if I didn't bother with place hitting at all. But today's game is not the big thing to consider. If a player can really place his hits, he has a long advantage over the man who cannot. He can cross up the opposing pitcher and outfielders almost at will. It's difficult, if not impossible, to work any combination against him. But the ability to do this thing is the most difficult problem which a batter ever has to conquer. It is a problem so difficult and so important that he is justified in devoting not only one game but his entire career to its mastery. That is exactly what I have done."

He did not underestimate the difficulty involved in placing his hits. "A batter needs continual practice," continued Ty. "That's one reason why I am now hitting for less than .300. When I came back into the game I was somewhat rusty from my winter's layoff. I have to limber up and acquire once more the nice ability to drive the ball. This ability doesn't return to a man over night. It requires a month or two of practice. During that month or two my batting average suffers. But later on, with the warm weather, when the diamond hardens up and the ball doesn't stick where it strikes but rolls and bounces across the field, when I have got into my swing just right and meet the ball fair, and step into it or away from it just as I aim to do, then I can begin to break up the fielding defence and will more than regain in July and August all the batting ground I lost in May and June. That's my system in a nut shell. If you don't like it you must at least admit that it has brought results."

When Babe Ruth upset all baseball standards with his terrific slugging, Ty Cobb was a bit critical. He once remarked, "If I had set out to be a home run hitter, I am confident in a good season I would have made between twenty and thirty homers. True, I couldn't hope to challenge Babe Ruth at his particular specialty, but I would have done much better in that line than I have done. I would naturally have sacrificed place hitting, which, to my way of thinking, is the supreme pinnacle of batting art. The slugger, needless to say, is almost never a place hitter. He can't be. It's not in the scheme of things. He hammers the ball and let's it go at that. While there's something to be said in favor of the man who can drive the ball over the fence, in my opinion it's a neater piece of work to be able to drive the ball between left and center field where there's no one to stop it. My idea of a genuine hitter is a man who can bunt, who can place his hits and who, when the need comes, can slug. I believe that a batter should use his brains and his feet as well as his batting eye and his shoulders."

Cobb's glory as a hitter passed with his ability to place his hits. Though still great, he was no longer supreme and regretfully he acknowledged this fact in a conversation I had with him. He said, "I can tell more quickly than anyone else when I am a little off my batting stride. I don't hit the ball just where I want to hit it. Somewhere down the stretch of twenty years I have lost perhaps a hundredth of a second in timing; a tenth of an inch in distance. It's those little fractions that mar a record when you travel at the speed I have travelled for twenty years."

Ty Cobb was right in claiming that place hitting is the most difficult thing in batting. He has also proved its supreme importance in his own experience. But to prove that a thing exists and is important does not tell the anxious beginner how to master it.

Edd Roush, for many years the best place hitter in the National League, laid down some fundamental rules on the subject. He said, "You can tell the theory of place hitting to any amateur, but he can master it only by long practice. Some batters, I venture to say, never could learn to do it at all. And there are others, I wont deny, who don't need to do it. They hit hard and are naturally such good hitters that they will drive a ball safe a fair percentage of the time by just meeting it on the nose and let it go where it will. But that is no argument against place hitting. No matter how good they are, they would be better still if they could place their hits.

"There are, theoretically, two ways that you can place your hits. One is by shifting your feet; the other by timing your swing. The easier of these two methods is by shifting your feet. You can step into a ball when it is on the outside of the plate or you can step away from it. Sometimes infielders will get on to you by the way in which you hold your feet. You can then fool them, if you are skilful enough, by changing the timing of your swing. If I stand up at the plate, a left-handed batter, and hit late at the ball, it will go to left field. If I hit a little quicker it will go through the pitcher's box or to center field. If I swing still quicker, it will go in the general direction of right field. This looks like splitting hairs. But I do it myself to a certain degree, so I know it is not impossible."

George Sisler said, "Except when I cut loose at the ball, I always try to place my hits. To my mind place hitting is the real secret of batting mastery. Place hitting comes only from long practice, but there are a few hints about the craft that everybody should know. The first essential of place hitting is a proper position at bat. Have your feet right and your arms will take care of themselves. At the plate you must stand in such a way that you can hit either to right or left field with equal ease. The secret of good strategy is to keep your intentions to yourself. I take up a position where the natural thing is to hit through the pitcher's box. Under such circumstances it is just as easy for me to pull the ball into right field as it is to drive it to left. I do not have to exert myself at the last minute no matter which I decide to do.

"The second important element in place hitting is the timing of your swing. If I wish to hit into left field, I swing a little more quickly. I delay my swing to center, and still more to left field. That is the whole story. To be sure the difference in the timing

78

of the swing can be measured only in minute fractions of a second. I have been told that these fractions are so small that the whole thing is an absurdity, but it is not an absurdity. I do it myself consciously and deliberately. It is an art that has been mastered by other batters. Ty Cobb did not follow this system. To my mind his very stand at the plate made him a left field hitter. I do not criticize him for this, for the batter who would criticize the greatest hitter who ever lived must have his nerve with him. Ty had his reasons. Like most left-handed hitters, he could hit harder to right, but he deliberately made himself a left field hitter because infield hits played so prominent a part in his schedule. He could beat out the slow roller that went to the shortstop or third baseman. He could not do this if that roller went to the second baseman because the latter's throw, so much shorter, would nip him at first."

The learner must recognize that even the masters of place hitting differ about the rules of their difficult craft. Ty Cobb, for example, used a moderately heavy bat and in general placed his hits by the position he assumed at bat and by shifting his feet. George Sisler, though using a similar bat, assumed a fixed attitude at the plate and placed his hits mainly by timing his swing. Edd Roush employed both systems with telling effect, but unlike Cobb or Sisler, he used a very heavy bat, 48 ounces, with one or two exceptions, the heaviest bat in use in the National League. And he justified this choice on logical grounds. He said, "Place hitting is in a sense glorified bunting. I take only a half swing at the ball. The weight of the bat rather than my swing is what drives the ball."

To sum up, place hitting is an art so difficult that some great batters even deny that it exists at all. Others will admit that it occurrs, but claim that it is poor dope, that in giving direction to the ball the batter inevitably cuts down on velocity, and velocity is more important than direction. Most batters admit the existence of place hitting, but use it themselves only sparingly. In general sluggers rarely or never attempt to place their hits. For the few, however, place hitting is the chiefest of the batter's accomplishments. Ty Cobb, George Sisler, Edd Roush, all champion batters, admitted that place hitting was the foundation of their successes.

The Art of Bunting

THE bunt to the batter, is like infighting to the boxer. The pugilist, when his bone crushing wallops go wide or are blocked, can wear down his opponent by a rain of short jabs to the ribs. The batter, when he finds the opposing pitcher with too much smoke or too sharp a break to his curve, can stop swinging, hold the bat loosely in his hands, poke at the ball, and if he is skillful or lucky, beat out the puny rap to first base.

There would be more great hitters in baseball if the bunt were better developed. Most sluggers have no use for this important play. And sluggers set the pace. Batters who are not sluggers follow the universal example. If they spent the needed time in mastery of the bunt, they would equip themselves with a much more versatile attack and add many points to their batting averages.

George Sisler said, "There is no reason why a Major League batter should not be able to bunt. But too many of them fail. This is largely because they dislike to bunt and won't take the trouble to learn. How any one can undervalue the bunt is beyond me. The bunt was the cornerstone of many of Ty Cobb's batting championships. It's an important play quite apart from its value in the sacrifice. It's the best possible weapon to break up speed pitching which you can't hit. It's always on ace in your sleeve at a critical time. I bunt perhaps fifty times a year. I have never kept accurate tally, but it is safe to say that five or six times a year I make a really bad attempt to bunt. But it is much easier to lay down a bunt than it is to make a safe hit. Dangerous as it seems, I favor bunting the third strike under certain circumstances."

John Tobin said, "Theoretically bunting is easier than hitting, and yet there are not so many players who are good bunters. I know in our spring training down south, a number of boys who thought they needed to brush up on the bunt, practiced a good deal. And yet I doubt if they improved much. To my mind bunting and dragging the ball are plays that ought to be featured more. Occasionally a team faces a pitcher who seems invincible. Inning after inning goes by and perhaps the entire team has collected only a hit or two. If the team then starts bunting or dragging the ball, they often upset the pitcher, break up his cast iron defence and very likely secure one or more runs before he gets the game in hand. Rarely you meet a batter so good that he can slug and do nothing else. But he's a onesided batter. To be able to fall back on bunting when straight hitting doesn't work is a good test of a well rounded batter."

Larry Gardner said, "Just slugging, slugging all the time with never a thought of a bunt is a triumph of brute strength and ignorance."

To be sure there are players who plead guilty to continual slugging, although they might not admit the ignorance. For example, Hy Myers once said, "Zack Wheat has bunted twice in five years. If he would bunt oftener he would be a much better hitter. He could mix bunting with straight away hitting and give his batting average a twenty point boost."

Zack Wheat speaks for himself on this point. He said, "In the Minor circuits I used to bunt often. Now I bunt rarely. Perhaps if I would bunt oftener I would be better off. There is something to be said for a diversified system of attack . These fellows with nimble feet, who bury the ball in the dirt just in front of the plate and then beat the throw to first are all right in their place. They bat with their feet. I bat with my shoulders and wrists and eyes. Every man for his own style is my motto."

Harry Heilmann, another fearsome slugger, was inclined to agree with Wheat. He said, "I can not consider myself a successful bunter, even though I once beat out two intentional bunts in one game against Waite Hoyt. When it comes to bunting my own lack of speed and the good supply of third basemen totals up a heavy percentage against me."

The bunt marks a distinct advance in batting science over the old days of pure slugging. John McGraw said, "Willie Keeler and some of the rest of our old Baltimore Orioles were rather short and light. The big mastodons of pitchers laughed at us when we stood at the plate and threatened to knock the bats out of our hands. But they presently began to laugh out of the other corner of their mouth, for we bunted the ball and they were so big and cumbrous they fell all over themselves. We got to first base time after time and then proceeded to make life miserable for them on the bases."

Ernest Shore said, "The batter hasn't changed much with the passing of years while the pitcher has developed wonderfully in skill and mastery of the game. The batters' opportunities to improve are strictly limited. Outside of the bunt there are not many new quirks to batting which have come to light since the game was young."

Cactus Cravath said, "I don't bunt much myself for I like better to drop them over the wall. But I can tell any one else how to do it. You stand at the plate as though you were going to hit the ball a mile. When the ball is on the way, shift your feet, choke up on the bat, hold it loose and just meet the ball. Try to drive it toward third base or toward first, just far enough but not too far. Make a quick get-away and then run like the Devil."

This epigrammatic description congeals the science of bunting into few words. Cactus elaborated his remarks by stating that "The bunt has three main uses, the sacrifice, as a method of attack against tight pitching, and as a useful factor in diversified attack."

Ray Chapman, one of the greatest bunters who ever lived added another useful feature to the credit of bunting. "Bunting improves your batting eye," said Chapman. "When you are up there trying to bunt, it follows that you are sizing up the pitcher and getting valuable batting experience."

Jake Daubert, also one of baseball's greatest bunters, added yet another credit mark to the bunt. He said, "The bunt is a good thing to use when you are in a batting slump."

Elaborating on his bunting lesson, Cactus Cravath continued, "When the batter bunts, he holds the bat loosely in his hands. When the ball hits the bat, the bat gives and the ball doesn't travel very far. That is the whole science of bunting. Occasionally you will see a batter or a weak hitter up there trying to bunt who will drive the ball clear to second base. Now bunting is just contrary to ordinary hitting. A bunt is a kind of back handed hit."

Grover Alexander said, "Jake Daubert had the bunt down perfect. You have no idea how it bothers a pitcher to face such a play. Speed and stuff can fool the average batter but they won't prevent the fellow who knows how from laying down a little teasing bunt. In some ways a bunt bothers a pitcher as much as an extra base hit."

Milton Stock, a third baseman, echoed these sentiments. He said, "A perfect bunt can not be fielded by anybody. Max Carey is a good bunter and has perfected a bunting offense that is a winner.

He aims to bunt exactly down the third base foul line. He bunts literally on the run. Half the time he is holding the bat in one hand after he has made two strides toward first base. If the bunt is safe he has such a start and is so fast he will beat it out. If it isn't safe, he has merely lost a strike which he might well have lost anyway had he swung at the ball."

"Jake Daubert," continued Stock, "was the greatest bunter I ever saw. In his prime be could bunt almost at will. I don't know exactly what he did to the ball, but he seemed to put reverse English on it in some way so that it would stop just where he wanted it to stop."

Daubert illustrated his own system. He said, "You can not bunt effectively when the infield is playing in for you. You must pick your time, but that is not so difficult. They won't play for you all the time. There's one time in particular when you can depend upon their playing well back. That is when the pitcher has two strikes on you. You know the batter is out bunting the third strike if the ball rolls foul. Most batters dislike to take this risk but it is sometimes a good play.

"In 1914 when I led the League I bunted a third strike in three straight games. The first of these games was against the Giants. There was a man on first at the time I bunted the third strike. I advanced the runner to second and beat out the throw to first. The next man up hit safely, scoring the winning run from second base. Next day, with no one on and two strikes on me, I beat out a bunt and finally scored with the winning run. That night we went to Boston. Next day Bill James was pitching and had a lot of stuff. I laid down a bunt that was just about right on a third strike but it rolled foul.

"The successful bunter must dump the ball on fair ground in front of him. But that is not enough. The ball must roll away from the catcher and the pitcher toward third base, but not too far. You have to place the ball within a few feet of where you want it to go and with a speedy pitcher that isn't so easy as it looks."

Lee Fohl said, "When I was manager at Cleveland I used the sacrifice play a great deal. And why not? I had a man on the club, Chapman, who was almost sure for a sacrifice, and besides, he beat out the bunt fairly often."

Jake Daubert was equally successful in beating out the bunt. For that reason he usually batted second on the list, simply because of his unequalled powers to advance the runner while reaching first himself a fair percentage of the time.

Max Carey said, "A good bunter can help the base runner in a variety of ways. The most obvious, of course, is the sacrifice play, but there are others. I have often wished, for example, that Jake Daubert could have batted behind me. Jake was a wonderful bunter. It is easier to bunt than to hit, but it isn't always easier to bunt where you want to bunt. Besides, batters do not study the play as they should. Good hitters are often not good bunters. They prefer to swing. In consequence they get little experience so when called upon to bunt they are not there. If I were a manager I would train my players to bunt and keep on bunting. But that is a different story. Daubert could dump a little roller toward third base, get it to stop just about where he wanted it to stop, and be off like the wind. If he had batted behind me I believe I could have stolen third base at least 50% more often than I ever have done. I wouldn't have asked him to bunt much either. A bluff bunt on his part would have been enough to have sent the third baseman running in and give me my chance."

Walter Lutzke said, "I have made a specialty of bunts which is natural at my position, third base. I believe I am right in saying that every batter gives you some unconscious signal when he is going to bunt. Since the batter wants to fool you with his intentions, it is important not to give him the chance. The only time I am crossed up on such a play is where the batter makes a bluff to bunt. However, I usually play well in so I am in a good position to handle the bunt all the time."

Inability to handle bunts has impaired many a pitcher's usefulness. It drove at least one pitcher out of the Major Leagues. Said Allen Sothoron, "I was always a fair pitcher, if I do say it myself. But the bunt was my hoodoo. I could generally get my hands on the pesky thing, but I was always so hurried and anxious to get my man at first that I would throw wild. This bad fault, I believe, really drove me out of the Major Leagues for a time."

From a batter's viewpoint, the quick get-away is important in bunting. Ross Young is a past master at this detail of the batter's art. He said, "I have practiced the quick get-away so much that I start full speed for first base before I even meet the ball. The get-away is even more important for the bunter than speed. A fast man who makes a slow start is up against it. Even a slow man can learn to make a quick get-away and have a good chance."

Ty Cobb probably never mastered the bunt with such a degree of technical nicety as Ray Chapman or Jake Daubert, but he used it with even more telling effect, for it was always a potent weapon in his versatile attack.

George Burns said, "Ty Cobb does some curious things. I remember once when he was trying to bunt and failed to come through. He kept right on laying down bunts until he had appeared at bat twenty one consecutive times without making a hit. Then finally he laid down a perfect bunt, beat it out handily and having accomplished what he set out to do, resumed belting the life out of the ball and soon regained all the ground he had lost. Later that same season he made eleven safe hits out of thirteen times at bat and not one of those hits went out of the infield. Whatever Ty decides to do he plugs at doggedly until he has succeeded. You simply can't discourage him.".

There is a method of diversified attack which has crept into batting which combines some of the pecularities of the bunt and the hit. Players call it, "dragging the ball."

John Tobin, most successful of American Leaguers at this play, thus described it. "You can not always drag the ball any more than you can bunt. Conditions must be fairly favorable. Some pitchers offer less opposition than others. The same is true of infielders. A slow second baseman is a continual invitation to drag the ball for if the play works right, the second baseman should field it. Dragging the ball is simple on paper. Before the ball even gets to the plate, you start full speed for first. As the ball crosses the plate, you hook the bat around it and drag it past the pitcher. You hold the bat precisely as if you were going to hit the ball through the infielders. If you execute the play properly, you will have a grand lead to first base. You will be running full speed. The ball will hop along the ground faster than a bunt, but not so fast as the ordinary hit. The pitcher won't be able to stop it and the second baseman, if he gets his hands on it, will not be in a good position to make the necessarily hurried throw. I pull this play,

I should judge, about forty or fifty times a year and it generally works."

Carson Bigbee, who mastered this play more perfectly, perhaps, than any other National League batter, said, "It is a good play for a diversified attack. I do not care particularly whether the pitcher gives me a curve or a fast ball. I like a slow ball best of all for the "drag play." I also like a slow ball in bunting. I use the drag play perhaps fifty times a year. It's a neat little play when properly executed."

The Hit and Run and the Sacrifice

THE standard methods of advancing the base runner, aside from plain hitting, are the familiar sacrifice and the less often used but even more dangerous hit and run play. Lee Fohl, in a sketchy manner, outlined the advantages of both plays. "For years John McGraw used the hit and run play. But McGraw had a club of fast players who were reasonably good hitters as well. Hugh Jennings has gone on record as criticizing the sacrifice hit when the hit and run play could be used. But he would be the first to admit that some players are good on the sacrifice while others are hopeless, that a few players can negotiate the hit and run while most players can not. The sacrifice hit has grown in favor. Baseball has become more of an exact science and there is less disposition to take chances. Most players can learn to sacrifice properly while there are few players who are good on the hit and run.

"I admit, the hit and run looks fine when it goes through. You have sent the base runner from first to third, it may be, and have another runner on first. You are in a fine position to score one run, maybe two. That's when the hit and run succeeds. But generally the play fails. That means that your batter does not get on, or that if he does, the runner was retired. Very often there has been no advance. Nothing has happened but the retirement of the batter or the runner. Sometimes there is a double play. The hit and run is merely a gamble. There is also a risk in the sacrifice, but this risk is much less pronounced, while the benefits, if not so great, are very much surer."

Joe Gedeon, counted one of the best hit and run man in baseball before he was banished from the game as a melancholy aftermath of the Black Sox scandal, once discussed his favorite play.

"The hit and run is usually a combat of wits between batter and catcher. If the latter can cross you, he can usually spoil your play. I could illustrate from an experience that came to me in Cleveland. I gave the signal to Austin to go down on the next pitched ball. I then saw O'Neill, who was catching, reverse his former signal and call for a pitch out. Such a wide ball would probably be impossible for me to hit and Austin would be headed off at second base. So I immediately stepped outside the batter's box, the universal signal in baseball that the hit and run is off. O'Neill promptly matched me by calling for the type of ball he wanted in the first place. I was sure, in my own mind, that he wouldn't call for a pitch out again, so I again gave Austin the sign. But sure enough, O'Neill had read my intentions and stayed with me. He got his views to the pitcher via the signal route and the next ball instead of being somewhere within reach, was so far off the plate that I couldn't even hit at it. Consequently Jimmy Austin, who had faithfully followed instructions, was caught by a mile. The hit and run play is one of the finest pieces of strategy in baseball. But it's always risky."

Naturally players need a good deal of coaching in the hit and run play. As Ralph Works said, "The player generally should not be criticized for failure to execute the hit and run play. Most of the blame goes to the manager. It is his place to coach the man how to execute the play. In the absence of coaching, the player's natural instinct is to whale away at the ball as hard as possible. It is only human for the player to do this. Consequently he will take his swings unless ordered to do otherwise."

Robert O'Farrell, the star Cub catcher, said, "One of the most important things a catcher can do is to break up the hit and run play. This is a paralyzing play when it goes through and puts the defence in an extremely shaky position."

Doubtless the hit and run play is criticized more by the thoughtless crowd than any other play in baseball. Where the play fails and makes the runner look foolish, the crowd is prone to consider that the player has merely indulged in a stupid bit of base running.

As a matter of fact, he is only the innocent victim of circumstances beyond his control.

Max Carey said, "In my opinion some managers engineer this play on a wrong principal. They keep the runner close to the bag because they reason, the pitcher won't waste a ball. He will pitch to the batter, because it will be evident to him that the base runner isn't going to steal. I always follow exactly contrary methods. I start with as big a lead as I can get, then, even if the batter fails to come through, I may make second on a steal. Besides, in my opinion, it is better dope to allow the pitcher to pitch out to the batter and get himself in the hole. The more you worry the pitcher, the more likely he is to take a balloon ascension."

Some of the finest examples of inside strategy and daring base running have hinged on the hit and run play. Ty Cobb said, "There was one play in particular that I studied a long time. I never had the right opportunity to spring it and yet I think it was a legitimate play. Very likely I shall never have the opportunity to try it now, so I don't mind outlining what it was.

"I planned to engineer this play with the help of Donie Bush. He was to get on first base. Then I was to give him the hit and run sign and try to score him from first base. The hit and run will generally advance a man from first to third, if the batter drives the ball to right field as he should. But to try to score the runner from first on a mere single was an achievement that might rouse the ambition of anyone. At first sight the play looks impossible, assuming that no error were made. As we planned it, however, it was possible, though admittedly difficult. The execution of this master hit and run play was simply this. I was to give Bush the sign. He was to take a long lead and start full speed for second. By the time the ball reached me, he would be very nearly there. He was a fast man and with that lead, nothing could prevent him from reaching third, provided that I came through with my part of the program. By hitting the ball into right field, the right fielder would naturally throw to second base to prevent me from taking that bag. But there would be no particular incentive for him to hurry the throw as he would naturally assume that I wouldn't be so foolish as to try to make second on a single. He certainly wouldn't even imagine that Bush would try to score. But that is just what he would try to do. He would round third base and keep on to the plate. I would round first base and keep on for second. The play required me to sacrifice myself, if necessary. It would be simple to put me out at second. But the shortstop or second baseman, whichever took the throw, would be disconcerted to see me tearing into second. And by the time he discovered Bush making for the plate, it would require a perfect throw to catch him. Probably, however, he would not be in a position to make a perfect throw and with a break in the luck, Bush would be safe. It would have been a pretty play."

The sacrifice and the hit and run are brilliant contrasts. The sacrifice is methodically drab and generally sure. It advances a base runner while eliminating a batter. The hit and run requires for its proper execution a bit of successful place hitting. Even sluggers who never think at any other time of giving direction to their wallops, try to place their drive on the hit and run. If it succeeds, the hit and run is perhaps the most effective of offensive plays. But few players are capable of executing it properly and it is always dangerous.

Making Good in the Pinch

THERE is a time element in batting which is all important. Mere ability to hit is not enough. That rarer ability to hit when hits mean runs is what counts.

The Championship of the World may rest upon a single hit. Said Bill Killifer after the World's Series of 1918, "The thing that sticks most in my memory is the particular ball that Ruth hit off Lefty Tyler, a hit that decided the Series. That shows the importance of a hit in the pinch."

Making good in the pinch naturally suggests the pinch hitter, the relief batter who is sent in at a critical moment to take the place of some less competent regular. The particular requirements of a pinch hitter were thus set forth by Eddie Murphy, himself one of the greatest pinch hitters who ever lived. He said, "A good pinch hitter needs to have the same qualifications as a good all-round batter, with a little something extra thrown in. That something extra I would call coolness under fire, or if you prefer, ability to rise to the occasion. There are some men who never do themselves justice in a crisis. They seem to get flustered and go all to pieces.

There are others who re-act to an emergency and do even better than common. They are the men who are natural pinch hitters. I consider that my experience as a lead-off man has helped my batting in the pinch. A lead-off man is supposed to look them over, to make a pitcher work and not to bite at bad balls. To be perfectly fair, I must admit that luck plays an important part in pinch hitting to an even greater degree than it does in ordinary batting. For the pinch hitter faces the pitcher only once and his trial is quickly over. The thing which I most object to in pinch hitting isn't the tense situation with men on bases and important results at stake. It is rather that I am called upon to act pretty closely under manager's orders. It is difficult enough to hit safely under any circumstances. To do so under orders is still more of a task."

Cactus Cravath, a formidable pinch hitter, made these sage remarks, "Some hitters are nervous when called on in the pinch. Others hit somewhat above their usual form. A good pinch hitter is a valuable man to have on a ball club and can win a lot of games, provided he is lucky enough to come through with a hit. One good pinch hitter might even win a pennant for a ball club that was reasonably strong elsewhere. It is perfectly possible for a pinch hitter to win half a dozen ball games, and less than that number might cinch the pennant. But I do not wish to give the pinch hitter more credit than is coming to him. Even if he does make good, he shouldn't get chesty. Perhaps the man he displaced in the line-up would have done equally well. Poor hitter as he doubtless was, even his batting average in the pinch would not have been an unbroken succession of goose eggs.

"The thing which handicaps the pinch hitter is the fact that he is usually never called upon till late in the afternoon when the sun is lower and the ball correspondingly hard to see. Besides, he has had no opportunity to face the pitcher and size him up. For all that, I rather like to hit in the pinch."

The pinch hitter, however, is only one interesting phase of a larger field. For there are many regulars who seem to have the ability to come through in a tight place, although their averages may not be high, while more than one good hitter on paper has been correspondingly weak at critical moments.

George Whitted said, "The manager would prefer a mediocre player on his team, a man who is always trying and improving himself, always working for the club, to a batter of much larger natural gifts who was lazy or indifferent or dissipated and who wasn't living up to the full possibilities which were in him."

Some batters of this type have become famous. Jack Coombs said, "On the old Athletics when I was a member, Jack Barry was known as a timely hitter. But," added Coombs. "Why shouldn't he have been? There were usually men on bases when he came to bat. If he came through with a hit, he was pretty sure to advance or score some one, for the runners were there. It was his position quite as much as his ability which made him a timely hitter." Evidently then, opportunity sometimes makes the timely hitter.

There have been examples of ball clubs with weak batting averages that were nevertheless good in the pinch. Fielder Jones said, "They called the White Sox the hitless wonders. It is true their batting was light, but they hit at the right time,"

Carl Mays reminds us that even sluggers are not necessarily good in the pinch. He said, "There's many a slugger who can drive out long hits with nobody on bases. In a tight game when a hit means everything, he's likely to strike out. The responsibility is too much for him."

On the other hand, some sluggers add to their values by the timeliness of their wallops. Frank Navin said, "Sam Crawford was without doubt one of the greatest natural hitters who ever lived. And he combined with great hitting strength a timeliness in delivery which made his batting doubly effective."

The player of this type does not always receive the publicity which is due him. Walter Johnson said, "Duffy Lewis is a man who gets about one tenth the publicity which Babe Ruth does. But the players all recognize him as one of the greatest hitters in the game. He can hit anything and is doubly dangerous in the pinch."

Some times the odds are decidedly against the pinch hitter. That is particularly true when he faces certain pitchers. Dazzy Vance said, "I have faced about forty pinch hitters in two years and just two of them connected with hits. That gives the pinch hitters an average of about .050. But don't think I take any liberties with those birds. The very next one I meet may break up the game with a whistling triple. That's one of the well known uncertainties of the grand old pastime."

Although the batter in a crisis may figure that the cards are stacked against him, there are really some things in his favor. Ty Cobb said, "I find it easier to hit the ball with the bases occupied. The pitcher is worried. The infielders are worried. When you do connect the flying runners rattle the fielders. Besides, with a runner on first or second, the pitcher is not allowed to take his wind up and that bothers some pitchers greatly. Whenever you can figure that the pitcher has something on his mind besides trying to fool you at the plate, you can figure a break of luck in your favor. Many pitchers without their windup are considerably less effective."

It isn't always logical to figure that a batter should be taken out at a critical moment simply because he hasn't made a hit all day. Moose McCormick, who was kept by the New York Giants for a number of years solely in the capacity of a pinch hitter, once said, "Many people reason that because a batter hasn't hit he is weak and it would be an advantage to put another man in his place. I would reason that because he hasn't done a thing all day he is about due and all the more apt to come through with a bingle."

Occasionally a batter gets the undeserved reputation for being weak in the pinch. There is a disposition to rate a batter's effectiveness somewhat on the number of runs he drives home. Jake Daubert said, "I am not claiming that I am a good hitter in the pinch. I don't know and anyway it would be better for some one else to talk on that point. But at least there has never been any proof that I was a poor hitter in the pinch, for the mere number of runs a batter drives in is no proof. The clean-up hitters will always drive home the runs because they are in the proper position in the line-up to do this.

Ability to rise to the occasion generally gets the rookie a job. Sometimes opportunity is long delayed. George Whiteman, the star of a World's Series, was himself an aged rookie. He said, "I had about given up hope when this chance came. I said to myself, 'It is the last chance you will ever have, so it is up to you to make good.' I worked hard. I did my best. I am not sure I could do so well again. But it will always be a satisfaction to know that I was able to do good work for once in my life."

The hard row of the rookie who is waiting his chance was thus described by Hans Lobert. He said, "When the young player is having the crudeness ground out of him and the polish of the Big League player substituted instead is really the turning point of his career. If he has natural ability and faith in himself and spirit enough and perseverance enough to stand the knocks and the sarcasm which are heaped upon him by other players, he is bound to make good. If he becomes disheartened and discouraged, he loses his nerve and has no prospect but a speedy return to the Minors."

The quality of mind which enables a man to make good in the pinch is a study in psychology. Ty Cobb said, "You would think that a player would react in a certain way under given conditions, but you would be wrong. The reaction would depend entirely upon the man. When the pace gets hot, some players rise to the occasion and do all the better for the added stimulus. Some, however, are inclined to wilt. I won't say they are quitters, although I would probably have used that word at one time. They just don't react as I would have them. Instead of getting up on their hind legs and battling all the harder, they give in. This is a trait that is foreign to my make-up and it grates on my nerves. I came to Detroit with the reputation of being a fresh Busher. In truth my only wish was to make good. Instead of finding friendly co-operation, the older men tried to make life miserable for me. They didn't confine themselves to cutting remarks, but they played tricks on me. They seemed determined to get me off the club. I didn't feel friendly toward those fellows at that time, but in the light of experience, I feel that I owe them a vote of thanks. In those formative years when I couldn't decide just what was best to do, they decided for me. I made up my mind I wouldn't be put off the ball club. Their opposition was just the stimulus I needed."

The more difficult the task, as Ty points out, the greater the stimulus to the player with grit, ambition and the determination to succeed. In fact, Ty once told me that he considered one of the most favorable factors of his brilliant career was the keen competition he had encountered all along the way. He said, "I was born with a restless desire to do a thing as well as it could be done. That meant doing it a little better than the other fellow. When I entered baseball Lajoie was still great. He was a wonderful batter and extended me to the limit to beat him. Eddie Collins was a good pacemaker at times, and Joe Jackson forced me above the .400 mark to keep ahead of him. Roger Peckinpaugh had a great season one year and made me hustle. Tris Speaker was a worthy foe and once he beat me. There was never a time when I could feel that I could afford to let up and take things easy. That driving competition was, to my way of thinking, one of the best strokes of luck that ever came my way."

Batting Spurts

THE batter who has his periods of black despondency when he's in a slump, has also red letter days when he can hit anything the pitcher gives him.

One of the commonest forms of batting spurts is known as the "morning glory" average. Zack Wheat described this batting vagary when he said "Rookies often start at a fast clip in the spring, before the pitchers settle down. But their averages melt in hot weather. A good batter often starts slow, but he improves against good pitching and is going strong at the finish, when the race is close and hits count for the most. You know, a morning glory looks fine when the dew is on the grass, but you don't see it so well when the sun comes out bright. These May batting averages don't amount to much. The test of a good hitter comes later in the season. The morning glory average is generally a false alarm."

Joe Gedeon said, "Why do I hit well in the spring? It's in the books. I have studied the reason and think I can explain it. In the spring I am generally in fine form while the opposing pitchers are not. They haven't developed the gilt edge control they master later in the season, so they can't pitch to my batting weakness so well."

Most batters sometimes in their career encounter a streak of favorable days when they hit at a record clip. Duffy Lewis said, "During that best season of mine at Salt Lake City, I hit safely in thirty three consecutive games, I made just sixty five hits. That's about two hits per game on an average for we will say a .500 average or a bit better. Once in a while you will see a batter break loose with one of those spurts but he can't keep it up. In fact, that's just what such things are—spurts. A runner can go about two hundred yards at top speed, but he can't keep up the pace for five miles. When you are enjoying one of these hitting streaks, you are in luck. Your line drives are going straight and you are batting out a lot of fluky hits. Your batting eye is clear and you are meeting the ball just right. Everything is coming your way. But it's only a question of time when something happens to spill the beans, for you are just as likely to fall into a slump as to enjoy a spurt. Once in a while a star hitter like Hornsby or Sisler will go at a .500 average for a month maybe, but they can't keep that pace throughout a season. And even when they are having a spurt, they seldom hit above .500."

Roger Peckinpaugh said, "Sometimes you can't seem to help is when things are coming your way. A batting streak is a great thing while it lasts, but it begins to wear on you. You try to keep it in the background of your mind and you might succeed if people would let you. But every body you meet speaks about it, wishing you well. But the net result is that you have that confounded batting streak in your mind all the time. Naturally it makes you a little nervous and not until you have made at least one safe hit, can you breathe easily. When the spurt is over, you are pretty sure to strike a reaction. In my case, I went into a slump the minute I stopped hitting safely. And a slump gives you just the reverse of a spurt. When you are in a slump it seems as though the whole diamond is crowded with infielders and you couldn't bat a ball through with a shovel."

Pep Young said, "One season I went four days without making a hit. That was my worst slump. On the other hand I hit safely in twelve successive games. That shows how things even up. If you get a bad break, you're bound to meet a good turn sooner or later. What happens is easy enough to figure. In a slump you are not hitting up to your true form. In a spurt you are hitting considerably above it. That's the story."

The Official Scorer sympathizes with a spurt. Said Ty Cobb, "While Sisler was having his great string of consecutive hitting games (it lasted forty one games) the Browns visited Detroit. There was one contest in particular where Sisler hit in hard luck. He hadn't succeeded in getting one safe all day. Then, in the final inning, he hit a roller to the infield which was fumbled momentarily, and he beat the throw by an eyelash. Fortunately the Scorer viewed the matter as he should have done and as the rules declare, when he gave him the necessary hit."

I interviewed Zack Wheat the day his string of twenty six consecutive hitting games was broken. "To tell the truth," he said, "I am glad it is all over. It's a fine thing to be in a winning stride and belt the old ball, but when you have taken a big spurt and come somewhere near equalling a record, then the strain grows too great and the farther you go the harder it is to hit safely. This may not sound like good sense, but it is true. When you face a pitcher in an ordinary game, you are inclined to wait him out or try to get him to feed you the kind of a ball you want. But when you are trying to establish a record, you can't take any such chances. So as a result, you start swinging at almost anything that offers and naturally hit at bad balls."

Hugh Duffy, champion batter of the National League, had perhaps a seasons spurt in the year that he hit .438. Explaining that record performance, he said, "It's very evident that when a batter has a bang up season he must begin just right, find conditions favorable and go straight ahead through the season full speed. That was what I did back there in '94. I got away to a good start and I held my advantage. But don't think I didn't have to hustle to keep ahead of Delehanty. He was a terrific slugger and one of the greatest hitters who ever lived. He chased me across the .400 mark himself. But I beat him by a comfortable margin."

John McGraw said, "There is a good deal of psychology mixed up in a spurt. That goes for a club just as it does for a batter. When a club is winning, everything seems to break right. The pitchers are going well, the fielders are full of pep, the batters are hitting and the team is getting the breaks. A club, under such circumstances, enters every game with supreme confidence. On the other hand in a losing streak, the club is already half defeated before they begin. They expect to lose and do lose. It is difficult to explain this mental influence for defeat or victory, but every manager knows what I mean."

Phenomenal batting spurts sometimes last for a few days. For example, Ed Konetchy said, "The best record I ever made was against Brooklyn. I rapped out twelve straight hits. And to show the uncertainties of batting, the next time we met Brooklyn, I had the hardest kind of work to make three hits in four games."

Many a batter has a red letter day that stands out in his batting average. George Cutshaw explaining the day that he made six safe hits said, "I didn't think much about it until I had come through with four hits. Then I happened to remember that I had broken my own record. I was pretty well keyed up when I came through with the fifth hit. When I faced the pitcher for the sixth time up, I admit I was weak in the knees, but I gave it a hard rap and beat the throw. It's all over now, but there's one satisfaction. I know how it seems to have a real day at bat, even it I never have another."

The freakiest of all spurts, and the hardest to explain, is that sudden batting frenzy which attacks a club and is called a rally. George Stallings said, "You have seen many a club go along against an opposing pitcher for several innings doing little or nothing. All at once the men seem to find their batting eye. They start to hammer that pitcher all over the lot. When a manager has another twirler warmed up and yanks out his battered veteran, the substitute fares no better. That is a fine example of the spirit that wins on a ball club. So long as the flurry lasts, any pitcher may well dread to meet those batters."

Every pitcher has experienced batting rallies. I remember seeing Old Cy Young, when the opposing club had belted him out of the box. But Cy was philosophical. He said, "If I had let a little thing like that worry me, I never would have lasted long as a pitcher. I learned twenty years ago that when a club is really hitting, no pitcher on earth can stop them."

Hollis Thurston said, "The pitcher is always worrying about a batting rally and he has reason, for that's when the game is trembling in the balance. What can he do? That's a hard question. When one of those rallies start, I aim to stall around in the box, take plenty of time and do something different. If they have been hitting my fast ball, for example, I give them no more fast ones. You have to jab in the dark, hoping to strike the winning combination that will fool them."

Christy Mathewson once attempted to explain a batting rally. He said, "Many people have wondered how it is that a pitcher can go on inning after inning without a hit being scored from his delivery, and then all at once, without warning, three or four solid drives will go shooting into the outfield. Possibly the pitcher has begun to weaken a trifle. Possibly the batters are beginning to solve his delivery. But not infrequently it is merely an example of the mathematics of baseball. According to the laws of probability, the average batter will hit safely about once in four times. This will give him an average of .250, which isn't far from the mean, including pitchers and other weak hitters. Now it stands to reason that some times hits will appear about once in four times at bat, sometimes there will be a much longer stretch of no hits, and sometimes several hits will follow one another. On such occasions a pitcher is said to have a poor inning, whereas he may have been at his very best in that unlucky frame. But the accumulated chances were percipitated on him all at once. That this explanation applies to many a batting rally is proved to my mind by the fact that where the pitcher is left in he will frequently pitch just as air tight ball after such an inning as he did before. Undoubtedly the batting rally is one of the most curious of the many strange phenomena of baseball."

Spurts are enjoyable while they last, but the batter who can eliminate both slumps and spurts, so far as possible, is the greater hitter. Said Rogers Hornsby, "Consistent hitting, in my opinion, is just as important as good hitting. A streaky hitter is always difficult to classify. You never can tell just where he belongs. From his general average you might claim that he was a .300 hitter. But that average is based on streaks when he hit .350 mixed up with slumps when he hit .250. Such hitters are always a problem. The manager may put one of these fellows in clean-up position one month and have him on the bench the next. The manager doesn't like to shake up his batting list, for it is fooling with a mighty delicate piece of machinery. Hence, these uncertain batters are always gumming up the works, for they are always either better or worse than their position on the batting list would indicate. I believe the thing which has given me the most satisfaction is my consistent hitting. I generally hit about as well at the beginning of the season as I do in the middle or at the close. And my average has varied little for some years."

Batting Slumps and How to Cure Them

SLUMPS are the bane of the batter's life. They prove a continual source of worry to the greatest stars; they wreck many a batting average. And every season they send many a rookie back to the Bushes, his prospects blighted, his hopes in ruins. The study of slumps, their varieties, their obscure causes and above all helpful remedies, comprises one of the most important chapters in a batter's experience.

Hans Wagner one remarked, "The thing which bothers the batter more than anything else is a slump." Cy Williams, the home run slugger, modified this statement in the interests of accuracy. "Slumps," said Williams, "worry a batter more than anything except actual injuries."

Slumps are of two kinds, prolonged and transient. Upon the former variety Walter Johnson once made the following interesting observation. "Some times," said Walter, "a batter who has been in the game a long time will slump for a few seasons. Then, when every one begins to believe that he is about through, he will blossom out with the best season of his career. Sam Crawford did this in 1911 when in his thirteenth year he hit for .378, the best mark he ever made. Tris Speaker slumped a number of seasons, then came out of it with a rush and beat Ty Cobb for the batting championship. Nap Lajoie fell under .300 for two seasons running, then came back strong. Such feats, however, are rare among batters."

Such reversal of form for so long a period of time is not a slump, according to the commonly accepted definition. The slump, as the batter thinks of it, is relatively transient. As Eddie Collins says, "Slumps, the worst of them, pass in time."

If we investigate further, we will discover that transient slumps are also of two kinds. Edd Roush has clearly drawn the distinction. "Slumps are of two kinds," said Roush. "One kind is when you're merely unlucky; the other when you are off your form. I do not call a slump when you are merely unlucky, a true slump. There are times, however, when you are not hitting the ball hard or true. Then there is something wrong with yourself. That is a true slump."

The first of these types, what we may term the unlucky slump, was well illustrated by Jake Daubert some years ago. Said Daubert, "I went to bat twenty-five straight times without making a hit. Almost every time up I met the ball square but drove it right at a fielder." That slump was due to bad luck.

Ball players readily recognize this form of slump. They excuse their unfortunate team mate by saying that "He's hitting in hard luck." The second type mentioned by Roush, as caused by something wrong with yourself, is the true slump, the mysterious malady which causes sleepless nights to the greatest hitters in baseball.

Hans Wagner said, "There doesn't seem to be any way to explain a slump." In a sense he is right. George Sisler some years ago encountered a most disastrous slump which he described. "I was breezing along in great shape," said Sisler. "The latter part of the season I was hitting for .360, but I struck a slump, for no reason that I could discover, which cut that average to .318 in two week's time. My all round work also seemed to suffer. I am at a loss to explain that slump. It was a heart breaker while it lasted. On other occasions I have been injured or wasn't feeling just right. But this time I was in tip top shape." Sisler added, "Slumps are curious things anyway."

Rogers Hornsby said, "I can not explain slumps. If I could explain them, and what is more outline a quick cure for them, I would not have to play baseball for a living. I would earn much more by coaching other batters."

Oddly enough, Ty Cobb once expressed somewhat the same idea. Said Ty, "I believe it would pay every Major League club to have a man do nothing but coach batters. A trained man who knows batting could help batters out of a slump."

Tris Speaker, in analyzing slumps, said, "Sometimes they are due to the way a batter stands at the plate. Sometimes they are due to the way he holds his bat. In my own case, I have found that I was hitting weakly because I was off balance at the plate. A lot of slumps are caused by worry or overanxiety."

Things which cause slumps, while an interesting study, are not of so much importance. All authorities agree that slumps are inevitable. As Miller Huggins said, "Sooner or later every batter is bound to strike a slump. If he gets going real bad and hasn't nerve, he may not recover his true form." Slumps, it appears, are a universal disease and particularly in the case of the young player whose reputation is not yet established, a dangerous disease. Since the malady is unavoidable, the cure is important.

Edd Roush clearly depicts the difficulty of laying down any general rule. He said, "I believe what helps one batter in a slump would be useless or worse than useless to another batter in a slump." He adds to this pessimistic statement the cheering advice, "A slump is like a mild sickness. You will recover from it in time, if you give yourself a chance."

The most famous batting authorities are divided into two antagonistic groups when it comes to the treatment of slumps. Eddie Collins, one of the wisest players who ever lived, ably champions one of these two prevalent theories. He said, "I have no set rule for climbing out of a slump except to 'bear down hard.' I always give myself a careful self analysis. I try to put my finger on the hidden cause of my slump. And when I think I have located that cause, I exert myself to get out of the slump." In other words, Eddie contributes to the list of helpful hints on overcoming slumps, the slogan, "Bear down hard."

Some batters agree with Eddie in his contention, but more do not. They rather side with the opinion expressed by Rogers Hornsby. "Admitting that there are batters who study themselves closely when in a slump," Hornsby said, "this seems to me like poor dope. A man who studies himself in a batting slump is keeping his mind on his troubles. Dwelling on trouble only makes it worse. My advice to a batter in a slump, is to forget it. Just go up to the plate as naturally as you can and work out of it. You'll soon discover that you are stinging them just as hard as ever."

There you have the extreme views. One famous batter says, "Bear down hard," the other says, "Forget it."

Tris Speaker in discussing slumps, agrees with Hornsby in theory and Collins in practice. Speaker said, "Every slump is made worse by over anxiety. The more anxious the batter is to overcome his slump, the more difficult it seems for him to hit. I have observed that batting, to be done effectively, has to be done naturally. The less exertion a player puts into his hitting, the more likely he will be to hit naturally." Speaker, like Hornsby, advises the batter to keep his mind off his troubles, but he goes on to say, "If I were in a slump myself, I would be inclined to go out in morning practice and have a pitcher throw the ball to me and keep on throwing it until I got back in my strike once more. Practice would be my way to overcome a slump."

Cy Williams treated slumps as a problem in psychology. He said, "When I'm not hitting right, I try to wipe everything out of my mind that might bother me. When I go to the plate I resolve deliberately not to think about my physical condition or my luck or whether I'm in form or even whether I can see straight. Once I get the right mental attitude, I start hitting as well as ever." In Williams's scheme of things the proper treatment of a slump is sheer effort of will; a triumph of mind.

George Sisler agreed with Hornsby's fundamental principle, that making any unusual effort to overcome a slump is bad. But he counsels the unfortunate batters to seek advice, and he cited an interesting illustration. "Some years ago," he said, "I watched Speaker when he was in a bad slump. I could tell easily enough what was wrong with him. He was overanxious, was swinging too eagerly and hitting the ball with the handle of his bat. I could tell what was wrong with him, he couldn't. Nor can I tell what is wrong with myself when I am in a slump." Sisler then goes on to advise the slumping batter to get some team mate to watch him carefully and tell him what is wrong.

Harry Heilmann was inclined to belittle Sisler's suggestion. He said, "I was in a prolonged batting slump and I didn't have to wait for any advice. It came to me from all sides. If there were twenty-six players on our club, then I got twenty-six different kinds of advice as to what I should do to work out of that slump."

Heilmann's commentary was suggestive enough, though perhaps a bit overdrawn, but it does not dismiss Sisler's treatment, although it seems to do so. Advice is of two kinds, good and bad. There are batters who are competent to give advice in the case of a team mate's slump. It is their advice which should be sought.

Heinie Groh who though never a League leader, was doubtless one of the most scientific hitters who ever lived, said, "Nine times out of ten when I am in a slump I find I am swinging a bit too soon. My cure for a slump is to delay my swing a little. I believe many batters are guilty of the fault I mention. The mere fact that they are usually overanxious to hit makes them swing too soon."

Hans Wagner said, "Whenever I am in a slump, I look at my feet. Almost always I will find that I am not standing right at the plate. That's the cause of the trouble."

George Burns, the first baseman, not the outfielder, had much the same comment. Said Burns, "If a batter could drop down from an aeroplane and land exactly right in the batter's box and stay just where he landed, he probably never would get in a slump. But many batters start digging their feet into the ground, move around unconsciously and before they know it, are in an awkward position which makes it difficult for them to hit the ball true or hard."

Ty Cobb, who knew more about batting than any one who ever lived, added his bit of advice. "In a slump, raise your elbows. You'll be more likely to swing the bat parallel with the ground, more likely to meet the ball fair. You may be unconsciously cutting up at the ball because your swing isn't right. Raise your elbows and you will get back into your stride."

Jake Daubert counseled overcoming a slump by avoiding the issue. "If you can't hit," said Jake, "bunt. Keep on bunting until you find you can hit once more. Any fast man who knows how to bunt can bunt himself out of a slump."

Bib Falk advised still more drastic methods. Said Falk, "The best thing to do in a slump, particularly when it gets on your nerves, is to take yourself out of the game. Take a vacation. Sit on the bench a few days. The rest should cure you. And when you come back to the lineup you'll probably be as good as new."

When Lee Fohl was managing the Browns, Ken Williams, the famous home run slugger, fell into a slump. "This was due," said Fohl, "to the heavy bat that Williams used. He couldn't get the bat around. He was so eager to make home runs that his general work suffered." Here is the suggestion of another possible remedy. Batters in a slump often shift bats. They find in a lighter or perhaps a heavier war club at least a temporary relief.

Many other batters might be quoted on this singular subject, but those whose opinions have been presented have covered the field. They comprise most of the greatest hitters of modern times.

Their opinions vary widely; are often contradictory. There is, as Roush said, "No general rule that can be laid down." All that any batter or any authority can do, is to offer some possibly helpful suggestion.

Striking Out

"I NEVER worry when I strike out," said Walter Johnson. But then, he was a pitcher and didn't need to worry.

The average batter strenuously objects to being retired on strikes. In general it means that he has been shone up by the pitcher and is a blow to his dignity. Moreover, the spirit of the fans reaches its lowest ebb when a favorite slugger strikes out in the pinch. "Casey at the Bat" still remains the classic among baseball tragedies. "The best batters in the world strike out once in a while," said Ed Walsh. He was 100% correct in that statement..

Doubtless the public is inclined to exaggerate the importance of a strikeout. Ed Reulbach said, "The fans don't seem to understand strike outs. Such a man as Hans Wagner, a great batter at all times, is much more likely to strike out than a fellow like Willie Keeler for instance. This does not mean that Keeler was a better hitter than Wagner but is a mere evidence of a different temperament and a different type of batting."

Walter Johnson, long known as the strike out king, who certainly knew something of strike outs if any man ever did, was also inclined to belittle one of Keeler's favorite exploits. Said Johnson, "When Keeler went an entire season without a strike out he merely showed what could be done by a clever batter with a certain batting style. Ty Cobb could do the same anytime he wanted to. But the good batter has something in mind very different from avoiding a strike out. He is either trying to advance the runner or to get on base himself. In order to do this to advantage it is often necessary for him to take two strikes before he even swings at the ball. At that stage the pitcher has him at a disadvantage and it is sometimes possible to slip over a third strike. If his intention was merely to hit the ball somewhere, anywhere, he could almost always do it, though in the majority of cases he would not hit safe. Personally I have little respect for such records which are mere showy performances made at the expense of a batter's own club and are directly contrary to the proper aim of legitimate batting."

An occasional strike out is not necessarily a disadvantage. Babe Ruth struck out more often than any other batter. But in the early days when Ed Barrow managed him, he said, "I don't object to having Babe strike out. He has to do something at bat and if he isn't coming through with a hit he might as well strike out as fly to the outfield. I had much rather he would strike out than to hit into a double play."

Ed Konetchy said, "A strike out once in a while does a batter good. Suppose he is in the midst of a streak hitting .500. All pitchers look easy. He grows overconfident. It seems all he has to do it to step into the box and wave his bat ferociously. A strike out shows him more plainly than a curtain lecture from the manager that a man has to work all the time in baseball and that it never pays to feel too sure of himself."

Sometimes players under certain circumstances are encouraged to strike out. This occasionally happens when a game is due to be interrupted on account of rain and a manager is in a hurry to retire the side. It occasionally occurs when a team is rushing to catch a train. More often, however, it is confined to the work of the pitcher. Jack Coombs said, "The pitcher would hit much better if he would put his mind on the job, but he has other things to think of. I remember a double header in which I worked against New York, years ago. I was at bat four times in the first game and twice in the second. I struck out exactly six times, that day. Why? Every time I went to bat Connie Mack would say to me, 'Strike out this time. Don't even take your bat off your shoulder.' He wanted me to save my energy entirely for pitching."

Certain pitchers specialize in strike outs, particularly speed pitchers like Walter Johnson and "Dazzy" Vance. Naturally batters who face these pitchers will strike out more frequently than common. The average pitcher endeavors to strike out a batter only at certain stages of the game, where a runner is within threatening distance. As Val Picinich said, "Most catchers know where a ball should be placed to fan a batter. But owing to a pitcher's mediocre control, they often signal frantically to have the ball so placed only to see the pitcher groove it and be slammed for a hit, or reach full length to grab for a wild one. This is discouraging work and hard on the catcher."

It requires usually the burning up of a good deal of speed and energy to fan a batter. Nevertheless, some pitchers can, almost at will, fan a certain batter if they set out to do so. For example, "Dazzy" Vance once struck out seven successive batters, tying a world's record. After the game he said, "If I had known I was that close to a world's record, I would have fanned the next fellow if I broke my suspenders doing it."

Striking out is the peculiar penalty of two entirely different types of batters; the waiter and the slugger. The waiter is trying to work the pitcher for a pass and usually allows himself to be put in the hole with two strikes. Often he will take the third, thinking the umpire will call it a ball only to be retired on strikes. The slugger, pursuing altogether different methods, and seeking to drive the ball out of the lot, will often miss a third strike because he is exerting himself to hit it hard. The fans, however, are very prone to forgive the slugger even when he fails. As Rogers Hornsby said, "Even when you swing yourself clear off your feet, in that moment of disappointment you will hear some fan's voice in the stands, 'If he'd ever hit that one it would have travelled.'"

The strike out, though unpleasant, is certainly no disgrace. It is an inevitable part of the batter's experiences.

Getting the Pitcher in the Hole

THE swift moving drama when the batter faces the pitcher passes quickly through various phases. From a point of rough equality, the pendulum swings violently now in favor of the pitcher, let us say, then in favor of the batter. Both are seeking an advantage. And it is the batter's two-fold objective to get the pitcher in a hole and to avoid that unpleasant predicament himself.

Claude Williams, once with the White Sox, said, "I do not consider myself in the hole even with the count of 3 and 2. In such a case I do not cut down on my speed nor do I groove one. I try to put the ball about where I would naturally put it. The batter may wait it out, but if he does so, the umpire is likely to retire him on strikes. He knows this, so if the ball is anywhere near the plate, he is apt to take a swing at it. Whatever the merits of the 3 and 2 count, there is little doubt that the pitcher who has two strikes on the batter at any stage of the game, occupies a strategic position."

Ty Cobb said, "Many batters have the mistaken idea that the pitcher is working on them and that there is nothing they can do in self defence. This seems plausible for they reason, 'We have to hit what he gives us.' That's only partially true, however. The batter is seldom compelled to hit any particular ball. He has a choice. Unless the count is 3 and 2 and the next one is over the plate, he can either hit at a ball or refuse to hit. Even when his back is against the wall and he is forced to do something, he can vary his attack. He can punch at the ball. He can slug from the handle of the bat. He can pull the ball to one field or the other. Oftentimes he can work the pitcher much more effectively than the pitcher can work him. He may brow beat the pitcher into giving him his base, or if the pitcher is uncommonly tough, he can bunt. There are a variety of weapons at hand and he can always choose that particular weapon which seems best suited to the needs of the moment. A batter is supposed to be in the hole when the pitcher has two strikes on him and not more than two balls. That's purely theoretical, however. I never consider myself in the hole when the pitcher has two strikes on me. He might have a shade the advantage, but I would proceed to off set that. Above all things I would guard the plate. I would crowd up close and watch everything he gave me very carefully. I would bite at no bad balls. He would be forced to put the ball over to tempt me, and I figured that if he did put it over, it was just as easy to hit that ball as any other."

The batter seeking for the particular ball he likes, sometimes delays until he finds himself in the hole. For example, Joe Jackson said, "In a general way when I am given a free hand, I aim to wait until I get a ball I like. That's the kind of a ball you can pickle. But you don't always get the sort of ball you like. When you're in the hole you have to hit at anything that comes over."

Burleigh Grimes said, "A pitcher has an overwhelming advantage when he can tell what the batter is going after. Dick Rudolph used to say he could do this. I do not question his word. I can do it myself very often on most batters. They have a way of tipping you off to their intentions. When a batter begins to see red, he starts cutting up at the plate. He shifts his shoulders or bends his knees or kicks the dirt with his hind foot or does something different. These are signs of battle, that the batter has made up his mind to hit the next one. So that when you see the gleam of conquest in his eye, you can bear down a little harder on the next one. If you have sized up the situation correctly, you can then lay back and listen to the pleasant sound of his bat as it swishes through the air six inches high while the ball ducks across the plate."

Getting the batter in the hole isn't always easy, however. Fred Marberry said, "I am a relief pitcher and have good luck. But when I go the distance I am not so lucky. Evidently I can fool the batters for a few innings but they get wise to me before the end of a regulation game. It's the same Old Abe Lincoln statement, 'You can fool some of the batters all the time and all the batters some of the time.' But I for one can't fool all the batters all the time."

Rogers Hornsby had a simple formulae to avoid getting in the hole. "Take your swings, all three of them. Have your cut at the ball. Don't let them call you out on strikes or get you in the hole. Have your three swings and you will hit."

Many a batter has found that the pitcher will get himself in the hole if you will give him a chance. Joe Gedeon said, "In April or May when the pitcher is wild, he will get himself in the hole and then have to lay one over the plate that you can hit. Later in the season when his control is good, he will just as readily get me in the hole instead and then I will find myself hitting at bad balls in self defence. It's the old story of pitcher versus batter. When either one of them has the other in the hole he has a big advantage."

Naturally the waiter type of hitter is most successful in getting the pitcher in the hole. Bert Shotton said, "A good waiter can worry the pitcher more than a little. The waiter doesn't hit at bad balls. He doesn't even hit at good balls until he has to. Consider the effect of such tactics on the pitcher. Suppose he puts one over the plate. The batter merely looks wise. The pitcher wastes one, hoping the batter will bite. But he doesn't. The pitcher curves over a strike. Still the batter does nothing. But he looks threatening. The pitcher fears that if he puts another one over, the batter will hit it so he wastes that ball. The count is 2 and 2. The pitcher decides the time is ripe to end the agony. He puts over another. The batter fouls it off. The pitcher gets crafty. The batter has shown a disposition to hit. He gives him another almost in the some place, but not quite. It is a ball. The batter let's it go by. The pitcher is now more in the hole than the batter is. The count is 3 and 2. The pitcher at least must get the ball over the plate. The batter doesn't necessarily have to do anything. Besides, the pitcher, in the effort to get the ball over the plate, is apt to cut down on his speed. That ball is threfore much easier to hit. The pitcher knows this so he may put all the stuff he can on the ball, hoping the batter will hit anyway. But the ball breaks away from the plate. The batter does nothing and gets his base. The pitcher has had all his hard work for nothing. For the moment at least he has completely lost confidence in himself."

Cactus Cravath remarked, "When the pitcher is in the hole, he is apt to do one of two things. He will either be a little wild and thus pass the batter, if he'll wait him out, or else, in the effort to get the ball over the plate, cut down on his stuff so that the ball is easier to hit. I like to see the pitcher in the hole. That's a situation which fattens batting averages."

Dick Kerr once remarked, "To my mind the worst hole a pitcher can possibly be in is to work in an extra inning game where the first man up hits a triple. In an extra inning game you can't afford to allow any runs at all and where the first man triples there are too many ways for him to score."

Eppa Rixey once said, "The worst hole a pitcher can be in is to have the bases filled with nobody out." This is indeed a psychological moment, but not a few pitchers escape from that tight place without a score.

Dutch Reuther went Rixey one better. "The worst hole a pitcher can be in is to have the bases filled, three balls and no strikes on the batter up and then be asked to go in and retire the side. I had that job once," said Reuther, "when I was pitching in Canada."

The Batter's Weakness

PERHAPS no theme in baseball proves more engrossing to pitcher and batter alike than the so-called batter's weakness.

Ed Reulbach said, "Every batter has a weakness. He may fight against it and refuse to admit it. He may even fail to recognize it as such. But it is there and the pitcher's cue is to discover it and make the most of his discovery. A batter's weakness consists of his inability to hit a certain type of pitched ball. For example, he may find it difficult to hit a low ball, though he may thrive on high ball pitching. Perhaps it is a ball on the inside of the play that bothers him. Perhaps it is a certain type of delivery like a curve or a slow ball. Depend upon it, no batter ever lived who did not detest certain kinds of pitched balls. He might be able to hit them, but they bother him none the less. It is difficult to estimate how much a batter's weakness will affect his average, but I believe where the pitcher takes full advantage of this weakness he can easily cut that batter's average in half. In short, I believe that the average batter will often hit as high as .350 when the opposing pitcher is not taking advantage of his weakness, while in cases where the pitcher does take advantage, his average will shrink below .200."

Claude Williams, once with the White Sox, said, "All batters have their weaknesses but now and again some master slugger will appear who throws all rules to the winds and seems to hit anything you can give him. Such a man is Babe Ruth. Off-hand you would say that left-handers should bother Babe, and they do. But he hits home runs off left-handers just the same. We held a consultation of war over Ruth one summer. We discovered, or thought we did, that Ruth lifted the ball when he hit it and therefore must like low balls. Armed with this information one of our pitchers gave Ruth a hot one off side which he couldn't possibly lift. Ruth met the ball fairly and drove it into our left field bleachers. So we decided that Ruth must like them outside of the platter. So another of our pitchers decided that a high one on the inside would be more advisable. He gave Ruth that kind of a ball. True enough, Ruth didn't knock it into the left field bleachers. He drove it clear out of the park over the right field wall, a stunt that had never been done since Comiskey Park was built. What is the solution to such a pitching problem? In my opinion there is no solution."

Beyond doubt the pitcher's study of this complex question is a problem. Jack Coombs once related an experience along this line. He said, "I gave Davis Robertson a curve which he missed by at least a foot. Well, thought I, that's a good thing to remember. I'll give you another one of those, old boy. Later in the game I did.

There were men on bases and it was quite advisable to retire Robertson, so I pitched exactly that kind of curve in almost exactly the same place and he drove it over the fence for a home run. A batter's weakness is all right, but you can't afford to bank on it too strongly."

"Dazzy" Vance held a somewhat similar theory. He said, "Batters' weaknesses are liberally discussed in the clubhouse and on the bench. There's one curious thing I've noticed about them. They seem to vary with the observer and I think I can explain the reason why. First impressions are always strong. If I am facing a young fellow I never saw before, I naturally have to work on him pretty much in the dark. Suppose I try him out with a curved ball and he looks weak. Consciously or unconsciously I am apt to set that ball down in my brain tablets as the one thing he can't hit. Another pitcher may decide that he looks weak against a fast ball. I don't say that a manager never changes his mind, but I do say that first impressions weigh altogether too much with him and they do with the rest of us."

Evidently the batter's weakness is often not clearly defined. This idea is tersely expressed in a rather illuminating comment by John Bassler. "I doubt," said Bassler, "if the public knows what a pitcher or a catcher really means by the batter's weakness. For example, it's questionable policy to give a batter many balls of the type he likes least. If you do so you will actually help him to overcome his weakness. Besides, a batter's weakness isn't a fixed quantity. It varies not only with the pitcher but with the stage of the game. It's something that is continually changing. And the catcher has to understand not only the batter's fundamental weakness but how that weakness becomes greater or less with changing conditions. Suppose, for example, Tris Speaker were at bat. Now Tris is one of the oldest and wisest batters in the business. Such a man is always a problem. Speaker has his batting points and like all the others, he has a weakness. If you pitched to Speaker waist high on the inside, he would drive out line hits all day long. But he isn't so good on a high ball. I don't say that he can't hit them, but he isn't so good. Last summer Speaker was at bat with two on, a critical time in the game. I tried to get two strikes on him as quickly as possible and had the pitcher put over two high, fast balls. Speaker missed one and fouled the other. Then the pitcher

111

wasted one. Speaker's greatest weakness is a slow, high curve. I had the pitcher give him one. Having already faced two high balls, Speaker was rather looking for another. He had a toe hold and was prepared. The curve completely crossed him up. He never even offered at it. He knew he was beat. But had I given him that curve at the first, he might well have looked for another and been in a position to hit it. Some pitchers can throw to a batter in a certain way and get by with it while others would be batted out of the lot for doing the same thing.

"There are pitchers, for example, who prefer to give the batter their strength rather than to pitch to his weakness. This is another way of accomplishing the same end. In his prime Walter Johnson was a pitcher of this type. His best ball was a high, fast ball. He would pitch them to a batter who liked high, fast balls on the theory that he would get so much stuff on the ball the batter couldn't hit it anyway. Naturally there are few pitchers who could afford to do this."

Grover Alexander mentioned a similar incident. He said, "Big Jim Vaughn used to pitch the particular kind of ball a batter liked best just to show him that he couldn't hit it. Nothing pleased him better than to strike a man out pitching to his strength."

While this was an occasional stunt, it was not Vaughn's steady policy, for he once said to me, "The older batters of the League are all carefully catalogued in the pitcher's mind. He knows the supposed weakness of every one of them and pitches to that weakness. That isn't to say, of course, that every ball pitched is to the batter's weakness. If this were so the batter would always know what was coming and in time would break himself of that weakness. But it does follow that in the main the pitcher tries to give the batter balls that he is known to have difficulty in meeting."

A batter's weakness is somewhat a matter of psychology. For example, Edd Roush said, "I don't know that I have any particular preference for one type of ball over another. Some days I can hit curves or fast balls or slow balls or spit balls and they all seem easy. Other days, for no apparent reason, they are hard to hit. I imagine the fault lies rather in the batter's mind than in the delivery he faces. On his good days he can hit anything. On his poor days he couldn't hit a watermelon with the side of a house. At least that is my experience."

In general, curve pitching bothers more batters than fast ball pitching. However, Ray Kremer said, "It's no use to look for batter's weaknesses in this League. They don't have them. On the Coast there were men who couldn't hit a curve very well. But in this league it is useless to look for batters who can't hit curves. You won't find them, except perhaps among pitchers and they don't count."

The pitcher's failure to discover a batter's weakness is the cause for some morning glory batting averages. Max Carey said, "Young fellows occasionally break into the League and bat in great style for a time. You think they are going to be world beaters. And then something happens. They slump and keep on slumping and slump right out of the League. The mystery is explained. They had some fundamental batting weakness. The pitchers didn't discover it at once, but when they did learn they drove the batter to cover."

George Dauss considered curve ball hitting the test of a good batter. "A good hitter," said he, "had rather meet a curve ball than a fast ball. The curve is the great bug bear of the mediocre hitter. Now the curve travels slower than the fast ball and its break, while greater, is not so sharp as the hop on the fast ball. Really good hitters like curves."

Vic Aldridge held much the same theory. He said, "Theoretically a curve ball would look harder to hit than a fast ball. I believe it is for the majority of batters. There are exceptions, however. Take Rogers Hornsby, for example. He hits a curve better than a fast one. There are other batters who thrive on curves. It's the same old story of what is one man's meat is another man's poison."

Jim Thorpe, the famous Indian athlete, might have been a great baseball player but for a batting weakness. He said, "I can't seem to hit curves. I believe I could hit .300 otherwise. But against curve pitching my average shrinks below .250."

The slow ball is a troublesome customer to many batters. Jean Dubuc once known as the master of the slow ball, said, "It seems odd to most people that batters can't hit a slow ball. But there is nothing odd about it. If you are sitting in a chair and a person went to hand you a glass of water, you would reach out and take it readily enough. But if that person dashed the water at you all at once you wouldn't be prepared and might get splashed in the face. The batter is in the same predicament. He sees the pitcher wind up and thinks from his exertions that he is going to put over a curve or a fast one. Hence, he is taken off his guard, is perhaps off balance, hits too quickly, is crossed up generally and even if he does meet the ball is likely to drive it only for a puny rap."

The slow ball is particularly troublesome to sluggers. Arthur Nehf said, "Sluggers break their backs reaching after slow curves. That is Babe Ruth's weakness, for after all, he is only a glorified slugger."

A batting weakness can often be overcome. Ira Flagstead said, "I used to be weak against a curved ball, but there is no reason why a good batter can not improve himself. Let him get pitchers on his own club to pitch to his weakness in practice and he can learn to thrive on the particular ball he thought he didn't like. Naturally some pitchers bother a batter. Williams of the White Sox struck me out twice in succession when I first faced him, but I watched him closely from the bench and the plate and soon got on to his style."

George Whitted had much the same experience. "When I broke into the League," he said, "I was nearly driven out on curve balls. I couldn't hit one of them with a canoe paddle. But fortunately I realized how rotten I was and I determined to hit one of those blamed twisters if it cost a leg."

Fred Clarke enlarged upon the same theme. He said, "When I was manager of the Pirates I knew every weakness and every strong point of every batter on the team. When they were not hitting right I knew why and could tell them so. But, and here is the rub, I never could tell what was wrong with my own batting when I was off stride. And there was only one man on the club who could. That was Beaumont. So I used to get him to look me over and diagnose my ailment.

"A weakness that is known, however, is different. You can cure that yourself, if you are willing to take the pains. I remember when Clark Griffith used to pitch. He was a foxy old bird and he fed me slow curves that made me look foolish. He had a genuine good time at my expense. But when his club had gone, I got a pitcher to throw slow curves to me by the hour until I could hit them. The next time Griff faced me there were two men on bases. He was full of confidence. He gave me a slow curve and I nearly knocked down the fence with it. I can still see the look of surprise on his face when that ball sailed over the outfield."

Cactus Cravath goes so far as to say a good word for a batter's weakness. "The best thing that can happen," said Cactus, "is for a batter to have a known weakness. Then you can be sure of what the pitcher is going to give you. This is a great advantage for you can get set for that particular kind of ball and murder it. Even if you do happen to be weak you can practice until you master it. I tell you, there is nothing like a batting weakness to boost the old average."

Dick Rudolph held that a batter's weakness was something, almost anything, that he didn't expect. "Most batters," said Rudolph, "try to foresee what the pitcher will give them, a majority of the time. And upon their ability to do this and make the most of their knowledge depends their success as batters. It follows that the most successful pitcher is the one who can most often fool the batter by giving him something that he isn't looking for. I would easily rate this talent as number one in the pitcher's list."

When is a weakness not a weakness? Lee Fohl said, "Often a good batter may have what would seem a weakness but it isn't a weakness for him. In may even be a source of strength. Some batters are graceful and some are awkward. Awkwardness is not a defect. Hans Wagner was awkward. In the last analysis it is results that count. The manager cares little and the public cares less how a .300 average is gained so long as it is gained."

Jim Bagby still holding tenaciously to his set theory, said, "I think Ruth has a weakness, because I believe every batter has a weakness. But I am frank to confess that in his case I don't know what it is."

John Bassler, however, was not so pessimistic. "Ruth has a weakness, of course," he claimed. "In general, a left-hander's curves bother him. He has certain peculiarities. He cuts up at nine out of ten balls. This would be a defect in most batters, but Ruth is the most dangerous batter in the League none the less. He hits

115

every ball so hard it's a possible safety. I once saw him make a home run at Detroit swinging the bat with one hand."

Hornsby, as he reached his prime, stated that he had no weakness. "Dazzy" Vance discussed this point. He said, "I have known Hornsby when there were two strikes on him to go after a ball that was high and a little off side. So personally I would figure that a pretty good ball to give him with two strikes. But don't overlook the necessary first step in that little program. You're passing over a lot of ground hurriedly when you discuss what you will do after you get two strikes on Hornsby. Of course, other pitchers would figure Hornsby different. That's just the point. If we all laid our heads together and cut out day dreaming, we'd probably admit in sober sense that he didn't have any weakness and we'd be about right."

And still opinions about great hitters differ widely. For example, H. L. Constans, Secretary of the Pittsburgh Club, said of Hans Wagner, when the latter was in his prime, "He has no known weakness at bat. Wherever the ball or whatever the delivery makes no difference to him, so long as it is over the plate."

And yet, Ed Reulbach took issue with this view. He said, "Hans Wagner was perhaps the most consistent hitter and surely one of the greatest hitters who ever lived. But had Wagner been obliged to bat against Old Jack Taylor all through a season his average would have shrunk to .150. No other pitcher had Wagner's number as Taylor did, but he would make Wagner so sore that the Dutchman frequently shifted and tried to hit left-handed. Honus simply could not guess Taylor right and he knew it.

"Ty Cobb is perhaps the most versatile batter who ever lived, and yet if Ty had to hit against Mordecai Brown an entire season he would not hit over .200. This is no criticism of either Wagner or Cobb. It merely shows that a pitcher with a certain type of delivery can stop any batter on earth."

The Use of Signals

EVERY ball club has its signals. They are quite as important as good management, in fact, they are an intricate part of good management.

The catcher continually signals to the pitcher. Base runner and batter have their system of under ground communication. Many an order is flashed in visible code from the bench. These signals are zealously guarded, but occasionally they are interpreted by the opposition. Advance information of this kind is always valuable and in baseball, legitimate. A ball game is a minature battle and many of the rules of civilized warfare are allowable.

Eddie Collins said, "The study of pitchers is an important part of batting. When I was with the Athletics we used to watch signals very carefully. This was an open secret at the time and no secret at all nowadays. We were fairly successful in catching signals. Being able to tell what the pitcher was going to throw gave us a decided edge in batting."

Eddie Plank corroborated this view and gave a concrete illustration. He said, "The Athletics profited a good deal from signal tipping. It was specially useful to the batter to know whether he could expect a curve or a fast ball. Stuffy McInnis, who was not naturally a good hitter, was able to hit over .300 solely through the benefit he gained from this inside dope on the pitcher's stuff."

Max Carey said, "Some times it is easier to detect a curve on the way from first base than it is at the plate. The coach at first base can sometimes fathom the pitcher in this way and flash his information to the batter. Ordinarily a pitcher holds a ball differently when throwing a curve than he does when throwing a fast ball. Ty Cobb has been particularly successful in telling when curves were coming, and I believe that is the secert of some of his success. Not all pitchers, however, can be analyzed in this way. Wilbur Cooper, for example, holds a curve exactly as he holds a fast one."

Where signals are most in evidence, of course, is in the work of the battery. Steve O'Neill said, "I signal my pitcher for every ball pitched. Some catchers signal only for fast balls or curves. I also signal for slow balls. I very seldom have a disagreement with my pitcher, certainly not more than once a game on an average. The catcher and pitcher must work together, in perfect harmony, or you will soon find the pitcher growing unsteady. A catcher can restore a pitcher's confidence more quickly than an air tight infield."

John McGraw uses more signals than any other manager. Babe Ruth once criticized this in a signed article. Confronted with this statement, McGraw made no effort to deny it. "What if it's so," he said. "It seems to get results."

John Rawlings explained this system. He said, "McGraw controls team play mainly through catcher and pitcher. He will give the catcher the signal on almost every ball pitched. As a result McGraw controls the pitching of his club, which is half the battle."

Chief Meyers once undertook to jolly Fred Luderus. When Fred ambled to the plate Meyers was ready for him. He fixed his fingers in a fake signal and said, "Look down into my glove. The best hitters steal the signs, you know." Luderus did not move. The pitcher shot one over the outside corner. Fred's bat swung with a crack and he ambled easily around the bases. "I don't need to steal signs to hit that pitcher," he told Meyers as he crossed the plate. "Besides, they pulled that stuff on me in the Bushes, long ago."

Infielders, particularly shortstops, get the catcher's signal for a certain kind of ball and play accordingly. Walter Gerber said, "The secret of playing short field is to lay for the batter. You get the catcher's signal. You know whether the pitcher is going to throw a fast one or a curve and act accordingly. When the batter swings to meet the ball you start either to the right or left. If he connects, you know where the ball should go and you are already on your way."

Signals are not altogether for the opposition. The batter and the base runner have their signals also and both are in continual communication with the bench. Eddie Collins said, "It is most essential for a player to have his mind always on possible signals. It is not an uncommon thing for a base runner to strike up a conversation with an opposing player when he is temporarily resting on a bag. But take it from me, there is many a signal flashed from a batter to this same base runner that escapes the latter's notice simply because his attention is not centered where it should be."

The famous hit and run play depends largely upon signals. Steve O'Neill said, of this play, "The batter has signalled the base runner to go down to second. He must hit at the next ball pitched. Therefore the catcher should signal for a ball that the batter can not hit. The batter, however, sometimes gets this signal and in turn flashes his intentions to the base runner. In fact, the hit and run play is a continual warfare between catcher and batter in which both are trying to get the other's signals and profit by the knowledge. Eddie

Foster and Joe Gedeon," continued O'Neill, "are the best hit and run men in the American League. But they can be crossed by a clever catcher. And when they are, they look as foolish as anybody else."

Some players endeavor to throw prying eyes off the scent by elaborate and meaningless signals. For example, "Dazzy" Vance said, "Deberry will sometimes signal for a certain kind of ball. I will look wise and solemn and shake my head. He'll signal again and I'll shake my head again. The batter, digging his spikes in the dirt and fooling with his bat, will naturally wonder what fearful concoction I am going to give him next, after all that playful interchange of thought waves with Deberry. So he'll be all set for some freak monstrosity and then I'll generally breeze over a fast one and have him looking foolish. Deberry and I have our little signals, but they are not quite so obvious."

When Not to Hit

THE fan's idea of batting is rather primitive. The number of times the player hits safely, compared with the number of times he takes his position at home plate is that player's batting average. All very simple, is it not?

But the student of baseball, the player who really thinks, discovers quite speedily that batting isn't so simple. He learns that there are other ways of showing batting ability besides the crude and obvious one of leaning on the ball. And he comes to the conclusion in time that these finer, more subtle methods are even more effective than lambasting the horsehide to the far corners of the lot.

John Evers graphically illustrated this point when he said, "I am convinced that in my own career I could usually have hit thirty points higher if I had made a specialty of hitting. Some lumbering bonehead who does make a specialty of hitting and nothing else may forge well across the .300 line and everybody says, 'What a grand hitter.' The fact is, the bonehead may have been playing rotten baseball when he got that average and someone else who didn't look to be in his class might be the better hitter of the two. Of course there are plenty of times when there is nothing like the old bingle. But there are plenty of other times when the batter at the plate should focus his attention on trying to fool the pitcher. In my own case I have frequently faced the pitcher when I had no desire whatever to hit. I wanted to get a base on balls."

Bert Shotton was even more outspoken in his praise of the waiting policy. He said, "To me the particular thing which baseball suggests is the base on balls. It is the corner stone of the game. The very name baseball is almost the same as base on balls. The spectator at the game is likely to look upon the base on balls as a mere incident; a momentary wildness on the part of the pitcher, or a gift to a dangerous batter. This opinion is often justified, but just as often the base on balls is a real tribute to the batter's skill in working the pitcher. Obtaining a base on balls is just as much an offensive detail of the game as a double or a triple. In many cases it is more destructive to the opposing defense than a hit, for it goes straight to the heart of the pitcher's confidence in himself.

Slim Sallee expressed the pitcher's viewpoint of the base on balls. He said, "A good bit of batting is knowing when to wait the pitcher out. There are a lot of good pitchers who defeat themselves through their lack of control. They have plenty of stuff, but they are wild. If the batter is foxy he will let those pitchers get in the hole simply by standing at the plate and looking wise."

George Sisler said, "When I was a pitcher myself, I always figured that when I had the batters swinging I had them beat. It's the waiting batter that worries a pitcher. Then you have to keep on getting the ball over the plate. That is a continual strain on a pitcher and the very thing he likes least of all."

Gladstone Graney, one of the best waiters who ever lived, said, "Not only does waiting a pitcher out impair his confidence and his control, but it also makes him work harder. A safe hit may be made on the first ball pitched. A pass is much more wearing on the pitcher's arm. It requires at least four balls and generally one or more strikes. Including fouls, I would say that the pitcher who issues a pass averages at least six pitched balls. Often he uses eight or nine. Besides, this extra work imposes a severe strain on his nerves and control. He is burning up a lot of strength and tiring the old soupbone. And in spite of all his hard work, he fails in his object, to get the batter.

"I believe that the waiting game is the most effective batting system that could possibly be devised. The batter can do the pitcher far more damage by waiting him out than he can possibly do by hitting safely. And isn't that what the batter is supposed to do; disrupt the pitching defense in every legitimate way?

"I frequently try to work the pitcher for a pass even with a man on first base. If I am successful, I advance that man to second quite as effectively as a sacrifice hit would do. Moreover, I have advanced him to second while getting a base myself. To be sure, waiting the pitcher out is not the common method of advancing the runner, but it is an effective method. Even a run is occasionally forced in by a base on balls."

Ed Reulbach confirmed Graney's opinion when he said, "A base on balls bothers a pitcher more than the average hit, for he knows that in the run of the game the batter is going to connect safely once in a while and he views a hit as an unavoidable accident. But the batter who works him for a base on balls has beaten him at his own game, and what is more, impaired his confidence in himself."

The ability of some players to work the pitcher for a pass is no less famous than the ability of other batters to slug.

In 1919 Babe Ruth received 101 passes, Graney 105. With men on bases and Ruth at bat the pitcher saw but one path to safety, and he chose it. Better an extra runner on first than a battered baseball skipping over the sunbaked outfield. Ruth's many passes to first were a tribute to the heaviest bat on record. But could any contrast be clearer than the contrast between the massive, fence-smashing Ruth and the unimpressive, slender and meagre hitting Graney? Ruth's passes were gifts. Graney's passes were earned.

How can the batter work the pitcher for a pass? Graney himself explained the system. "It doesn't occur to most people," he said, "that the batter has anything to do with it. He merely stands at the plate and takes what the pitcher gives him. But I can assure the public that the batter is working every minute of the time. Theoretically, if the pitcher had perfect control, you couldn't work him. But who has perfect control? The pitcher is trying to work you, your cue is merely to let him work himself. He will usually do this, if you give him a chance. No pitcher will willingly put the ball through the center of the plate. He is trying to keep the ball to one side or the other. In this effort he is apt to over-reach himself and put the ball a little offside or a little too high or too low. The waiter lets these balls go by. The batter swings at them, if they are to his liking. That is the difference between the two. If you swing and connect you are either safe or out and the pitcher is through with you. If you let them go by, the pitcher will be in the hole and you will still be a big problem in his mind. Then he gets nervous. He tries to cut the corners with the next one, but he is a little too careful. The ball breaks outside. Soon the count is, let us say, three and two. If he cuts the plate you are in a fine position to hit him and he knows it. If he tries to cut the corners he may miss again and pass you. He is likely to lose out either way. I never feel so comfortable as when I have the pitcher with the count of three and two. Usually I am that lucky at least once during the game.

"Contrary to some people's opinions," continued Graney, "I believe it is really harder to wait them out than to hit safely. For consider what the waiter has to do. If the ball comes anywhere near the batter, he intends to drive it out of the lot. The only thing that concerns him is whether the ball is going to approach the plate. His whole mind is centered on hitting that ball. But the waiter has a far tougher job. He doesn't know that he will even try to hit. He surely will not unless the ball is to his liking. He won't bite at any bad balls. His mind is set on avoiding batting, if possible. But, and here is the hard part, he may find himself obliged to hit to prevent being retired on strikes. So he has to make up his mind in the very last half second whether or not to swing at any given ball and from that time on his job is just as hard as the batter's ever was for he has changed at a moment's notice from a waiter to a batter while the batter was never anything else. In other words, the successful waiter has to play two entirely opposite systems every time he goes to the plate and he has to shift from one system to the other with lightning rapidity. Therefore I say the successful waiter has a harder task than the mere slugger whose mind is occupied with hitting the ball and nothing else."

The difficulties of the waiting game are well understood by wise batters. Like all good things, working the pitcher has also its disadvantages. "The waiter," says Ty Cobb, "is somewhat at the mercy of the umpire. He may think the fourth ball was off side and the umpire may call it safe. Hence, the waiter strikes out rather often. But at that I don't believe he strikes out as often as the slugger."

Undoubtedly playing the waiting game hurts the individual batting average. Max Flack said, "If they gave a fellow some credit for a base on balls it wouldn't be so bad, but they don't do this. At the best they merely don't penalize him with a time at bat. It is good baseball to work the pitcher for a pass, and it's evidence of good batting ability. Then why should the batter be called upon to do this at the expense of his own average? Owners say they pay little respect to the records, but they do just the same. I know that from experience. When I have had a pretty good season and mention that fact, the owner is quick to come back at me with the dope that I have hit only .260."

Though perhaps the finest exhibition of adroit batting, the base on balls is unpopular from the spectators' standpoint. Hank O'Day recalled how baseball was fundamentally changed by the modified foul strike rule. "This was one of the best things that ever happened," said Hank. "The rules stopped the tireless process of the batter always trying to get his base on balls. People like to see batters hit. They don't want too much waiting them out."

One of the most unpopular plays in baseball is undoubtedly the intentional pass where the pitcher shirks his responsibility by giving a dangerous batter free transportation to first base. This is, of course, an obvious tribute to a slugger's batting power. Numberless rules have been suggested to penalize the intentional pass. The inherent difficulty of the problem seems to lie in that word, "intentional."

Hollis Thurston said, "Occasionally you will pass a man deliberately, but more often you are working the corners in the effort to get him to bite at a bad ball. If you don't quite do this, or if the umpire gets dust in his eye at just that moment, you pass the batter."

George Dauss said, "I can understand the agitation against the intentional pass. But I consider it foolish. It sounds all right to give the slugger his chance to connect, but when the game is in the balance it is the game that counts. The crowd wants the home team to win. Naturally the only reason a pitcher passes a certain batter is because he is trying to win. If he didn't do this, he would be false to his trust, for he is supposed to use any lawful device to win his game."

Steve O'Neill said, "The intentional pass has made a lot of noise, particularly in the case of Babe Ruth. I realize the pass makes the spectators mad, but it's a part of baseball, so what are you going to do? I can see no way of reading it out of the game. I doubt the wisdom of leaving the decision to the umpire. Every time the batter got a pass, you would have a young riot on your hands for of course the pitcher would swear that he was trying to put the ball over the plate. Even though you thought he was a liar, how would you prove it? I have seen pitchers do mighty funny things. I have seen them miss the plate by two feet when I knew they were trying to locate it."

Lee Meadows said, "The intentional pass is exaggerated at best. If I give seventy passes during a season, maybe thirty of them will be partly intentional. A pass is a good thing with a man on second base and a dangerous hitter up for it offers the chance of a double play. Most passes, however, are merely careful working of the corners for some slugger where the pitcher's control wasn't perfect."

John Morrison clinched the argument with the cynical statement, "There is no way to prevent a pitcher from passing a batter. At the worst, he can hit him and thus compel him to take his base."

Ivy Wingo emphasized this point still more strongly. He said, "A pitcher who has determined to get rid of a dangerous batter could hit him with a pitched ball. Of course he wouldn't intend to injure the batter. He could hit him on the arm or the leg, but he surely would try to hit him if there were a severe penalty for passing him. Such a rule would be bad for baseball, in my opinion."

To sum up:—Good policy often demands that the batter refrain from hitting. Working the pitcher for a base on balls does more injury to the defence than a slashing hit. Waiting the pitcher out impairs his confidence in himself, unsettles his control and by making him work harder tends to tire his pitching arm. A good waiter must possess a keen eye and a cool judgment. Successful waiting is often harder than successful hitting. The knack, however, may in a measure be acquired.

The intentional pass is a tribute to a batter's slugging power. It is unpopular from the spectator's viewpoint. There seems no just way of legislating against the intentional pass, for it is difficult, if not impossible, to determine when the pass is intentional. Furthermore, as a last resource, the pitcher could hit the batter and make him take his base.

Mental Qualities That Influence Batting

"AN aggressive spirit is the best start toward a good batting average that I know anything about," said Wild Bill Donovan.

Ty Cobb emphasized this statement by a concrete illustration from his own experience. He said, "Throughout my career, if I had not developed the determination to succeed at all costs and possessed the ambition to go the other fellow one better, I doubt if I would have hit .320. In other words, my life-time batting average has been increased at least fifty points by qualities that I would call purely mental."

Determination, or, as it might be called, persistent courage, has another name in baseball. Miller Huggins said, "The very best characteristic a player can have, the strongest possible foundation for his success, is guts. I do not know another word which conveys so clearly and concisely those qualities of earnest, courageous, aggressive, good sportsmanship as that short, rather ugly monosyllable. Let a player of brilliant attainments lack that quality and he will never be more than a disappointment to his associates and to himself. The characteristics which the fiction writers call red blooded strength of purpose, ambition, decision, the scorn to be discouraged, all these and many other virile and commendable qualities are wrapped up in that blunt little word of four letters."

The aggressive ball player is not always amiable. For example, Joe Birmingham said of John Evers: "They claim he is a crab. Perhaps they are right. I have often wanted to know what a crab was. I wish I could find out. Above all, I wish I could get some on my ball club. I would like to have twenty-five crabs playing for me. If I did, I would have no doubts over the pennant. They would win hands down."

Mere mechanical ability means little without the mental traits which should give those talents their driving force. Carl Weilmann said, "A scout can often detect unusual ability in a young player,—that is mechanical ability. But he can't tell how much that young fellow is endowed with the determination to succeed or how hard he is willing to strive for success. That's the big unknown quantity in rating a youngster."

Not a few ball players have told me that they consider Ty Cobb's supremacy over all rivals was not due to his undoubted natural talents, but rather to his sheer determination to succeed. Ty himself remarked: "I was endowed by nature with a restless ambition that would acknowledge no superior. If I felt that another fellow had me beat, I was never easy in my own mind until I had surpassed him. No doubt this temperament of mine acted as a continual spur to make me hustle and accounted in no small measure for what I have learned of the difficult art of batting. The batter starts with a certain equipment which has been given him by nature. A good batting eye is an undoubted part of this equipment. Then there is a free swing, the punch behind the swing, the manner in which he stands at the plate. He can improve these things by observation of other players or by studying his own tendencies and defects. I would not minimize any of these things. They are important. But above and beyond the purely mechanical there is a wide field to which the batter may attain and where he may develop powers quite beyond those to which nature has seemingly limited him. This field I would call mental as contrasted with more physical gifts. Batting is unquestionably mental as well as physical. That is, it should be, though I must confess many batters use their heads little, if at all. The most important factors in batting are concentration and determination. Devote all your energy to the one thing of hitting properly and then everlastingly keep at it by sheer force of will. Determination is all the stronger if you get mad about it. Before going up to the plate I have deliberately tried to develop a grouch against the opposing pitcher. I have ransacked my brains to discover faults in him which I did not like. I have tried to develop a state of mind where I was burning up with eagerness to hit anything he could possibly give me."

Determination sometimes engenders a passing ill will among ball players. Joe Tinker, however, considered this of little consequence. He said, "Some people make a great deal of differences among ball players. This amounts to little. You can not expect to be on intimate terms with every player on the ball club, and there is no reason why you should be. I would like to see a player have a little more of that aggressive spirit myself. I think it is a good thing. Baseball is no game for mollycoddles. The man who makes a successful player is the man who has the most spirit, the most aggressiveness. He must have this spirit to make good."

Like all good things, however, aggressiveness can be carried too far. It is particularly unfortunate when it gives the player the reputation of being a trouble maker. John Evers said, "The thing that has held me back and hampered me at every turn is the prevailing sentiment among baseball men that I was too much of a scrapper; too likely to prove a disturbing element on a ball club."

No ball player can succeed all the time. But even failure may be made a stepping stone to success. For example, Carl Lundgren said, "Determination to win next time is the way to overcome discouragement and defeat. But," he added, "I consider a certain amount of discouragement is positively beneficial."

Frank Chance doubtless had the same idea in mind when he said, "Don't get discouraged over mistakes. A mistake is often the most valuable lesson a player can have."

The determined player never lets down on the job. Lee Fohl said, "I don't mean to say that ball players lay down on the job. There's not much of that in the Big Leagues, at least. But there's a big difference between doing work that is merely good and hustling at the top of your speed. It's the hustling spirit that wins. In fact I will say that any time a Major League manager has every man on his squad hustling, he has a prospective pennant winner."

Patience is a mental quality that the wise batter must cultivate. This is particularly true, of course, in the case of the batter who plays the waiting game. Gladstone Graney said, "There are players who can not seem to wait. They are impatient and if restrained by the manager they fall down completely. But the majority of batters would, in my opinion, be adding substantially to their value if they developed the patience to wait the pitcher out."

Waiting for an opportunity is a test of the player's nerve. Fred Mitchell said of the early part of his career, "My share in the proceedings was to sit on the bench and watch the other fellows play ball. But the bench warmer has his place in the scheme of things. We have all been bench warmers."

Discouragements come to all players. The unfortunate Phil Douglas once said to me, "A player will get discouraged easy enough, if he lets himself. But there is only one thing to do. Keep pegging away knowing that sooner or later something will break."

Stanley Harris who gave Washington its first Championship, said, "The manager who keeps the boys encouraged and on their toes is doing the best work possible for his club. The pace is a little hotter the higher you climb. But I am certain it is more difficult to manage a dispirited club than one which is in the running."

Sam Crawford once sagely remarked, "A man can not play baseball very long without becoming something of a philosopher." A philosophical poise is indispensable to the successful batter.

For example, Cactus Cravath said, "A man must be a good deal of a philosopher to get very far in this game. If he goes along day by day doing his best work and minding his own business, that isn't enough. Let him get into a few fights with the umpires, however, and other players, and people begin to say, 'Well, that guy is an aggressive cuss. He's a live wire.' And he gets his name in the papers and all the reporters want interviews with him, and the public swallows the bunk as usual."

Cravath was pessimistic when he said all that, but there was an element of truth in his words. The aggressive player who is too aggressive is quite certain to be colorful and color appeals to the public.

Worry is bad for the ball player. For example, Zack Wheat in a close pennant race, said, "I used to get up in the middle of the night and smoke a cigar so that I could calm down and get some sleep. It's a great strain on a player."

All players, however, condemn worry and some evidently practice what they preach. For example, Jack Bentley said, "One thing I have learned is not to worry. When I was with the Army in France I never worried. When I was under fire, sleeping on the ground, listening to exploding shells, I used to say to myself, 'Well, I might be in the hospital or the cemetery.' You have to take things as they come in baseball as elsewhere."

Babe Adams pitched well into the forties because, as he said, he didn't worry. "Mental attitude," said Babe, "has much to do with playing form. Excitable players are apt to be in and outers. A man shouldn't easily be upset by little things or he will be in hot water all the time in baseball."

The player's philosophy will vary quite as widely as the individual. But after all it rests upon certain fundamentals. It recognizes the basic fact that the batter's mental attitude is a compelling factor in his success.

Confidence

ZACK WHEAT once explained his greatest batting season in the terse statement, "I developed a contempt for pitchers." Ty Cobb called that statement the best short definition of batting ability he had ever heard.

Zack Wheat enlarged his definition a bit further when he said, "I have hit uncommonly well all season and the exact cause might be hard to find. True, I have felt well physically, but I have been in even better physical condition other seasons. Somehow I seem to have developed a lot of confidence. I felt like elbowing a pitcher out of the way when I met him. I could hit anything he had. I knew it and he knew it. That's the real explanation."

Most ball players rate confidence high among a batter's talents. George Whitted said, "It seems to me that almost everybody has tried to explain batting ability. The general opinion holds that it is in the eye. No doubt the eye has much to do with it. But my personal opinion is that batting ability, like all other ability, is in the brain. It's the knowledge of how to bat and the confidence that counts. The player when he goes to the plate can often tell when he is going to hit. He swings at a ball knowing that he will hit and he does. At other times he may have a doubt and he pops up a fly or misses altogether. To show how much confidence counts in batting, let me mention an experience of Dode Paskert's. Paskert once had a slump when he went for twelve full games without a hit. Finally he got so discouraged that one day when he was sitting on the bench he told the manager, 'If I tried to hit a fungo I don't believe I could get it past the infield'. Of course he woke up from that bad dream and started hitting again. Anybody with the physique to be a Major League ball player and the determination to make good, can make good, if he has confidence in himself."

Rogers Hornsby said, "The spirit that wins games is built on confidence. The lack of confidence and the fear of failure has just the opposite effect on a batter. I will go on record that if I did not have confidence in my own ability to hit any kind of pitching, I would never have led the National League nor hit even .300. If some manager had got it into my head that I couldn't hit certain kinds of pitching, and I had brooded over that idea and come to accept it as true, like a lot of batters I could mention, such success as I have gained would have been impossible".

Ty Cobb admitted that confidence was the keynote of his own unparalleled success. He said, "Over my twenty years of Major League experience, I have seen many batters. Most of them were mediocre. Some of them were good. A few were great. I have seen batters who had a better natural hitting talent than I possess. But I have never seen one that I would acknowledge, even to myself, that I couldn't beat. For that has been my motto throughout my career and I have never deviated a hair's breadth from that motto."

The player is very careful to retain his confidence in himself and to avoid doing anything that may impair that confidence. For example, Pie Traynor said, "Up to the time I joined the Major Leagues, I had seen a top notch ball club in action only twice. And one of those games I left in the fifth inning. Do you know why? I was afraid if I saw more of those fellows, I would become discouraged. They could play better than I and I didn't want to think that it was hopeless to compete with them."

The value of confidence is difficult to exaggerate. It follows that the lack of confidence is a painful handicap to the batter. Ty Cobb said, "My first season was the only one I failed to hit .300. Many people have wondered at this, but to me it is easy to explain. I came up from the South young—I wasn't over eighteen, and altogether inexperienced. I had a natural awe of Big League pitchers. They had me buffaloed. I was only a rookie looking for a steady job, not even certain that I could make good. Naturally I wasn't a regular. I played only when I was called upon to play. The second season, however, I gained confidence in myself. I found out what I could do and my real start dated from that time. The first year doesn't count in my scheme of things, thought of course it stands in the records."

Stuffy McInnis said, "There are times when it seems as though the ball player were working in a trance. I know I have made a peg to third base when I felt sure I was going to throw wild, and I invariably did throw wild when I felt that way about it. It was merely a momentary lapse of confidence."

Confidence, like every good thing, can be overdone. Over-confidence may become a worse fault. Jimmy Lavender said, "Over-confidence is never a good quality to have in baseball. Mere success should not make a man over-confident. If he is honest with himself he must admit that luck played a big part. I realize that I owe my own career, such as it is, to the blind chance which put the Cub pitching staff on the bum and gave me my long delayed opportunity. It takes a mighty little thing sometimes to change a winning career into a losing one."

Ball players are anxious to avoid suspicion of over-confidence. Benny Kauff, accused of this undesirable trait, said, "Perhaps I do talk too much at times and give a wrong impression. But to my way of thinking I am not swell-headed. I don't aim to be too confident, but I wouldn't give much for a ball player who didn't believe in himself. I am aggressive and confident on the diamond because I consider that I ought to be in order to be a good player."

What is confidence in the player's meaning of the word? Let us summon a little expert testimony on that point. John Evers said, "Confidence is a thing you can't describe very well, but you can feel it and see what it does. I never saw a clearer case of confidence than the Boston Braves showed in 1914. Their World's Championship was entirely due to confidence. In the early days of the season we were losing a lot of games by close scores. Such games are heart breakers. The boys got discouraged. It seemed as though they couldn't win. And then they got started and the pendulum swung the other way. We were winning games by close scores. Once we got started, nothing could stop us. It was confidence. That's all."

Miller Huggins said, "Confidence is the mental tonic which added to physical ability wins so many ball games. It is impossible to overestimate the importance of such confidence. Every winning club has it. No losing club has it. Lack of confidence can disorganize a ball club quicker than a series of accidents. Players get discouraged and they lose. They feel the breaks are going against them. It's the old story, you can't swim so well against the tide as you can with the tide."

Confidence, according to Jake Daubert, is an evidence of clear vision whereby the batter obtains a proper perspective of his own talents as well as the ability of the oposing pitcher. "Confidence," said Jake, "is the foundation of all batting. I have gained confidence in myself, otherwise I would not be able to hit .200. By confidence I do not mean that I expect to make a hit every time I step to the plate. I do, however, expect to make a try for a hit and generally I at least meet the ball. I have learned that all pitchers, even the greatest, are merely human and can be hit. I remember the first time I ever faced Christy Mathewson. He looked as big as a house. Young batters exaggerate the pitcher's ability and underestimate their own. The cure for this is confidence."

George Stallings said, "I have been in the club house when things were going badly. Some of the men may have been injured; we may have been meeting a club that looked to have a decided edge. And yet, I have sensed an air of confidence, a great enthusiasm on the part of the men that impressed me far more strongly than any bad luck or combination of unfortunate circumstances. It was the feel of victory in the air. With such men I have never been afraid to face what seemed like hopeless odds."

Every batter wishes he could hit. That is a mere hope. Confidence is a much stronger word. It is faith. Leon Goslin said, "I always figured I was a good hitter, but there's a lot of difference between believing a thing and knowing that thing. When I was an amateur I could hit some kinds of pitching, the kinds we were called upon to face in the Bush Leagues. But I didn't know for sure that I could hit Big Leaguers. When I broke into the Big Leagues I found I could hit pretty well, but it took me some time to really find myself. In time I was convinced that I could hit Big League pitching. From that date I have been successful."

Experience, by teaching a man what he can do, promotes confidence. There are, however, other aids. Ray Schmandt considered a good education helpful. He said, "A college won't make a good player out of a poor one any more than it would make a good banker of a man who had no ability in banking. But I do think a college education is useful in baseball just as it should prove to be in any other profession. It adds something to a man's confidence in himself."

Confidence is sometimes a matter of temperament. A sheer lack of nerves is often a good substitute. I once asked Jeff Tesereau, on the eve of a World's Series, if he felt the extra responsibility of the Big games. "Why should a ball player get rattled?" said Jeff. "I won't speak for the others, but I know myself. What is there to get rattled about? All I am supposed to do is to go in there and do my best."

Confidence is the ability to make the most of your ability. As Hugh Jennings said, "It isn't enough that a player should have talents. He must use those talents, otherwise he is merely a mechanical workman. The successful player has energy, perseverance, aggressiveness, ambition and confidence. They are all important and they enter just as much into his success as ability to field a hard grounder or to sting the ball."

Rogers Hornsby undertook to explain the part confidence played in batting. He said, "If a man doubts his ability to do a certain thing, the chances are he can't do that thing. If he has no doubt of his ability the chances are he will succeed. There is a certain mental attitude which I always try to maintain when I am batting. This mental attitude is merely this—to get in the frame of mind where you don't care who is pitching or what he gives you; whether he has an elaborate wind-up or a simple step and throw; whether he pitches a curve or a fast ball, high or low, inside or outside; to know that all you have to do is to meet the ball when it crosses the plate and feel within yourself that you have the ability to meet that ball."

Outguessing the Pitcher

OUTGUESSING the pitcher is a big question mark in batting. Is it the chief aid in successful hitting, as some experts affirm, or is it a quite useless incumbrance, as others claim, or may it be a positive hindrance to batting as still others would have us believe? Let us see what the batting authorities say on the subject.

For example there is Willie Keeler, one of the greatest of batters. He all but identified successful hitting with successful guessing. He said, "When you are hitting, it means that you are out-guessing the pitcher. When you are not hitting, it means that he is outguessing you."

Hugh Jennings said, "I know when I was a player myself and making a very fair record with the stick I always tried to figure out what the pitcher would give me. True, I was wrong a big percentage of the time, but the occasions when I guessed right were usually when I came through with a hit. I am convinced that had I not tried to guess what the pitcher would give me, I would not have hit .100. I know I used to lay for Amos Rusie's curve ball. He had a beautiful curve that broke like a bullet. Quite frequently he would get two strikes on me, but I would wait for that curve ball. I don't know that I would have even offered to hit his fast ball had he given it to me."

Tris Speaker backs up Jennings' statement. He said, "Personally I try to figure in advance what the pitcher will give me. I attempt to guess him right at least once in three times, though I do not always hit safely even when I have guessed right."

Bert Shotton said, "Ability to wait them out no less than ability to hit, requires a careful study of the pitcher. You have to bank on what the pitcher will give you on getting your base on balls no less than you do when trying to hit. You must know his tendencies at wildness and be able to predict his mental attitude. In short, you have to foresee what he is going to do and cross him or outguess him."

Sometimes guessing becomes a species of knowledge. For example, Ty Cobb said, "Much has been written about outguessing the pitcher. This is a practice I would not recommend. But the batter cannot observe pitching for many years, as I have done, and not know what some of those boys are going to do under certain circumstances. For instance, with two balls and no strikes, there are many pitchers that you can gamble will put over a fast one. Very often in a game you won't need to guess what a pitcher is going to give you. You will know."

Cy Williams said, "Most of the experts agree that guessing the pitcher is bad dope. I am with them in that opinion. And yet, perhaps a quarter of the time I am guilty of guessing myself, consciously or unconsciously. At certain stages in the game you can almost count upon certain pitchers doing certain things. The habit grows upon you like all habits and you have to fight against it. At least I do. Perhaps in guessing the pitcher I am right 50% of the time, but I know it is not a good practice. Most of the time I set my mind resolutely against it and merely wait for whatever the pitcher may give me."

Hans Wagner said, "Outguessing the pitcher? That's a hard proposition. Once in a while I will figure that a curve is about due or may be a fast one. Not often. Most generally I aim to be ready for whatever comes. That's the only safe rule in the long run."

Eddie Collins substantiated Ty Cobb's view. He said, "Off hand I would say that outguessing the pitcher is a mistake for the batter. Occasions arise, however, when guessing becomes almost a certainty. Long experience, familiarity with a pitcher and knowledge of what he does under certain conditions, sometimes give you an insight into his future operations so that you can sense what the next ball will be. In such a case you are foolish not to take advantage of your knowledge. Never try to outguess the pitcher, but figure him when you have the figures, is my batting policy."

Not infrequently the batter has the "figures." For example, Heinie Mueller said, "Sometimes the Giants' pitchers will give you nothing but curves. You know just what you are going to get and still you can't hit them. But I believe," added Heinie, "it's poor dope just the same."

Heinie is backed up by no less an authority than Christy Mathewson. He said, "It is mathematically poor dope for the batter to outguess the pitcher. The odds are heavily against him. There are too many things the pitcher can do if he chooses. Even if there were only a choice between two things, the odds would still be against the chooser. For example, if you call heads or tails on the toss up of a coin, you would figure you had an even chance. But the odds have been worked out as somewhat less than even, simply because you call the turn."

Most great batters as I have known them entirely repudiate guess work. For example, Lajoie once said to me, "The pitcher's thoughts are his own. I am no mind reader. I don't know what he is thinking about and I don't care. It doesn't matter to me whether he throws a curve or a fast one so long as he gets the ball over the plate where I can reach it."

Sam Crawford said, "Outguessing the pitcher is too deep for my blood. There are long odds against it. Often the pitcher himself doesn't know until the last few seconds what he is going to throw, so how should the batter know?"

Jake Daubert said, "If I had to depend on my ability to foresee what the pitcher had in mind, I would be lucky to bat .200. There may be batters who have this kind of head work, but I have no such ability myself. I have a notion that when I am at the plate, my main job is not to hypnotize the pitcher but to hit the ball."

Here are some brief bits of advice from famous hitters:

Clyde Milan—"Most good hitters are players who can hit anything and don't try to guess."

George Burns, formerly of the Giants—"I never try to guess the pitcher. I wait until I get a good one and then hit."

Jacques Fournier—"If the pitcher is trying to outguess me, he is wasting his time. I am not doing any guessing myself, so how can he outguess me? It's a contradiction in terms?"

Casey Stengel—"I don't try to outguess them. I let the pitchers do all the work and the worrying. I wait for a good one and then try to paste it."

Heinie Groh—"I never try to outguess the pitcher."

Harry Heilmann—"When it comes to outguessing the pitcher, I pass. In fact, I very rarely even try to outguess him. It is true that some pitchers follow a particular system most of the time and you can occasionally foresee what they will do under certain circumstances. With the count 2 and 1, or 3 and 1, there are pitchers who nearly always throw a curve. Others use a change of pace. If you call this guessing then every batter who uses his eyes is guilty."

Zack Wheat is even less friendly toward guessing than Heilmann. He said, "There are batters who watch the pitcher's hand and try to foretell what he is going to throw. Some of these batters claim to be able to predict from the way a man delivers the ball whether it will be a curve or a fast ball. Perhaps they can. I don't even try to do this myself. This is observation and is a little different than guessing, but I don't think it's good dope and I never try to guess what the pitcher is going to throw even when I have a hunch that it's a fast ball, for instance. I don't like to dwell on the thought. I want my mind on the ball and nothing else. And I want to feel that I can hit it no matter what happens. If batters would concentrate on that one thing and forget all the other frills, I believe they would be better off."

Most batters admit that pitchers try to outguess them, but some even criticize that. For example, Cactus Cravath commenting on outguessing the batter said, "Any time a pitcher does this, he is playing into your hands. As things are, he has odds of four to one against you, for the average batter doesn't hit safely more than once in four times. But when the pitcher tries to fool you by just guessing you have roughly as much chance as he of being right. And that looks to me like a big come-down for a pitcher."

At this juncture it is well to remember that some experts claim that it isn't the pitcher but rather the catcher that you must guess. For example, Fred Mitchell said, "Most of the war of wits that you read about between pitcher and batter is really between catcher and batter. It is the catcher who calls for curves or fast ones and determines when the pitcher is justified in wasting a couple. Most good hitters pay more respect to the catcher than they do to the man on the slab. They know the fellow they face is merely acting under orders and that the man they must beat is the man who is giving those orders. The batter knows this and takes advantage. Some catchers will not call for a fast ball under certain circumstances. The batter learns this. The catcher in turn realizes that he is being studied so he retaliates by often giving the batter something he wasn't looking for."

Along the same line George Sisler said, "The batter studies the catcher quite as closely as he does the pitcher. I know I do. It's useful knowledge. Not infrequently the catcher is the brains of the battery. He's the man you have to beat."

Some batters go so far as to claim that the effort to outguess the pitcher is not only useless but injurious. Zack Wheat said, "Poor batters generally try to outguess the pitcher. I won't say positively that is the cause of their poor hitting, but I do know that good batters generally don't try to outguess the pitcher."

Rogers Hornsby said, "Many batters are not content to hit the ball. They want full particulars about what it will do. They are the boys who give rise to the popular fable about outguessing the pitcher. Now this can be done theoretically in two ways. First, you can study the pitcher's delivery, the way he holds his hands and get some idea whether the ball will be a curve or a fast one. I consider this information as worse than useless for at best it is fragmentary. You simply haven't enough knowledge to go on and you are led to depend upon a false basis of reasoning. The other way is pure guess work and is still worse. To figure that just because a pitcher has thrown two successive fast balls it's about time for him to put over a curve, is all wrong. When the batter is in the box, he has enough on his mind to watch the ball closely and meet it. If his mind is cluttered up with theories and diverted by a lot of side issues, he can't concentrate on the problem which confronts him."

Big Ed Konetchy summed up the situation as it applies to Major League batters, fairly and concisely. He said, "There are just two ways to bat at all. One is to follow the ball with your eye from the instant it leaves the pitcher's hand. The other is by knowledge of the pitchers' peculiarities and his style of delivery, to try to figure what he is going to throw next and be prepared for it. Following the ball with your eye is much the more important of the two. But still I do not believe there is a good batter in the game who does not occasionally try to predict what the pitcher will give him next."

On Being Gun Shy

FEAR of being hit by a pitched ball is one of the least obvious but still important factors in batting. This fear impels the player to commit both mental and physical batting faults. In the mental field it shakes his confidence in himself and disturbs the calm, concentrated mind which is the proper mental attitude of the batter at the plate. Physically it is a constant urge upon the batter to pull away from the plate and, as the saying is, to hit with "one foot in the water bucket."

This natural apprehension is doubtless increased in the case of the batter who has been "beaned." The picturesque career of Frank Chance as a player was hastened to a close because the peerless leader was hit on the head several times by a pitched ball. Chick Fewster had his career much handicapped, if not entirely disorganized, by a similar painful accident. And it was a bean ball which brought sudden death to Ray Chapman in the very midst of a brilliant career.

Sometimes the approaching ball seems to exert an almost hypnotic fascination on the batter. Ed Walsh once related the following painful personal experience. He said, "I was at the plate. The count was 3 and 2, the psychological moment the batting sharps talk about. I was gazing out over the scene in a peaceful sort of way, wondering where that ball would go as it sailed out over right field fence, when zip, something happened. I was sure that "Mule" Watson, the pitcher, would cut loose with a fast one over the plate. He made good on half that prediction. The ball he pitched was fast enough, but it wasn't over the plate. It came straight for my old bean with the speed of a bullet. They say that a bird is hypnotized by the eye of a serpent. I don't know how that may be, but I was hypnotized by that ball. I tried to get out of the way, but I couldn't to save my salary. The most I could do was to turn my head and take it where the bone was thickest. There was a crash that sounded like the explosion of a Howitzer shell, a shower of sparks and rockets and then the curtain rung down. I dropped to sleep for a nap of several hours and awoke feeling like the morning after. My head may be hard, all right, but it isn't too hard to ache."

Hack Miller the strong man rather gloried in sheer physical force as a protection against injury. He said, "John Morrison hit me on the head with a pitched ball. The grand stand began to turn around like a top. I heard organs and angels and all kinds of queer sounds. But I didn't really lose myself. That showed the players that my head was tough."

John Collins said, "Some seasons ago I got hit in the head with a pitched ball. That's an accident that most players encounter sooner or later. I don't want more experience in that line myself. And I was lucky at that. I wasn't dangerously hurt, but I had a first-class headache that lasted a long time. And," added John meaningly, "you have to fully recover from such an accident before you know definitely that nothing serious is the matter."

In the season before his untimely death, Jake Daubert was laid up for some time with a bad case of "beaning." When he got back in uniform he said, "This is the eighth time I have been beaned since I joined the National League. There are seven pitchers who have the honor or distinction of bouncing a baseball off my cranium. I say seven because Big Jeff Teserau, when he was with the

Giants, did it twice. Either I am getting old or few rivets have worked loose in my skull, or Sothoron put more steam on that ball than I thought. Anyway, this eighth experience of mine was the worst of the lot. For several hours I couldn't see. And when my sight did return, it kept coming and going like switching an electric light on and off. Besides, blood oozed out of my ears and I developed a first-class headache which lasted for three weeks. I tried various remedies, but the thing which seemed to produce the best results was a simple massage."

A player can be seriously hurt by getting hit elsewhere than on the head. Cy Williams recounted how he was injured primarily because of the confused bleacher seats in the Philadelphia Ball Park. He said, "I suffered a broken arm some years ago simply because with the bleachers back of the pitcher full of fans, I absolutely could not see the ball at all. It struck my arm above the wrist and broke the bone."

The prime cause of hit batsmen is, of course, pitching wildness. Dazzy Vance said, "Look up my record. When I was in St. Joe I gave 110 bases on balls and I hit 25 batters, ten of them on the head. I had nothing against these batters, you understand. They simply couldn't seem to get out of my way fast enough. It always gave me the cold creeps to hit a batter on the head."

Wild pitchers are proverbially unpopular among batters. "Duster" Mails acquired his nickname because of his habit, in his early years, of dusting the batter off the plate. He didn't, however, do this deliberately. "Anybody," he explained, "who stood up to the plate when I was pitching in Brooklyn, was in danger. I was very apt to hit him if he didn't move and move quickly. But I was just as apt to put the ball ten feet away from him where he couldn't hit it with a broomstick. I didn't deliberately try to dust him off. I simply couldn't make the ball do what I wanted it to do."

Rarely a batter is dangerously hurt by a bean ball. Jeff Pfeffer, who nearly wrecked Chick Fewster's career, explained the unfortunate case. He said, "Nothing was further from my thoughts than what actually happened. While batters are hit fairly often by pitched balls, it is rare to see one hit on the head. A man can duck his head in the fraction of a second. But Fewster never moved a muscle while that ball came toward him. I thought at first he was hypnotized, but later he claimed that he never even saw the ball. It was a very unfortunate affair, but as I certainly had no intention of hitting this batter, I could not blame myself. It was merely my bad luck to be mixed up in such an accident."

The most famous incident of beaning was the fatal accident which cut short the career of Ray Chapman. What added to the tragedy was the maze of rumor and criticism which sought to hold Mays responsible for the affair. Mays himself explained his part in the proceeding. He said, "The death of Ray Chapman is a thing I do not like to discuss. It is an episode that I shall always regret more than anything else that ever happened to me. And yet, I can look into my own conscience and feel absolved from all sense of guilt. The most amazing thing about it was the fact that some people seemed to believe I did this thing deliberately. Now I am a pitcher and I know some of the things a pitcher can do and some he cannot do. I know that a pitcher cannot stand on the slab, sixty feet from the plate, and throw a baseball so that he can hit a batter in the head, once in a hundred times. But to kill a man it is not enough even to hit him on the head. Walter Johnson, with all his terrific speed, has hit batters on the head and yet they did not die. There is only one spot on a player's skull where a pitched ball would do him fatal injury. That is a spot about his temple which isn't half as large as the palm of my hand. Suppose a pitcher were moral monster enough to want to kill a batter with whom he can have no possible quarrel. How could he do this terrible thing? Christy Mathewson in the days of his most perfect control couldn't have hit a batter in the temple once in a thousand tries."

Walter Johnson said, "The bean ball is one of the meanest things on earth and no decent fellow would use it. I shall not attempt to judge anyone, but there are pitchers, I am convinced, who do resort to the bean ball intentionally. Such a ball to be effective must be pitched fast. The bean ball pitcher is a potential murderer. If I were a batter and thought the pitcher really tried to bean me, I would be inclined to wait for him outside the park with a baseball bat, or I wouldn't be averse to spiking him as I slid into first base when he was covering the bag. I don't think any treatment of such actions is too severe."

Pitching wildness and the resultant fear of being hit which it implants in the batter's mind, is a serious deterrent of batting.

Wilbur Cooper said, "One reason why pitchers are often weak hitters is because they are gun shy. Their batting eye is not developed enough so that they can protect themselves. They are not at bat often enough to learn how to dodge. Now I do not believe that pitchers deliberately bean batters. But take a pitcher like Dazzy Vance for example. Suppose he tries to put the ball high, on the inside, a good spot for some batters. Suppose he gets it a little higher or a little more inside than he intended, for he has a lot of speed and his ball hops. Such a ball might hit a man in the head when it was furtherest from Vance's intentions."

Not only pitchers are afraid of being beaned, the greatest batters sometimes have the same fear. Ty Cobb said, "Walter Johnson, for a long time, had me buffaloed. I wouldn't admit it to anyone else, and I don't think I ever showed it. But I had a dread amounting almost to positive fear of his fast ball. I have a vivid recollection of how it seemed to me when I faced Walter. That accursed fast ball of his used to whistle when it shot past. I found myself unconsciously speculating on just what would happen if that ball hit me on the head. It wasn't a pretty picture."

This natural aversion which even Ty Cobb admitted, may, however, be overcome. Ty went on to say, "I took myself resolutely to task for all this. I reasoned with myself. I said, 'I am up here to make a success. I must overcome this foolish fear. The worst that can happen to me is that Walter Johnson will hit me. If he does hit me that is all a part of the risk I assume playing ball, a risk that is peculiar to my profession. I won't be intimidated by anything a pitcher can give me. This fellow is human and while he is something of a problem, I must solve what he has to offer.' So I ignored my fears. I not only refused to back away from the plate, but I crowded the plate. I was determined to conquer Johnson's fast ball. And that season I batted nearly .700 against him, a higher average, I believe, than anyone else ever made at his expense."

Occasionally a batter will deliberately allow himself to be hit by a pitched ball. Fred Snodgrass was accused of doing this in a famous Word's Series. He did obtain his passage to first several times during this series by being winged by the ball.

While the fear of getting hit is a powerful handicap against batting, actually being hit sometimes helps the offensive. It is obviously equivalent to a base on balls and its effect upon the pitcher is even more disastrous. As Oscar Vitt remarked on the occasion when he was beaned by Walter Johnson, "Walter was so much upset by the accident that he couldn't locate the plate and we pounded him all over the lot."

We have also noted how Ty Cobb overcame the terrors of Walter's fast ball. Every batter has something of the same problem. Cactus Cravath said, "I have been hit on the head several times and believe me I felt it, even though my skull may be all that some people try to make out. But the bean ball itself isn't particularly dangerous, with all that has been written against it. A ball thrown directly at a player's head can be ducked easily enough. Those which are really more dangerous are balls which are thrown considerably lower so that in trying to duck the batter actually lowers his head to the line of approach to the serious detriment of his own skull. I have heard players say they would just as soon be kicked by a horse as hit by a bean ball. I cannot agree with them. True, I don't like to get hit any better than the next man. But I realize it is part of the game. If you get hit today, you can probably breathe easy until a week from next Thursday. The only safe rule is to stand up to the plate and take your chance. If you are shying all the time at what the pitcher throws you, you might just as well go over and sit on the bench."

Don't Let Them Get Your Goat

"DON'T let them get your goat" is homely advice that is whispered and spoken and shouted to literally thousands of batters from April to October. The indefinite "them" referred to are primarily the opposing pitcher, catcher and that much criticized individual, the umpire.

A batter's eye isn't clear when he's seeing red. And mental poise and self possession are quite as important at the plate as other more advertised talents. Beyond a doubt losing one's goat is a very genuine batting weakness.

Babe Ruth once illustrated this point. He said, "Some years ago a youngster went with us to Hot Springs to train with the Red Sox. He had made a great reputation for himself as a batter in the

Minor Leagues. He showed well in practice games in the south. He also got off to a good start in the regular season. Then the pitchers discovered a weakness of his. He was afraid of a high ball on the inside. Perhaps he had been hit by a pitched ball. At any rate he would step away from the plate when the ball was high on the inside. He appeared fearful that such a ball would hit him on the head. The result was that the pitchers took advantage of him by driving him away from the plate. His batting average fell away to a whisper and he was back in the Minors by July."

Benny Kauff said, "The main thing a batter should do, in my opinion is to study the pitcher. The pitchers in this League are wise old birds. They are lying awake nights trying to get something on the batter. Naturally they will succeed in doing this so long as the batter goes to sleep and lets them get away with it. I know they are getting me altogether too often and making me do the top act at the plate. Don't let the pitchers get you going is my advise to any young batter."

Not only are all pitchers scheming to take advantage of the batter, but he will generally find some pitcher whose slants are particularly difficult for him to solve. Ed Konetchy said, "Every batter has some pitcher who is a tough nut for him to crack. I believe if you would ask most of the good hitters to name the particular bad actor of their pitching enemies, they wouldn't speak of Mathewson or Rucker or Walter Johnson, but some unknown Bush League star just breaking into the game. The Busher puts everything he has on the ball. He is wild and you can't predict what he will do next."

Rogers Hornsby, while admitting the batter's dislike for certain pitchers, ridiculed this mental attitude. He said, "Most batters have the idea in the back of their heads that a certain pitcher is hard for them to hit. How foolish! They don't have to hit the pitchers. All they are called upon to do is to meet the ball. It's the same ball whether Alexander handles it or some unknown rookie. The eye can travel much faster than the ball and so can the bat. The batter can meet the ball no matter who throws it."

The left-handed batter's aversion to a left-handed pitcher is deep seated. Edd Roush said, "I object to the left-handers on principle. Southpaws have a bad habit of stinging me in the early innings of the game. Later on, if I am lucky, I manage to caress them with a hit or two. But the game is usually pretty well advanced, if not entirely over, before I can step up to the plate and face them with any degree of confidence."

Pitchers are often distinguished by their ability to beat certain clubs. The opposing batters surrender their goats before the first shot is fired. As an example, George Chalmers said, "I always did seem to have the Indian sign on the Giants. The Giants had a chance to get me, but McGraw thought I was through, so I signed up with the Phillies and the first game I met the New Yorkers, I held them to a brace of hits."

Carl Weilmann held a particular jinx against Detroit. He said, "I can't explain why I should be so lucky against the Tigers. Perhaps I am going uncommonly good when I face them. And perhaps they are not going so well. There must be some explanation besides the one the Detroit players give. They claim I am merely a big, lucky stiff."

Vean Gregg said, "I suppose every pitcher has some club that he can beat easier than others. I never thought the White Sox were weak. Certainly they wouldn't rank so on the records. But I have won twelve straight games against them and four of those games I was opposed by Big Ed Walsh."

The batter must not only be on guard against the pitcher. He must also consider the latter's battery mate, for the wise catcher is frequently a thorn in the side of the inexperienced hitter. Muddy Ruel said, "There is one important way in which a catcher can help his pitcher. That is by talking to the batter. I admit that all batters are coached to pay no attention to the catcher. But it is human nature to listen and still more human to be influenced to some extent by what you hear. There are batters in this League who can be talked to. Once you get their minds off their work, even for an instant, they are in a bad way."

Ira Thomas rated talk as one of the catcher's most important weapons. He said, "The backstop can often do much more damage with his mouth than he can with his throwing arm. The catcher who knows his business will keep up a rapid fire conversation with the batter in the effort to get his mind momentarily off his work. Sometimes he can even get his goat. Then he has him."

The umpire is a perennial problem. Rogers Hornsby said, "I suppose the umpires do their work as well as it can be done. And I can appreciate the difficulty of their jobs. But they certainly do make life rough for the batter sometimes and they're always a problem that you have to figure just as you try to figure the opposing pitcher."

The umpire bulks larger on the horizon of the waiting type of batter than he does with the slugger. Said Bert Shotton, "The waiter, much more than the average batter, must study the umpire. And to a degree he has to gamble with the umpire. Occasionally I tell an umpire I think he is mistaken, but I never argue. I believe arguments with umpires are bad policy. There isn't much excuse for an umpire's calling one that is wide of the plate. Where they go astray is on the height of the ball. Bear in mind, the catcher is crouching right in front of them and they can not follow a low ball very well. Besides, many batters crouch more or less and it is often a question whether a ball was above or below the line of their shoulders. I make allowances for the umpires, knowing that they are human beings like the rest of us, doing the best they can. The umpire, from the batter's viewpoint is a kind of necessary evil that he will be wise to accept with as good grace as possible."

Everett Scott said, "There is no excuse for umpire baiting and I have no taste for that sort of thing anyway. I believe I have been put out of the game just twice since I have been in the Big Leagues and there is a certain umpire who gave me the gate both times. He may have done his duty as he saw it, but I never had the least trouble with any other umpire. You can mark it down that a player is seldom put out of a game unless he gives the umpire pretty good cause to be sore."

No doubt the umpire should make allowance for an excitable player. Governor Tener, when President of the National League, once criticized one of his umpires for putting a player out of the game. The player happened to be Jack Smith of the Cardinals and he was thrown out at second on an eye lash play in trying to stretch a single to a double. He threw his cap on the bag and the umpire ordered him off the field. Said President Tener, "If I had been in the umpire's position, I think I would have picked up his cap and handed it to him. That, in my opinion, would have been far more impressive than ordering an excitable player off the field."

While many players object to arguments with the umpires, there are some who defend such arguments. Frank Chance said, "Avoid umpire baiting. The most successful teams are those who keep off the umpires. Don't kick needlessly, but at the same time, don't let anybody put anything over on you. It does no harm to let the other fellow see you are watching every move."

Even Old Nap Rucker, one of the easiest going persons who ever donned a uniform, sometimes got "riled" at the umpire. He said, "The crowd doesn't bother me with their yelling. But there is one thing that does bother me. And that is the umpire when he starts to go wrong. The pitcher can tell whether he has put over a strike as well as the umpire. Still, it does little good to rave about it. The umpire was put there to give decisions and no one can expect that he will be right all the time. So far I have never been put off the field by an umpire."

John Evers said, "It's getting pretty tough these days in baseball. I was fired out of so many games on my ear last summer by these human walruses in umpire's suits that I think my ears must have callouses on them. And instead of sympathizing with me, everybody seemed to sympathize with the umpires. They all took a turn at panning me. I began to think I must be some relation to the Kaiser. I have made up my mind that my mouth will be hermetically sealed this season. So far I have got along fine. I have been in two games already and haven't bawled anybody out yet. I believe I can keep on being a human Sphinx, though they say that steam under pressure exerts tremendous force and is liable to cause an explosion."

John McGraw, another vulcanic spirit, has had more than one altercation with umpires. After a verbal interchange which ended in a fist fight, McGraw said, "What was I to do, stand and be insulted by this umpire? I wouldn't think much of a man who wouldn't resent a personal insult."

No doubt some players have suffered because of their reputation as trouble makers. John Evers was one of these. He said, "Much trouble results from the fact that some players have a reputation for being bad actors and the umpires won't give them a chance. If I never spoke another word to an umpire, the public wouldn't get wise. They would still think I was an umpire baiter because I have that reputation."

Howard Ehmke said, "The umpires certainly figure a man a good deal by his reputation. I have the reputation of being a little wild, and what happens? The umpires never give me the corners."

It is a decided handicap when a batter loses his goat easily to pitcher, catcher or umpire. It is an even greater handicap when his reputation leads the umpire unconsciusly to give him the worst of the close decisions.

Grasping Sudden Opportunities

THE player who can take advantage of any slip on the part of the opposing ball club is the smart player. This requires an alert mind, a close concentration on the task in hand and a thorough knowledge of baseball.

Trick plays are the spice of an otherwise drab game. However, there is a distinct difference between plays that can be worked on an amateur diamond and those that would succeed in a high grade, professional league.

Fielder Jones said, "It is ridiculous to hear the old boys relate some of the tricks old timers used to pull off. Mike Kelly, for instance, would cut across the diamond from first to third base without going anywhere near second. If the people who called that stuff clever knew the difference between a baseball and a pumpkin, they would talk differently. Why such junk as that wouldn't get by now in a Class "D" Minor League. The fact is those tricks they rave so much about are a joke. They would be proof enough if other proof were wanting, that baseball thirty years ago was a pretty crude proposition. And why shouldn't it have been? Does any sport reach its prime at the start?"

Tricks are not so common as they used to be, because, as Fielder Jones says, "Baseball has developed to such a point that many of them would be ineffective." However, modern baseball of the highest grade is enlivened by occasional examples of daring and initiative.

George Sisler said, "Ty Cobb resorts to infinite tricks, legitimate, to be sure, but tricks just the same. For example, he often slides into first base. Other batters seldom do. Ty does this for two reasons. First, he makes the play look close and predisposes the umpire in his favor. Furthermore, he kicks up a cloud of dust which further complicates the play and is liable to disconcert the first baseman so that he fumbles the ball."

Ty Cobb himself has always been a champion of offensive play. He said, "After all, the offense has it on the defence every time. The Tigers didn't score more than any other team last year on batting alone. They scored part of those runs by demoralizing the defence. The daring player knows what he has in mind all the time. The defence doesn't. I take advantage of the psychology of the thing continually. The infielder can't handle himself so well when he is laboring under a cloud of uncertainty. Hurried work is poor work. I try to keep him in the dark as to my intentions and make him hustle when I disclose those intentions. The trick play is going," continued Ty sadly. "It will be too bad when it disappears for it is the one thing above all others that adds spice to baseball."

Hans Wagner once told me his impressions of Ty Cobb. He said, "I watched him in the games he played against us. He was trying all the time to take advantage of every opportunity that offered just as you would expect from a great player. I shifted around some myself to see what he would do. When I moved over toward third, he would alter his attack and try to drive the ball through the gap between short and second. True, he wasn't always successful, but I could tell what was on his mind. He was always looking for a weak spot somewhere that he could take advantage of."

This spirit which Hans Wagner describes so simply and yet so forcibly is a rare and valuable talent in itself. Lee Fohl said, "The player who is really doing the best work on the ball club is frequently a quiet, unassuming chap who doesn't hit .300, but is studying the opposition all the time and trying to win for the club."

Frank Chance said, "Don't encourage rough work, but insist that your players grab every reasonable opportunity."

Ability to grasp a sudden opportunity demands that rare and much discussed talent known as quick thinking. On this subject Eddie Collins said, "A favorite topic in baseball is so-called quick thinking. Probably there is no theme which has been more discussed or less understood. Some players possess the knack and some do not, though they may have even superior intelligence. It's not a matter of education. It's not even a question of brains. It's an example of mental alertness. Ty Cobb possessed this mental alertness to a degree which I believe has never been equalled. His mind worked like chain lightning. What his eye saw, his brain instantly resolved upon and his finely geared body instantly set in motion. Quick thinking demands not only insight into a problem, but the ability to make an instant decision. This is where most players lose out. They readily comprehend an opening when it offers, but they lose a fraction of a second in balancing risks. And in that brief delay all hope of success goes glimmering. Cobb saw, decided and acted all at once."

Ty Cobb had something to say on the subject of quick thinking which is of unusual interest. He said, "Quick thinking, so-called, is usually the result of a play that has been thought out long in advance. Later on it becomes second nature. Most of my so-called quick thinking plays have been the result of a lot of thought, much experience and a kind of baseball instinct which I believe is a product of the two. Certainly I would now perform almost any play that might come up on the diamond by second nature. My rule has always been to take the offensive. That was the rule of the German General Staff in the Late War. The best defence is an offense. The most disconcerting way to off set a boxing opponent is to get your blow in first. Hit, and hit some more and keep on hitting. Never mind what the other fellow is doing. Be so busy yourself that he doesn't get a chance to be busy. If you hit the ball there are a lot of things that can happen. It may go safe. The fielder may drop it. He may fumble it. He may throw wild. The infielder who gets the throw may drop it. A thousand different things can happen to that ball. Any one of them will put you on first base. Take chances. Get the pitcher up in the air. Rattle the catcher. Get the infielders throwing the ball around. Some of them are bound to throw wild. Whatever happens will be to your advantage. The man who holds the initiative in baseball holds the whip hand. And yet, most ball players follow exactly a contrary system. They wonder what the other fellow is going to do so much that they never get around to doing anything themselves. I could talk a lot about baseball, but I would rather act for an hour than talk for a week."

Never jump on a man when he is down, is a homely slogan of the rough and tumble school. Needless to say, that slogan has no place in baseball. The player who grasps opportunity is only too ready, figuratively at least, to jump on a man when he is down.

This is particularly evident when a batting rally starts. As Walter Johnson said, "Big innings come when the batter gains courage and confidence. The pitcher on his part, may contribute to the slugging match by getting rattled. It's a tough job, however, for any pitcher to stop a ball club when they are hitting."

Cy Young went a step further in a conversation I once had with him. He said, "When batters are hitting no pitcher in the world can stop them."

That is the big crisis when a ball game is wavering in the balance. As John McGraw said, "Most ball games are won in a single inning. Sooner or later by one move or another, you are able to launch an attack where it counts and by one vigorous assault win the game. A steady pounding away at the line and then an irresistible rush through the weakest place, that's the system."

Inevitably the ball player who suddenly assumes the initiative, who siezes an opportunity by a daring chance, must also assume a risk. But as Ty Cobb said, "The most you can do in baseball is to get the shade the best of the chances on your side. I am always scheming to upset the balance of the pitchers and get the infield up in the air. If you can shake their confidence you can detect it in the way they handle themselves. Get them rattled and it's a cinch they will leave some hole open somewhere. That's your chance only you must know how to take advantage of the chance and not waste a fraction of a second in the way you go about it. Speed is always important in baseball. But it's never quite so important as when you are trying to sieze a sudden opportunity."

Pulling the Unexpected

TY COBB once said, "There are various kinds of bad plays, but the unexpected play is always a good play."

George Sisler backed up this statement with the following terse comment. He said, "The bed rock of the defence is preparedness. When a play is expected, it is already half defeated. There is no sure defence against the unexpected play. That is why, dangerous as it seems, I favor bunting the third strike under certain circumstances. It isn't expected."

That this alert, original attitude may be an important factor in a batter's success, is indicated by Urban Shocker. He said, "The secret of Ty Cobb's success as a batter was the fact that he always established a mental hazard. He was always on the offensive and you never knew exactly how to guard against him. Sometimes he would choke up on the bat and punch a hit through the infield. Sometimes he would swing from the handle and slug. Sometimes he would bunt. The only thing you could depend upon in his case was the fact that he would give you something that you weren't expecting."

Bert Shotton said, "The best time to hit the pitcher is when he isn't expecting it. While he is trying to work you, he is really working himself. At such times he will put a ball across the plate, not putting all he has on it, thinking you won't offer at it and you hit it for a single. Next time you come up he doesn't know what to give you and you have him up in the air before he begins."

As Sisler says, the play that is expected is already half defeated. Ty Cobb emphasized this idea when he remarked, "Some batters have a weakness that isn't commonly listed under that head, and yet it's a weakness just the same. They are either sluggers who always hammer the ball or short hitters who roll to the infield. Both systems have this defect in common, that the fielders all lay for them and spoil a certain percentage of their hits. I always endeavored to offset this by giving the fielders something they were not expecting. They were never able to map out any defensive campaign against me."

Undoubtedly this quality increases a batter's ability immeasurably. Babe Ruth once said, "You don't need to be a .300 hitter to be a star. Eddie Foster, is seldom classed with the great batters of the American League. But he is one of the most valuable hitters on the circuit just the same. This is because he is always doing the unexpected. If you think he is going to bunt the ball, he will swing at it with his full strength. When you are laying back, expecting him to hit, he is likely to bunt the ball and beat the throw to first."

Unexpected plays are unexpected only to the defense. The man who pulls them must often have prepared them long in advance. Ty Cobb, most daring and original of ball players, gave this interesting reminiscence. He said, "In my younger days I used to work out a certain play a good while ahead. I would try it out several times just preparing the ground for some tight game when I could really use it in earnest. Suppose the score was 7 to 1 in our favor. Suppose I came through with a single. I would round first base and go tearing down towards second. Perhaps I would be thrown out. That would be all right. It made no difference for we needed no more runs. The play, let us assume, looked foolish and I got properly panned for making it. But that never bothered me. What I had in mind was pulling that play sometime where it would do us a lot of good. Perhaps two or three weeks later we would encounter a game with the score tied in the eighth inning. Suppose, under those circumstances I could manage to single. I had already plowed and planted the field. I was now ready for the harvest. Naturally I would go to first, but I wouldn't stop there. I would go charging down towards second. As I was running I could see the outfielder handling the ball. If he picked it up cleanly and was in a position to make an accurate throw, I could scramble back to first, even though I were half way down to second, and be none the worse for the chance I had taken. But if the outfielder were just a little slow, if he fumbled for only a half second, I could beat the play and be safe at second base. Then, if anything turned up, I could score. I have won many a close ball game by just such a play that I have tried out several times when it wasn't necessary just to get the hang of it."

How Batting Aids All-Round Playing

BATTING is undoubtedly the most powerful stimulus for good work in every other department of player activity. As Bill Killifer said, speaking of his best individual season. "I hit better than I have ever hit before and when a ball player is hitting he is playing a good, all round game in other respects."

Joe Sewell said, "I have been hitting pretty good all season. It's well understood in baseball that when you are hitting you play better. I guess the batting gives you confidence. You'll find that most ball players seem to have good all around years when they are hitting. When they are not hitting, they are apt to be something of a disappointment to themselves and to their club."

Even the work of pitchers is helped by good hitting. Connie Mack said, "Ed Rommel is a good pitcher because, first of all, he is a good ball player. He's a good, heavy hitter and he not only pitches well but he fields his position well. And he's a good man on bunts."

As hitting stimulates all round play, a falling off in hitting handicaps a player even though he may be naturally a brilliant performer in other ways. Max Carey said, "The fact that I have not hit as well as I should have liked to do, has injured my base stealing. For one thing, I naturally don't get on as often and therefore don't get the opportunity to steal. I believe that my batting has suffered also because I have specialized in base running. The energy that I have burned up in frequent slides to the bag, in steals that did not materialize and all the rest of it, have taken much of the energy I might have devoted to hitting. I make no claim that I should ever have been a world beater at bat. But I do know that I could have hit much better than I have done had I specialized in batting. In short, my entire career has been a problem of how to develop my talents and build up my weak points so that I might be the best player that I am capable of being."

Undoubtedly hitting ability keeps many a man in the line-up who would otherwise be benched or released for weakness elsewhere. Eddie Brown, the Brooklyn outfielder, said, "My throwing arm has been considered bad, or at least not good for years. And my fielding wasn't anything to brag of, though it has improved. But one thing I could always seem to do was to hit. That has kept me going in baseball. It has helped me to develop other things where I was weaker so that I can take my place among Big Leaguers now, even though it is late in the day."

Really great hitting usually make a great player. Ty Cobb said of Eddie Collins, "Collins is a great hitter. He'll be remembered for that probably more than anything else. But he is a great all round ball player, a wonderful fielder and base runner. He is one player whose ability in any given direction is obscured by his greater all round ability."

Dave Bancroft, struggling with the manager's problem of building up a weak ball club, said, "If a hitter is good enough, you can forgive him for a few fielding lapses. What the manager would like, of course, is to get players who are capable at both. I am inclined to believe, however, that there are more good fielders naturally than there are good hitters among the recruits in the Big Leagues. Some managers think that pitching is the big problem. On the whole, however, I believe it is easier to build up a pretty good pitching machine than it is to get a genuine batting punch in a ball club."

How the Batter Helps His Team Mates

THE success of a ball club demands that a player submerge his own selfish interests in the greater interests of his team. All players do this to some extent. Few players, however, even in the Major Leagues, consider as much as they should, how they may help a fellow teammate.

Ed Rommel had this necessary function in mind when he said, "The most important thing in baseball is winning games. If a player can't see the interests of the club superior to his own, he won't get very far."

There are many ways in which the batter can serve his fellow teammates. Bert Shotton outlined one of these methods. He said, "The leadoff man who is trying to work the pitcher for a pass is also helping the next man on the batting list. For the moment the pitcher has lost confidence in himself, the next man up will have an easier time because of the confused state of mind in which the leadoff man got the pitcher when he worked him for a pass. And don't forget that the leadoff man did work the pitcher for that pass and is entitled to full credit."

The batter may be of great assistance to the base runner, quite apart from hitting the ball. Max Carey illustrated one phase of this interesting proposition. He said, "If I were a manager I would teach my players the community of interest between batter and base runner. These players are in an ideal position to help each other and to help the team. The batter can help the base runner in a variety of ways. He can crowd back in the box, thus pushing the catcher back and making his throw longer and more difficult. He can sprawl around and bother the catcher in a variety of ways short of what would be called by the umpire plain interference. And he can also refrain from hitting at the first ball pitched, thus giving the base runner a chance to steal. Casey Stengel wasn't with Pittsburgh long, but he co-operated with me better than any other player I have ever known. He would generally wait until the pitcher had two strikes on him before he attempted to hit. That gave me the finest possible opportunity to steal. But it wasn't a one-sided proposition. I helped Casey quite as much as he helped me. I drew him many a pitch-out by making long leads and then darting back to the bag. I continually worried the pitcher and very often got him in the hole. As a result he would either pass Casey or lay one over where Casey could hit it. We had a neat little combination all to ourselves while it lasted."

Joe Birmingham said, "If the batter knows that the runner intends to steal and the hit and run play might be in order, it is his duty to aid the runner, if he can. He may swing at the ball in an attempt to confuse the catcher, but he must also remember that the swing will cost him a strike. For that reason the batter should exercise good judgment in determining just how far he can assist the runner."

With a runner on second base, the batter could often assist that runner to advance to third by a bluff bunt. Carey said, "If Jake Daubert had batted behind me, I will gamble I could have stolen third almost every time. All he would have needed to do was to give me the advantage of a bluff bunt."

There are more subtle ways in which a man may help his teammates or they may help him. One of these ways is competition. Carl Lundgren said, "The longer a man plays, the closer must be the competition to bring out his best efforts."

Competition shines at its best, of course, when two or more players are fighting for the same job. But it has a very real influence on batting quite apart from such a struggle for the survival of the fittest. Joe Sewell illustrated this feature of the case when he said, "I have enjoyed a good season, but I have had some great pacemakers. Speaker has had a whale of a year. So have Jamieson and Summa. I believe, when you are one of a bunch of good hitters, the influence gets in your blood and you hit better yourself."

A player's paper average often depends not only upon his own work, but also upon the co-operation of his teammates. This is particularly so in the case of runs scored. Oscar Vitt, when he led the American League in runs scored, thus explained his position at the head of the list. He said, "A man on base simply had to keep moving with that heavy artillery of Cobb and Crawford behind him. Many a time I was thrown out at third and home, besides scoring all the runs they gave me credit for."

John Tobin occupying somewhat the same position said, "The lead-off man naturally scores many runs. His position in the line-up accounts for that. And yet, while his teammates help him in a way, they hold him back in others. It's a rule that works both ways. For the lead off man follows the tail of the batting list and the slower runners. If one of these ice wagons is on base, the lead off man is handicapped both in batting and base running. Even a safe hit may be lost because the ice wagon failed to make the bag ahead of him. I know when Urban Shocker has been on second base and I have reached first, he has said to me, 'Don't step on me if somebody else slams it out.'"

Tommy Griffith one season when he was hitting hard but in poor luck, lost a clean hit because the runner on first loafed on the job and failed to make second. "That's the last straw," said Tommy. "It's bad enough to lose hits because they go straight at outfielders. It's the limit when you lose them because the base runner goes to sleep on the bags."

In a wider sense, even a player's reputation depends directly upon the work of fellow players. As George Sisler said, "You cannot judge a player's record by itself alone. It must be compared with the work of others. Take, for example, the experience of a player now disgraced, Joe Jackson. Joe was good enough to lead any league at bat. He made the record, unequalled so far as I know, of leading four successive leagues at bat on his first appearance in each of those four circuits. In the American League he hit over .400 at a time when it was commonly supposed that no batter would ever again hit .400. But throughout his whole Major League career he was overshadowed by Ty Cobb. People will remember Ty's unmatched record as long as the game endures. They will very likely forget that Joe Jackson was almost as great a hitter. That word almost makes a lot of difference in baseball."

Obeying the Manager's Orders

YEARS ago, long before he became manager himself, Ty Cobb said in a moment of petulance, "The managers have the game by the throat. Their cry is all for machine baseball. Perhaps the average player can perform better under a director, but surely his initiative and individual action suffers greatly."

Most batters have chafed at times under managerial restrictions. No doubt the influence of the manager has rested heavily on many a batting average. Hal Chase said, "One thing which has affected my record as much as any other is the trouble I have had with managers. As I look back now, I can see that part of the fault was my own. But I refuse to shoulder all the blame. The average ball player tries to overcome a sensitive disposition. But unless he has a hide as thick as a rhinoceros, he can not play his best game when he is at outs with the manager."

Sage Old Hans Wagner had some remarks to make on this subject. He said, "There are few things so good they haven't shortcomings. The system of modern managing is no exception. The system may be necessary, but it discourages a good player from showing what he can do. Good players are often bothered by too many instructions. This is especially true of good hitters. A natural born hitter can't follow instructions too closely. He must have his head. I saw some time ago where Joe Jackson claimed that his slump in batting was due to the fact that he was trying to follow instructions from the bench. Joe is one player who cannot follow instructions."

John McGraw, who more than any other one man has been responsible for the domination of baseball by the manager, once said, "There are few players with initiative now. Perhaps the manager is partly accountable for this. Baseball has tended to become a machine proposition. But the manager has really had little choice. In order to get results he has had to do the thinking for his club. There are players like Ty Cobb who are a law unto themselves. They take daring chances which the average player can't do. Cobb gets away with his stunts seven times out of ten and it pays. Other players might get away with them three times out of ten and it wouldn't pay. As a result the tendency in baseball is to play safe and avoid chances."

George Burns, when he was with Detroit, said, "Every manager has his own ideas. He is the boss and what he says goes. Now it stands to reason that in a bunch of twenty odd players, there will always be some who don't hitch with the manager. Perhaps it will be their fault, perhaps not. Now if you are working for a manager who is over you and has authority to do about as he pleases with you, and he doesn't like you, what are the odds that you will do your best work for him? Easily a million to one. One reason you won't is because you can't. It is humanly impossible. I defy any man in any kind of a job be it baseball or brick laying to do his best work for a boss he can't get along with."

Davis Robertson was an example of a brilliant career spoiled by friction with the management. He said, "My main criticism of McGraw is that he tries to run everything. I do not deny that his system has brought results, but I do deny that any player with some initiative and some intelligence should be forbidden all original action. The system is fine for a player who can't think. There are players in baseball of that type. But certainly the system would never develop a star. To be sure there are few stars. But players are not few who can do their best work only when allowed a certain latitude. And I am one of them."

I once heard Casey Stengel discussing a cynical newspaper article which accused ball players of lacking brains. Casey said, "Why need a player have any brains when so little is left to his judgment? If he has a natural talent for hitting to right field, the manager tries to make him over into a baseball machine that can grind out hits to any field. If he is good at slugging the ball, he is told to bunt. If he is sure he can whale some pitcher a mile, he is instructed to wait him out. Where did you ever hear a manager give a player instructions to try a certain system and then if it didn't come through, switch to something else? Suppose a batter has orders to hit to right field. He tries a couple of times. He misses and he gives away his intentions to the outfielder. Wouldn't it be good policy then to switch to some other field? But very seldom are such things left to the discretion of the batter."

Napoleon Lajoie terminated his great Major League career with a grouch at the management. He said, "I have no objection to working under a competent manager. I voluntarily resigned the management myself which ought to prove that I wasn't crazy about the job. I worked willingly enough for several managers, but when a Bush League player like Joe Birmingham tries to teach me how to play, it is ridiculous. Why he would even tell me how to hit, me who was batting .300 when he wore short pants."

Managerial disputes are not only bad for the player but for the club. Concerning the same Lajoie disagreement, Charles Somers, then owner of the Cleveland Club said, "Lajoie was a wonderful player, and in his prime I doubt if he had an equal. I will give him credit, he made the Club. But I made a fatal mistake in signing Lajoie to a long time contract after I had appointed a younger manager. Such a situation is almost certain to create friction. And you can not properly blame either man."

Ty Cobb is one player who has generally had his way, but when he was a rookie he, too, suffered from managerial restrictions. He said, "When I was at Augusta, Andy Roth was managing the club and we didn't get along any too well. Andy tried to put a bridle on me and every time I cut loose with something new he checked me up. Under these conditions I soon assumed an indifferent attitude and was just drifting along when George Leidy came to my rescue. He was our center fielder. He took me around to shows and told me of life in the big cities, so my ambition to see those things was roused and my work improved at once." It would indeed have been a misfortune if Ty's matchless career had been lost to baseball through early discouragement.

Many a trade has been the result of a managerial dispute. Richard Hobilitzell said, "My transfer from Cincinnati has been called many things. But to me it seems like a dispensation from Providence. To get away from Herzog and to get with a manager like Carrigan is about as great a contrast as a man could ask for."

Managers are criticized for various things. Bill Doak made a novel criticism of Branch Rickey. He said, "Rickey knows too much to be a good manager. He is smart, but he isn't a good manager."

Old Hank Gowdy, on the much discussed subject of McGraw, said, "He is exacting and successful. What more can be asked? He demands that a player submerge his individuality in the larger individuality of the club. As a builder of winning machines, he is right. Far be it from me to take issue with McGraw. He knows more baseball than I ever will know. I play his game and follow his system for that is what I am paid to do. But I can have ideas. A ball player, among other things, has personality. When you take that away from him, you leave him little else."

Some managers get along with little friction and win the respect and even friendship of their men. Eddie Collins said, "Connie Mack is a regular fountain of confidence among his players, with a pipe line of abundance leading to every one. He treats his players as he does his children, with kindness and firmness and ever lasting patience. It is a pleasure to work and win for him because you know he appreciates your efforts."

Even the hard bitted McGraw has numerous defenders among his own players. Larry Doyle said, "They give McGraw a bad name as a driver. But I always liked him myself. He is domineering sometimes, but that is because he is in earnest and wants to get at the heart of things in a hurry."

Schuppe, whose brilliant career as a pitcher was cut short, echoed these sentiments. He said, "McGraw is a driver and when things are not going right there are likely to be fireworks. But I have sat on the bench myself and seen somebody pull a bone and said to myself, 'Well, Old Man, if I were manager, that would cost you Fifty Dollars.' McGraw is all right."

John Rawlings, not too friendly with McGraw who traded him, said, "After all, his system is merely trying to get nine men to pull together. If you are driving a span of horses, you won't go far unless they pull together. Driving a team of nine players is much more difficult. It stands to reason it's a good system where the man who is pulling the wires knows what he is doing. And surely no one ever questioned McGraw's knowledge of baseball."

"Butch" Schmidt of the ancient Braves, said, "Stallings has been criticized as a hard manager. I never found him so. He is cross on the field during the game, but that is because he feels the responsibility of his position. Off the field he is a prince."

Naturally the managers themselves justify a close control of the ball club. Joe Tinker said, "Every manager has his own ideas about running a ball club. Right or wrong, that is the only way to run a club, have all the management in one pair of hands. Team play is absolutely indispensable to success in baseball. And team play is imposible unless the manager has authority to carry out his own ideas."

Harry Wolverton whose brief reign as Yankee pilot was not conspicuously successful, said, "I have no set system of management. True the manager must maintain discipline, but that can be done pleasantly and agreeable. I always aim to retain the respect of my players. I do not think it good policy to tie a player down by restrictions which are difficult, if not impossible, to enforce."

Frank Chance said, "Don't be unreasonable. But don't stand for indifference. A player must give the best there is in him to his club. Don't let the players run the club. Run it yourself."

Bill McKechnie said, "There are two ways of conveying an idea to a ball player. You can speak to him pleasantly and firmly, or you can knock him down with a club. I do not favor the club method myself. I have never seen a man who needed to be bullied."

George Stoval was a likeable manager, reasonably successful and extremely popular with his men. He said, "I suppose I am a rather easy boss. Ball players are pretty intelligent people and it is generally safe to trust their welfare to their own hands. The player who won't take care of himself is his own worst enemy, and it's doubtful if a manager can compel him to do so. When a man is in uniform I expect him to live up to certain rules. After the game is over, I believe in allowing considerable latitude." When he was a manager, there was a rumor that Stovall's slogan to his players in action was the rather startling one, "Two kegs of beer if we win and one keg anyway."

Miller Huggins believed that a manager's work is less valuable as a club leader than elsewhere. He said, "You can't make players do things who can't do them. The manager of a ball club is little better than a builder."

Beyond a doubt, the type of manager who has impressed his own vigorous personality, his own logical ideas most strongly upon baseball, is John McGraw. He said, in defence of his pet system which has revolutionized the game, "Napoleon, I believe, said that one poor general was worth more than two good ones. He was right. I have never had to defend my own ability as a manager by defending the system that I employ. Whatever my own personal qualifications my be, I am certain that my system is sound. Nine mediocre players pulling together under one competent head, will do better work than nine individuals of greater ability without unified control."

That is the system of baseball management tersely expressed. And Frank Snyder says, "Whether you like it or not, it has come to stay."

How Mental Impressions May Help or Harm the Batter

A CONTENTED mind is a continual ally to the batter. A feeling of dissatisfaction, a personal grudge against the manager, a rankling injustice in the mind may well prove more formidable handicaps than a sprained thumb or a sore tendon.

John Evers said, "Ball players are peculiar individuals—they are sensitive. Misunderstandings among themselves and with the manager cause more trouble than will ever be known."

George Burns of Cleveland and Detroit said, "More than one pennant has been lost through dissatisfaction on the part of the players. If a man thinks he is being mistreated, he can't do his best work, I don't much care who he is. And there are ball players on almost every club who are in that position. I suppose the public wonders why they are slipping and wonders still more why their work improves, as it usually does, when they are transferred to some other ball club. Such misunderstandings are inevitable. Most ball clubs," concluded Burns, "are weakened to a greater or less degree by internal dissensions."

John McGraw emphasized this point when he said, "The fact that a batter hit .300 this season is no guarantee that he will do as well next year. He may have been perfectly satisfied with life originally. He may develop a grouch, think he is being mistreated and assume that mental attitude toward his work and his club which makes it impossible for him to show at his best. The mental attitude of a ball player, quite apart from his mechanical gifts, is a prominent factor in the managerial problem. And that mental attitude undergoes far more rapid, unexpected and serious changes in the course of a single season than mere mechanical ability would be subject to in a life-time."

It was the mental attitude of Maurice Rath which sent him into the Minors when he should no doubt have developed as a Major League regular. He explained, "I felt that I had had a good year for Comiskey, and I set about chopping wood and taking a lot of winter exercise to get myself in tip top condition. So when, in due time, I received my contract with a meagre increase in salary, I was disappointed. I stopped chopping wood. True, I reported for spring training, but I didn't exert myself. I felt that I had not been treated fairly, and I determined to do no more work than I was paid to do. Later, when the season began in earnest and a player, no matter what his feelings, will naturally do his best, I found that I couldn't deliver. I had completely lost my stride and couldn't seem to get started. The result was a miserable season which branded me as a failure and dumped me into the Minors."

Even Rogers Hornsby, great hitter that he is, has felt the spell of mental turmoil. That was particularly the case in the so-called War Year. Of that season, Hornsby said, "I didn't make a good showing at bat. But there were reasons. The whole schedule was turned up side down by the war and the players didn't know whether they were playing ball or counting daisies. Last year wasn't a fair test. Next year will tell a different story."

Dissatisfaction often sets the mark of drab failure on an otherwise successful season. Occasionally it drives a promising rookie back to the Minors. Rarely it eclipses a Major League star who has won his right to be called a star.

Davis Robertson might have been one of baseball's super-stars. His brilliant career ended in failure because of mental dissatisfaction. "The so-called big money in baseball is no temptation to me," he said, "I would not take a job for twenty-five thousand dollars a year if that job were wholly uncongenial. I would not have continued to play ball at New York under that maniac infield for much more than twenty-five thousand dollars. The atmosphere on that club was impossible from my viewpoint."

Davis Robertson was not the only man who rebelled against what he considered intolerable conditions on a Major League ball club. But he is the most conspicuous example of a Major League player endowed with extraordinary talents whose baseball career, partly through his own pride and sensitiveness, partly through tactless treatment from his associates, proved a melancholy contrast to what it might have been.

The causes of player dissatisfaction are legion. Perhaps the most prolific, however, is disagreement over salary. Edd Roush said, "No one thing calls forth so much trouble in baseball as salary disputes between owners and players. No doubt blame is sometimes due the owner for his obstinacy or tight fistedness. At other times the player is guilty of setting an exaggerated value upon his services. Players are often accused of being selfish. I suppose they are. This is a selfish world. Players are just as selfish as fish pedlers and undertakers. Everybody, so far as I can observe, seems to have one eye open for his own interests."

Often the member of a hopelessly weak ball club will chafe and rebel at the unpromising conditions which mar his future. Joe Dugan was an example of this rather numerous class of player. He said, "I liked Connie Mack first rate. He was a fine man to work for. But there isn't much fun in digging grounders out of the dirt for a ball club that is always resting on the floor of the cellar." Hence Dugan was traded.

A ball player's friends often foment dissatisfaction in his mind. Even a player's wife may be the cause of much mental unrest. George Burns said, "Naturally a man's wife thinks he is fully as good as he is. When he criticizes some other player's work in her hearing, she may mention it casually to that other player's wife. The glad news spreads and grows and pretty soon there will be four or five fellows on the ball club looking at one another out of the corner of one eye and reaching for a bat when they meet on the bench. I remember one club where the manager sent away all the players' wives. They talked so much and created so much ill feeling on the club that he wouldn't have them around."

Occasionally, no doubt, a ball player allows his dissatisfaction to grow unchecked because he hopes to better his condition. Walter Johnson said, "Some players get dissatisfied. They have poor years and then are traded to New York where they get more glory and more money. Other players stick with the home club, work hard year after year and never get anywhere at all. Baseball is like life, I guess—a problem."

If mental dissatisfaction is a potent handicap to batting, a contented mind is an equally strong stimulus. Casey Stengel said, "There is one reason why my work this year is better than it has ever been before. I am satisfied with my job and doing my level best to make good. I have been told that I wasn't straining my suspenders in the service of several clubs with which I have been associated. However that may be, I can say without reservation I am wearing my suspenders threadbare in the effort to do good work for the Giants."

Successful business men all admit that the man who would succeed must love his work. Dode Paskert said, "One reason that I have been able to put up so good a game for Chicago is this. I thoroughly like baseball. True, most players like the game well enough. But after they have been in uniform for a few years they get into the habit of taking things too much as a matter of course. This has never been my experience. I like baseball from the first day of spring to the last day before winter sets in. I enjoy double headers. I believe that is one strong reason why I am still able to play ball at an age when most players are through."

The player who is satisfied and eager to make good is already on the high road to success. The same is true of the ball club. But it is much more difficult to arouse club spirit of this desirable type than it is to arouse a similar mental determination on the part of the individual. Fred Mitchell said, "What is the difference between the Boston Braves this year and last? There is a profound difference, but it isn't so much in the make-up of the club. The difference is rather in the spirit of the men. They are full of fight. They hang together and play well together. In short, they have life and pep. It is not easy to defeat such a club no matter what paper averages may seem, for such a club is a living thing. It is this spirit which puts life into what would otherwise be only a loosely assembled machine."

Mrs. Britton, what time she was President of the St. Louis Cardinals, once said to me, "If you could always depend upon a player to do his best work, you would have a different outlook on the prospects of the club. Unfortunately, the mental attitude of the men is subject to so many changes without notice that you can never feel certain about the situation."

After all, the player who allows his feelings to impair his work, injures himself more than any one else and the futility of it is too obvious. As Wilbert Robinson said, "There's nothing to be gained in baseball by being in the dumps. I don't care what stage the pennant race may be in or how hopeless the ball game may seem. There's nothing to be gained by going into the ninth inning with the score against you and your head between your legs. Anything can happen in baseball."

Where Other Interests Intrude

"THE batter," said Ty Cobb, "must concentrate on the task in hand. His mind should be keyed to a high pitch and every energy bent on getting the better of the pitcher and driving out a safe hit. I practiced concentration so much that when I was on the ball field, I would forget everything else. Mrs. Cobb, for example, might be sick. I might be worried about her. Now I care as much for my wife as any man, but when the game started all those worries would vanish. I wouldn't even think about them. Often I have gone to the club house and got half dressed before such troublesome outside ideas would occur to me. That was merely because I practiced concentration. It became second nature to me and accounted in no small measure for my batting success."

What Ty Cobb has so graphically portrayed as necessary on the ball field is also required to a considerable degree throughout the player's active career. A batter's work is sure to suffer if outside interests take too much of his time or energy. As Walter Lutzke said, "In order to succeed, a batter must make a specialty of his business. Even when I am not playing ball, in the off season, I spend a lot of time reviewing plays that have come up or that are likely to come up, trying to improve my work."

Jake Daubert, who was unusually successful in various kinds of business, aside from ball playing, nevertheless condemned mixing the two. He said, "There is one piece of advice I would like to give any ball player. Don't go into business until you are through with baseball. That is one rule I would carefully follow if I had my career to live over again. If I am as successful as I expect to be this season," continued Jake, "my outside business interests will net me twenty-five thousand dollars, a sum greater than I ever expected to have when I began playing baseball, a sum greater than I could save in several years of playing ball. Nevertheless, knowing what I do of the endless troubles which business affairs cause a ball player, if I could begin where I began years ago with Brooklyn and someone should offer me a gold bar worth a thousand dollars for ten cents, I would be strongly tempted to refuse the offer because I would not want to let anything get me interested in outside affairs. I well remember five years ago when I hit but .261. It was a big slump. The papers figured I was nearly through. What was the real trouble? I had a lot of money invested in things that weren't turning out specially well, and I was worried. I had sickness in my family and that bothered me. I couldn't get these things out of my mind, and got run down and off my feed generally. I was lucky to hit .261."

John Evers' long and brilliant career was marred by a complete nervous breakdown, the result of losing twenty-five thousand dollars, his entire accumulated capital, in an unfortunate business venture.

As Larry Gardner said, "A ball player is peculiarly situated. For more than half the year he must be away from business, if he has one and therefore leave it in the charge of others. Besides, since he can give only a limited amount of time to his business the chances are he doesn't understand it as much as he should."

George Dauss said, "I would welcome an opportunity to make some money in the off season, but what can I do? There are only a few months at best. I am not a salesman. I have neither the reputation nor the desire to go on the stage. So I take things easy, rest up and dream of the good season I am going to have. It's a simple pastime, costs no money and doesn't hurt anybody."

In view of Jake Daubert's stirring condemnation and such unfortunate examples as John Evers' business collapse, many players, nevertheless, seek for some employment in the off-season. And there are strong arguments in favor of their choice. Christy Mathewson said, "No doubt every one has wished to attain that degree of prosperity where he no longer felt obliged to work for a living. One winter I decided that I had a comfortable income and thought I would put in operation this pet theory which I suppose everyone has cherished in his thoughtless moments. So I loafed for the entire winter and it was the most unsatisfactory season I ever had."

Joe Sewell said, "It's my opinion that a ball player needs to do something in the off-season to occupy his mind. Besides, why should a young fellow loaf? I don't intend to myself and I don't think it is good policy. Business openings come to a ball player, if he is in a receptive mood and I believe he ought to be."

Ray Schalk said, "Finding out from experience that I could work during the winter months has been the best thing in the world. I think that if a ball player would start right in at some useful work as soon as the season closed, he would be doing a wise thing."

Ed Rommel said, "I am not one of those ball players who can afford to take things easy. I mastered the plumber's trade, but the business does not appeal to me. I picked out a more congenial job, selling paint. I don't know whether or not I am a good salesman, but I keep plugging anyway."

These opinions illustrate the mental attitude of many prominent ball players toward some serious employment in the winter months. Others who do not work for money develop some hobby which keeps their muscles occupied and calls for wholesale exercise in the outdoors.

Hans Wagner kept up the pace of a champion ball player long past forty by strenuous exercise in the winter time. He said, "I play basketball, have played it for years. It is great exercise and keeps a man in condition. They say it takes the wind, and I suppose it does. But that's a good thing. It also gives a man a few bruises, but they don't amount to much. Playing basketball keeps a man in shape so he doesn't have to train in spring. That is what hurts a player more than anything else, spring training. I always go on the trips, but I don't train much. I aim to be in condition all the time."

Football interests many ball players, though they are spectators rather than players. Joe Bush said, "I love baseball, but once you have experienced it, you never can shake the hold which football has on you. I am too old to play football now, of course, but if I were not, I believe about one football game a week would equal ten baseball games in interest."

Almost all players spend some time of the off season in hunting or fishing. Bob Shawkey's statement on this point is typical. He said, "I go hunting usually after deer and moose up in the northern country. Most ball players are pretty good shots. They have a steady hand and a clear eye. If they did not, they wouldn't be successful as ball players."

These things, however, though beneficial are purely recreation. Many players, however, have a more serious purpose and try to earn a dollar in the off season. A handful of illustrations will serve. Eppa Rixey said, "I am a life insurance agent. They told me it was a good job for a player and in a moment of weakness I yielded. The germs of a great salesman may be dormant in my frame and it's up to me to give them a chance."

Walter Gerber said, "The past two winters I have been working in the real estate business. I haven't made a fortune, but it gives me something to think of."

Dick Rudolph said, "I have a new chicken house that cost me two thousand dollars. It is good enough for me to live in myself. I can't give all the time I like to raising chickens for I play baseball on the side. But some day I am going to show the world the money there is in hens. I have got all the Government reports for the past nine years and have studied them more closely than National League batting averages. You can't make money sitting in the parlor with your feet up on the mantel piece. But if you're willing to work and have any brains to start with, you can make money in hens."

Perhaps the ideal winter occupation for a ball player is work on a farm. Zack Wheat said, "There is no sentiment in business. I am a ball player in summer and a farmer in the winter time. I aim to be a success at both professions."

Fred Merkle said, "Swamp land in Florida is uncommonly fertile. I have some land there that I am going to put into potatoes. The only drawback is I can't be up here scooping them out of the dirt and down there digging roots at the same time."

Slim Sallee, with the homely philosophy that characterized him, said, "I have a farm and a fellow feeling for hogs. I guess like enough I'll get a job feeding hogs. You can always get a job feeding hogs as long as there are any hogs and any feed. I guess the supply of both will last as long as I do."

Some occupations are distinctly unsuitable for a ball player. John Morrison said, "I reckon I must get another job for the off-season. Swinging the blacksmith's hammer is bad for the pitching arm. It gives a man strength, but it tightens up the muscles and ties them in hard knots. There is Babe Adams on our club, forty-two years old and his arms are as soft and as pliable as an Indian's. That's one reason he has lasted so long."

Charles Deal said, "I learned to be a machinist and am going back to it some time. But it's an easy game to lose a finger and a fellow needs his full equipment in baseball. Mordecai Brown got along with three fingers, but he was a pitcher."

Some players who work criticize other athletic sports. For example, "Pie" Traynor said, "In the winter I work as a checker on a pier in South Boston. It's a job which keeps me in the open air and I like it. I believe every ball player ought to do something in the winter time to earn his keep. But I don't think he should indulge in other athletic sports. Playing baseball one hundred and fifty-four games, with spring training and exhibitions thrown in is enough for anybody."

Not a few ball players have in mind something more far reaching than a mere winter job. They are planning for the future when they can no longer play professional baseball. Carl Lundgren said, "Even though a young man becomes a professional star he should choose another profession for his life work, always keep it in mind and work at it in the off-season."

Leon Cadore said, "The trouble with most ball players is this. While everything is going along nicely they are inclined to forget that some day they will be called upon to put away their monkey suit and let the younger fellows take the helm. I have known ball players to last twenty years or more. But that is exceptional. But I have never known a veteran, no matter how husky, who didn't have to quit the game some time. How many ball players are preparing themselves for the future? I would say perhaps one in ten."

Occasionally a ball player will have so many other interests even in his playing days that baseball may take a back seat. Babe Ruth was in this position in his season of greatest fame. His secretary, John Igoe, said of that season, "Ruth received as many as one hundred and forty-four letters in a single day. He was offered money for all sorts of far fetched ideas. He was paid several thousand dollars for making a phonograph record. The Chairman of the Republican National Committee offered him two thousand dollars for four short speeches. He received a moderate fortune for appearing in a moving picture scenario. Wealthy Cubans paid him twenty-six thousand dollars for exhibition games. He received a large sum for the use of his name on a book that proved a frost. His theatrical engagements netted him a huge sum."

One of the outside interests which has caused a storm of dissension is golf.

"Dazzy" Vance said, "Playing golf is good, at least for pitchers. It takes their minds off the game when they're not due to be called on."

Nevertheless, not a few managers have banned golf during the active season on the ground that it diverted the players from baseball and was too much additional exercise.

Amid conflicting opinions it is not so difficult to draw a median line. No doubt things which divert the player's mind during the active season are open to suspicion. A few far sighted players plan not only a winter job as such, but the foundation of a future means of livelihood. In the last analysis, baseball itself, important as it may be, is an episode in the player's life. He must determine its relative importance for himself. George Stovall doubtless had this in mind when he said, "I was born a farmer. I have had the honor to live on a farm most of my life. And I hope to die on a farm."

Various Batting Handicaps

EUGENE HARGRAVE, the capable catcher, said, "You would think that Major League pitching is the biggest handicap a batter has to face. This isn't necessarily true, even when you consider nothing but pitching. I know it is harder to catch a pitcher in the Minors, and on some accounts I think it's harder to hit, for the Major League pitcher knows what to do and does it, so you can count on his working according to Hoyle. But the Minor Leaguer has no rhyme or reason to his work. Besides, there are other handicaps which every batter knows about, such as the parks, the weather and so on."

It is these obscure, variable, but ever present handicaps that we would examine for a moment, for they exert a considerable, if minor, affect on the batting even of baseball's greatest stars.

I recall a conversation I once had with Ty Cobb in the spring. He said, "I am not going any too well this season. I think it is the cussed weather you have up here. You would probably call it a nice May day, but it isn't warm. If I were south now I would gamble I would feel a hundred per cent better. We may miss some things down in the Cotton States, but we have real weather there.

It is this chill, clammy substitute for weather that you have here near the Arctic current that I never can seem to get used to."

The climate undoubtedly affects batting. For example, Fred Nicholson said, "St. Paul is the only club I ever played with where I hit under .300. I guess it was the climate out there."

Ty Cobb complained about chill weather. Excessive heat is fully as open to criticism. Ray Caldwell once said, "I don't mind hot weather, if it isn't too hot. Ordinarily the steamy day is built to order, for baseball. But sometimes the weather in St. Louis actually makes you wilt."

Ed Konetchy said, "The weather in St. Louis is so hot, in the summer, and sultry, that many a fan goes to the ball game in his shirt sleeves and sits in the shade sipping cool drinks, while the ball player is running around out there in the sun. This intense heat affects the player's work. In a prolonged spell he loses a lot of sleep. You can depend upon it that weather plays a fairly large part in a ball player's record."

Some cities have prevailing winds that bother a batter. Eddie Collins cited a sample. He said, "I have found that the prevailing wind at Chicago seemed to favor the pitcher and handicap the batter. I can not say this is the cause with other clubs, but we have found it so at Comiskey Park."

John Bassler said, "Not a little of a ball player's success is due to his ability to guard against obscure details that seem to work against him. For example, at Fenway Park in Boston there are air currents which make it difficult to catch a high fly in right field. More balls drop there safe than in any other park. A player needs to know of these pecularities of different fields. But knowing them, he is better to ignore them, for nothing worse can happen to a batter than to feel that certain obscure things are preventing him from doing his best work."

Another prolific source of discontent is the shape and extent of the playing field, particularly the neighboring bleachers and outfield fence. These conditions vary greatly in most circuits. Rogers Hornsby said, "Many players claim that some ball parks help their hitting. I think this is true. It is certainly true of the high fly which even a poor outfielder would get if the fence didn't stop him. I have often thought I would like to play on an open field. Frankly I believe my average would hold up with the rest, home runs as well as singles. The outfielders always lay back for me. On an open field they would probably lay still further back. That would give a fine territory between infield and outfield to drive hot singles. And as for homers, a hard hit ball between outfielders can not be run down and returned before a fast man has circled the bases."

Short fences are a fertile field of dispute. For example, Cy Williams said, "It is impossible to discuss my home run record at all without mention of that short right field fence at Philadelphia. Yes, that is a fine fence and I am glad it is there. The fence produces a fine crop of home runs."

This is true, but short fences also spoil some legitimate home runs. For example, Chief Wilson who made the record number of three baggers, 36, in 1912, said, "A three base hit may usually be made only by driving the ball clear to the fence, particularly toward center field on most grounds. I made 36 triples my best year, but not a few of those long drives would probably have been homers had they not been stopped by the fence."

Cactus Cravath in discussing the famous short right field at Philadelphia said, "That right field fence was never any further away than it was when I joined the club. And while we are on the subject, let me make a point. That fence isn't always a friend to the home run slugger. It is often an enemy. I have hit that fence a good many times with a long drive that would have kept right on for a triple or a home run, if the fence hadn't been there. There are always two sides to every fence."

Not only the dimensions of the field but the nature of the soil affects batting. Fred Mitchell said, "One of the many curious things that upsets batting dope is the field itself. There are Major League parks that have what the batters call a "live" field. There are others with dead fields. The ball, when it strikes, seems to stay where it struck or rolls forward in a half hearted manner. The batter has not only the pitcher working against him, but the field is also working against him. At Boston our batting average have suffered for the team has played seventy odd games a year on a very punk field. The ground was filled in and is much like a gigantic sponge. It gives and has no tendency to make the ball bounce. If Boston has the poorest field in the country, St. Louis has the best. The sun out there has baked the field as hard as iron."

Differences in playing field have played a part in the winning of more than one World's Championship. When Brooklyn played Cleveland in 1920 William Wambsganss said, "I know the Cleveland diamond has bothered the Brooklyn fielders. It is the fastest diamond in the American League. When the ball is hit, it takes one hop and is at you. It bounces over that hard turf and sun baked soil like a bullet. Brooklyn has looked like a different team in Cleveland and I believe part of that difference is due to the playing field."

In another famous World's Series between the Yankees and the Giants, Bob Shawkey complained about a break which cost him the game. He said, "That little bounder should have started a double play. Instead it went as a hit. Before I could stop them the Giants had staged one of their big innings. That little bounder was due to the condition of the field. The diamond was in wretched shape after the wild west Rodeo, for it was cut up with the horses' hoofs. It was the condition of the field that decided that game."

A sun baked outfield helps the batter in two ways. The ball bounces more freely and the outfielders have difficulty in keeping up their customary pep. For example, Max Carey complained of the Brooklyn outfield one September. He said, "The ground out there is as hard as iron. Running around on spikes makes your feet sore. I'd give a five dollar bill for a good rain storm."

In some parts the outfield bleacher, directly in line with the batter's vision, works havoc with averages. When the new Polo Grounds were rebuilt, seats were eliminated directly in center field and a neutral green background placed there for this very reason. At Philadelphia, in particular, bleacher seats in center field have proved troublesome. Cy Williams says, "This is the only park in the circuit which has bleacher seats directly in line with the pitcher in center field. When these bleachers are filled with white shirted fans, it is very difficult for a batter to follow the ball, with his eye. I can detect a decided difference in my own work when these seats are vacant."

Some players have personal peculiarities which are handicaps. For example, wearing eye glasses was long considered an insurmountable barrier. George Toporcer said, "I can not understand why the prejudice against eye glasses should have kept players out of the Big Leagues so long. I know when I was a kid I had to wear glasses and I liked to play ball, but the outlook was discouraging. So I went to work at another job. I never abandoned hope, however, and when my chance came, I was quick to seize it. Eye glasses are no particular disadvantage to a player. Why should they be? If a player got hit in the eye with a ball he might consider himself unlucky. But if a player's going to get hit in the eye, he hasn't much chance in a professional league."

Oddly enough, that rare accident is just what happened to another eye glassed Big Leaguer, Lee Meadows. He said, "I was warming up in practice, just lobbing the ball around as players will, when another ball came from some unseen direction and hit me in the eye. It broke the lense of my glasses into a thousand pieces and imbedded some of those pieces in the eye ball. The doctor worked over me for hours, taking those pieces of glass out of that eye. I never imagined anything could hurt so much."

We have briefly noted some rather common batting handicaps. Most good batters, while they recognize these handicaps try to ignore them. For example, Sam Crawford said, "When you come to figure out air currents, atmosphere pressure on one side of the ball, the effect of a dry versus a wet field and all the rest of it, you have mapped out a nice sounding story. But that's about all. I pay little attention to those things. If I tried to dope them out, I would never make a hit."

Rogers Hornsby emphasized this point. He said, "I have often heard players express an appreciation of some parks and a dislike for others. I have heard the same opinion about certain ball clubs and particularly about certain pitchers. I try to go on the theory that I can hit any pitching—anywhere. The batter who gets his mind cluttered up with a lot of foolish nonsense that he can't do this and he can't do that, will pretty soon awake to the fact that he can't do much of anything. After all, a batter's average is made on eight different diamonds. If he gets the conviction that he can't do himself justice on one or two of those diamonds, that mental state will hurt his average. I thought this all out for myself and decided to ignore such things. I made up my mind that all diamonds and all ball clubs look alike and they do look alike. I won't admit even to myself that I have any preference."

How Batting Varies With the Position Played

THE position which a player is called upon to fill on the diamond has some effect on his batting. This is particularly true when he is required to fill a position to which he considers he is not naturally adapted.

Martin McManus said, "Some players find the position for which they are naturally fitted and there's no doubt about it. But there are many players who do pretty well but are convinced they would do still better somewhere else. For example, I am a second baseman. I suppose I shall continue to play second. But I have played third, and if I had my choice I should change at once."

Dutch Reuther said, "You will find a lot of ball players who are dissatisfied with themselves. They feel, and often with reason, that they would have done better at some other position. Don't think for a minute that a ball player invariably drifts to the particular corner where he belongs. He gets the job that offers, not the job that he wants or may be best fitted for. Take the two most talked of players in the National League—Hornsby and Frisch. Hornsby has played every position on the infield and claims he likes third base best of all. Frisch broke in as a shortstop and went to third. But both are now stationed at second base. When this happens to the two most famous players on the circuit, you can imagine where the smaller fry get off."

Rogers Hornsby, before he became a champion said, "I do not think my Big League career up to date has given me a fair test. I have been shifted so often from one position to another that I have hardly been able to get used to any one position. A player needs to do this if he is going to show his best work."

Most players dislike to shift from one position to another. Ray Caldwell said, "I used to play the outfield as well as pitch, but that is a mistake. There is a great difference in the throw from the outfield and the throw from the pitcher's slab. Besides, playing the outfield interferes with a pitcher's control."

Some experts, however, have held that a player should be versatile enough to do well at several positions. Jimmy Callahan said, "I played second base quite a bit but never considered myself an infielder. I liked to pitch and I liked to play the outfield. In the days when I was in my prime, players shifted about much more than they do today. In my opinion it was a good thing for the game. Specialization has made baseball a technical game of great difficulty. But specialization, like everything else, may be carried too far."

George Sisler believes that the fact that he was a pitcher before he became a regular first baseman, has improved his batting. He said, "There is one thing that I believe has helped me as a batter. I used to stand on the mound myself, study the batter and wonder how I could fool him. Now when I am at the plate, I can the more easily place myself in the pitcher's position and figure what is passing through his mind."

Most batters, however, believe that shifting from one position to another hurts their batting. John Collins said, "I fill every position on the outfield that nobody else wants to play. I will play left field one day and right field the next. The star infielder must stick to his position and an outfielder should do so also. But I have long since given up hope of ever becoming a star, so it doesn't make much difference where they put me. But don't think this constant shifting helps your record any. No man can play all positions as well as he could play one, provided he stuck to that one."

Even when a player doesn't shift, some positions favor batting more than others. Joe Tinker said, "It is a question how much playing a difficult infield position interferes with a player's batting. To my mind it cuts a considerable figure. As you glance through the lists, you will see that many shortstops are rather poor hitters. There are few .300 men among them, while there are many such names in the outfield and at first base."

Jim Delehanty said, "I have played every position on the infield. I played third base when I broke into the game and also at Cincinnati; shortstop at Allentown; second base in various cities, and first base especially with the Tigers. It is odd that I have played the outfield so much when I consider myself so little fitted for that position. Second base is where I belong. Even though I don't get there often, I can play better and hit better when I'm on second."

Stuffy McInnis, long a first baseman, was once shifted to third. He said, "My record suffered at once, not in fielding, but in batting. It took so much of my time and attention to try to fill a position I was not accustomed to fill, that I got into a bad slump. In fact, my present unsatisfactory average is entirely due to my playing third. Once I returned to first base, I began hitting over .300 just as I have always done."

George Sisler said, "The fact that I play an infield position may hamper me somewhat in my batting. I believe it goes without saying that the infielder has more to occupy his mind than the outfielder and is therefore unable to devote his attention so much to batting."

Outfielders have less exacting duties than infielders and are therefore expected to hit better. On this point Hal Chase once said, "Cobb was fortunate in one particular. The position he filled helped his batting. It enabled him to keep fairly free from injuries and give him time to devote his full talents to the offensive."

If outfielders are expected to hit, however, more consideration is shown the battery. The pitcher and catcher have so much to do aside from batting that their records are seldom impressive. Bill Fisher said, "One reason why batting records will always suffer is this. There are nine fielders on a club cutting down hits. There are only seven batters making hits. The pitcher and catcher are mostly pretty useless with the willow."

Doubtless this is the prevailing rule, but there are exceptions. For example, Babe Ruth, when pitching, said, "The pitcher who can't get in there in the pinch and win his own game at bat, isn't half earning his salary. I am a pitcher myself and I like to pitch. But if there is one thing that appeals to me more than winning a ball game from a tough rival, it is banging out a good clean three bagger with men on bases."

Hugh Jennings summed up the situation when he said, "Outfielders must hit and so must first basemen. Their positions are not so difficult in a fielding sense and give them opportunity to develop their batting eye. Other infielders should hit, but you can stand for one weak hitter on your infield if he is good enough as a fielder. Generally you will get that weaker hitter at short stop. You can forgive a catcher for not hitting, for he has so much else on his mind, and you hardly expect a pitcher to hit. Sometimes, in fact, the manager will not even allow the pitcher to offer at the ball, preferring to have him save his strength. The position a player fills on the diamond has a direct connection with his batting. At some positions he is expected to hit because those positions offer him the opportunity to develop hitting. At others comparatively weak stick work is excused or even expected."

How the Batting Order "Colors" Batting

JOHN McGRAW once said, "Every ball team is capable of being arranged in a way to produce the maximum batting punch. You need a fast man who is a good waiter for lead off, another fast man good at the bunt and the hit and run in second place, then a massing of your heavy artillery in the next three or four positions so as to deliver the hardest blow with the least possible slowing down in speed. A slow footed runner, for example, will often cripple an attack. He must hit uncommonly well to be placed high on the list. Naturally your pitchers come last, for even if they are good hitters, they change too frequently for a settled batting order."

Jack Coombs said, "Every manager models his batting order on a scientific basis. He has so many batters at his disposal. He wishes to align those men so that their combined efforts will appear to the best advantage. How can he do this? Few managers agree on the precise details, but all agree on certain essential points. For example, number one should be a good hitter, but above all a good waiter. If he is short of stature so much the better for he will be harder to pitch to. All managers agree that the second man on the list must be a foxy hitter and fast on his feet. They agree also that third, fourth and fifth positions should be filled by good hitters who are preferably sluggers. I believe the three most important positions on the line-up are first, fourth and seventh place. First is obviously important. He is the entering wedge of your attack. Fourth is the logical clean-up man, the fellow who drives home that entering wedge. Seventh is a kind of clean-up man, but I cannot afford to put too good a hitter there. If I do, the opposing pitcher will pass him to take a chance at the tail of the batting order. Rather I must station a hitter at seventh who is not easily excited but is cool and always likely to come through with a hit."

Miller Huggins said, "An attack which is distributed through six or seven men rather than centered in one or two is much more effective. The team with a bunch of good hitters is usually consistent in its stick work. It is the steadiness of the pace which counts. On some clubs the batting punch is supplied by a renowned hitter like Hans Wagner or Nap Lajoie. On other clubs there is no such individual star but a better balanced attack of several men who are all good hitters. I prefer such a batting attack for your one or two stars may have an off day. The average work of six or seven men doesn't vary so widely. Besides, it is difficult for the pitcher to side step such an attack. In a pinch he can pass one or two men, but he can't pass half a dozen in succession. Furthermore, the strain of pitching to a number of men who are always dangerous is cumulative. The pitcher gets no breathing space as he would when he had retired one or two formidable stars and then faced mediocre batters."

Not all experts agree on the relative importance of the various positions on the line-up. Most of them would rate the lead-off man as important, and the clean-up sluggers as even more so. Hugh Jennings, however, thought differently. He said, "The neck moves the head and what the lead-off man accomplishes depends pretty much on the follow-up assistance he gets from the second man in the line-up. I believe it is a bigger job to locate a man who can play second properly than it is to find a good lead-off man. The talents which the lead-off man must possess are well understood and everybody realizes that the clean-up man must be a slugger. But the second place man hasn't been studied so thoroughly. This batter must be a good bunter. Good bunters ought to be common, but they are really less numerous than good hitters. The second place man must have a good batting eye and be a good waiter. Above all, he must use his head. In general he should hit to right field for his main object is to advance the lead-off man who has presumably reached first either through hit, pass or error. By driving the ball to right field he can send the runner to third base. If he hit to left field, that runner would be held at second. Above all the second place man must have the peculiar knack of knowing whether the second baseman or short stop is going to cover the bag. Then he must be able to hit in a manner to break up their defensive play. This is very important. In fact I consider it the prime qualification for the man playing second position on the line-up. Moreover, the second place hitter should be fast. Then he won't get snarled up in a double play. There are times when he will retire the base runner in spite of himself. Then his thoughts are bent on saving his own scalp. That's largely a matter of speed in getting to first base."

Arthur Fletcher once played Cy Williams, his heaviest slugger, in second place. He said, "Cy isn't much of a bunter, I will admit. But he has some qualifications that you can't overlook. First of all, he's a right field hitter. That's what you want, a man to advance the runner. Then Cy seldom strikes out. You can generally depend upon him to hit the ball and hit it hard. Thus he advances the runner even though he is thrown out himself. And that's as good as a sacrifice. Besides, Cy is always likely to come through with a hit which may be a homer. Placing him high in the batting order you get more of his work. He'll go to bat five times in many a game where he would appear but four times if he batted farther down the list."

Even the despised tail of the batting list may be a source of strength. Wilbur Cooper said, "I am convinced that a pitcher adds much to his effectivness by his own good hitting. I believe that my batting and fielding have won seven or eight games a season for me that would otherwise have been lost."

Bill McKechnie said, "In all my experience I have known just one batter who liked to play the lead-off position." Bill thought this an inexcusable attitude, but it's not difficult to fathom. Batters don't like the lead-off position because it interferes with their hitting. It cuts their batting average many points. For example, John Tobin said, "The man who bats number one on the list and hits for .280 is doing well. He must forget his own hase hits in an effort to get on and of course his average suffers. How much it suffers I couldn't say, but I believe it will drop twenty to thirty points. Of course, some one has to play that position, but I think the records ought to make some provision for lead-off man and not rate his batting on the same basis as that of the slugger who comes fourth or fifth on the list."

Max Carey said, "In fairness to myself, I shall claim special consideration for my batting. I would have done much better had I not been lead-off man for several seasons. It is well known that lead-off man can not expect to have as high an average as he could get lower down the list. There are two reasons for this. In the first place he often has to wait out the pitcher and try to work him for a pass. In the second place, the pitcher, when he faces the lead-off man, usually has no one on bases to bother him. He is able to take his full wind up and concentrate on the batter."

Batting languishes at the tail of the list. The catcher is out of the game frequently while the pitcher appears only once in three or four days. As Babe Ruth says, "No man can get in the games twice a week and do himself justice at bat as he would do were he getting daily practice."

Some managers shift their batting lists infrequently, even though one or two positions are open to criticism. They prefer to suffer this disadvantage rather than the greater disadvantage of a general disorganization. Not a few managers, however, particularly on losing clubs, shake up their batting lists rather often in the effort to hit upon a better working combination. When they do, the batting of the various players on the list is apt to fluctuate widely, for there is a definite connection between a batting average and the particular position in the batting order which a player is called upon to fill. In general lead-off man is handicapped by orders to wait out the pitcher, second position is handicapped by orders to sacrifice. The tail of the batting order is handicapped by a variety of adverse conditions among which infrequency of batting practice ranks rather high. Only at the clean-up positions does batting flourish at its best, for those players are usually called upon to "hit it out." There is also a noticeable psychology in a batter's position on the list. Let the man, for example, who has hit seventh, be raised to fourth or fifth place and his new responsibilities often act as a tonic on his batting average.

To sum up, a batter's work is colored to a considerable degree by the particular position he is called upon to fill in the batting order.

The Importance of Health

"HEALTH," said Rogers Hornsby, "is important in any line of work. But it is absolutely essential in baseball. When the season is on, I think nothing but baseball. I eat it and sleep it and have my mind concentrated on the subject. I do not smoke nor use tobacco in any form. Nor do I drink. Fortunately for me, I have never taken up any of those habits. I do not criticize them in others and I admit they may not be serious impairments to condition. But none of these things help an athlete any and I am glad I let them alone. I also keep regular hours and manage to get my assignment of sleep every night."

Sam Crawford said, "A long time ago I realized that the player must take excellent care of himself if he would continue in the Big Leagues. And I determined that I would never allow any senseless dissipation to undermine my health and strength. I was naturally strong and gifted with a great deal of endurance. But the regular hours I have observed and my steady habits of life have left me no older physically than many players considerably my junior."

Billy Sunday once said to me, "Baseball has demanded of her champion athletes that they live clean lives and let the booze alone. It has brought an increasing appeal to the college man, to men who have an ambition to succeed in life. It has shown the greatest athletes the value of clean living and the example of great athletes to the young of the Nation cannot be exaggerated."

Hugo Bezdek was even more pronounced in his views on this subject. "What is the foundation of a Nation's greatness? Health. What has done more to promote health in this country than all the doctors combined? Athletic sport. Health is the true foundation of success. The doctors strive to produce health by banishing disease. A better method suggests that we promote health rather than discourage disease. Fifty years from now the man who honestly enters the profession of athletic sport will be honored as much as the man who enters the profession of medicine. In the Army athletic sport did more to discourage drunkenness and immorality than all the available chaplains. In short, athletic sport performs the three-fold function of promoting physical well being, mental tone and proper moral sense. Need the man who recognizes these important services apologize for devoting his career to so useful a field?"

George McBride once said to me, "From the time I first began to go to school, I looked upon baseball as a clean and healthful occupation and a means of preparing myself for a business career, whether or not I ever developed enough ability to play the professional game. I believe the work that baseball has done among the boys of the country has been one of the strongest influences ever known for the development of good healthy bodies and strict principles."

No doubt baseball has been a tremendous influence in promoting health. But on the other hand, health is essential to baseball success. Ken Williams said, "One reason for my successful hitting is the fact that I always keep in good condition. I live in one of the greatest game countries in the world, Western Oregon. But I seldom go hunting or fishing. I'd rather drive a car. I went all the way home in my car last fall. Then I went down through Southern California, through Texas and up to Kansas City. I travelled several thousand miles over all kinds of roads and averaged twenty-seven miles an hour on the trip. Driving a car trains your eyes and hands and keeps you in the open air. That's the main thing, to keep in batting trim."

Doubtless other forms of exercise, as Williams suggests, promote good trim. But Bill McKechnie reminds us, "The secret of athletic success is to keep in good condition. But you can not train for baseball by swinging dumb bells in a gymnasium. You have to train on the field."

Surprising results have been attained by ball players who made physical condition a specialty. Joe McGinnity said to me, "I have pitched for thirty years and I believe I have averaged thirty games a season. And in all my experience I have never had what I could truthfully call a sore arm. It makes me smile to hear young rookies complain about their ailments. Not that I don't sympathize with the rookie, but his troubles seem so unnecessary. They must be due to faulty methods or lack of condition."

Hank Severeid used to claim he never got tired from catching the longest double header and laid his splendid condition to a rigorous course of training. "The Norwegians are used to physical exertion. They lead a healthy life mainly in the open. When they want to go anywhere, they walk, or if it is winter, travel on skiis. They eat simple wholesome food without the sugar and nicknacks which spoil the teeth and ruin the digestion of Americans. I inherited natural physical strength, good blood and good habits. The rest I have done for myself."

Some batters take unusual precautions to retain the fine edge of their batting skill. Nap Lajoie once said to me, "The secret of batting is in the eye. I never read at night, for I believe it is bad for the eyes. When your eyes go back, even a little, you are done."

Jack Bentley said, "I pay a great deal of respect to my batting. There is one thing I cannot afford to take chances with and that is my batting eye. I like reading better than most things. But I haven't read a book through for five years. I read the newspaper sparingly and an occasional magazine. I read as little as possible. That is solely to save my eyes. The batter can't have any too keen vision. The only difference between hitting .400 and sinking into a slump is in meeting the ball a fraction of a second too late or too early, a fracton of an inch to high or too low. Batting is in the eye and I am going to take just as good care of my eyesight as I know how to do."

There is much truth in this view, but several batters have done well in spite of eyesight which left much to be desired. Homer Summa said, "I have astigmatism in my eyes. Theoretically this should bother me in hitting, but I doubt if it does. At any rate I have not yet succumbed to wearing glasses."

In spite of the obvious benefits of careful living, some players ignore the simpler training rules and still excel. The use of tobacco, for example, has been prohibited on more than one ball club. However Hans Wagner once said, "Tobacco may shorten a man's playing life and interfere with his baseball career, but I guess it hasn't shortened mine to any extent. I have noticed that when a player starts to quit hitting, it shortens it a great deal quicker than tobacco. So long as you can rap out a hit once in a while, other things don't count for so much."

Babe Adams said, "While I am on the road in the summer time, I go to bed rather early. Sleeping is my long suit. Thomas Edison says four hours sleep is enough, which may be all right for inventors, but it is bad dope for ball players. Some time ago I was approached by a man who wanted to know if my ability to play Major League ball at the age of forty-two wasn't due to the fact that I left tobacco and coffee alone. I told him that I couldn't see how this explanation would answer as I always drank all the coffee I wanted and smoked most of the time when I was awake. True, I seldom smoke anything but cigars, but I do smoke a lot of them."

Zack Wheat, who made his best record on his sixteenth season as a Major League player, also took a few raps at the sticklers for careful training. He said, "I don't pay any attention to the rules for keeping in physical condition. I think they are a lot of bunk.

I have always worked hard all my life and am in the open air practically all the time. Let a man do that at my age and he can forget all about medicine and not even keep a speaking acquaintance with doctors. They say, for example, that tobacco hurts a person. I don't believe it. I smoke as much as I want and chew tobacco a good deal of the time. I don't believe that a ball player ought to go out and get soused. But during the active season I take a drink when I feel like it and I drink anything I want to drink. Generally I have a couple of drinks after the game is over. I believe a little stimulant is good for a player after a period of exhausting physical exertion like a ball game. I don't believe it hurts a player in good condition, no matter what the Life Insurance Companies claim about it. At least it hasn't hurt me. During the off-season I practically never take a drink. I don't even have it in the house. I don't feel that I need it. I am working on a farm and sometimes I do hard work. When I am not working, I go hunting. I think the Prohibitionists are crazy. I have known ball players for twenty years. Very few of them refrain from taking a drink now and then, and outside of a few old soaks who sopped it up by the keg, I have never known drink to hurt any ball player. Anything in moderation is my motto. The less you worry about the effect of tea and coffee on the lining of your stomach, the longer you will live and the happier you will be."

Hank Severeid said, "Ball players, as I have known them, seldom take good care of themselves. I don't mean that they are dissipated. They are more often just foolish. I go to bed at regular hours and get my sleep. I never use liquor or tobacco in any form. I take plenty of exercise. I don't know of any better exercise than swinging an axe on an oak log. It's fine for the arms and the shoulders. In the summer I take things pretty easy. I just play ball. Sometimes I will get up and walk several miles before breakfast, but that's just an appetizer. I am always in good condition so that I recover quickly from injuries."

However a player guards his health, he cannot ward off indefinitely advancing age. Sam Crawford said, "A ball player begins to grow old when his legs go back on him."

Terry Turner said, "A ball player starts going back when his arm fails him so that he can no longer snap the ball over to first base quickly enough to beat the runner."

"Doc" Hart, the Brooklyn trainer, said, "Ball players, aside from pitchers, feel advancing age first of all in their legs. The sudden start of going after a ball and the still more sudden stop jars the muscles. The younger player of twenty-five doesn't notice this, but the old fellow feels it. Ball players, particularly older players, are subject to a peculiar condition of the muscles known as a Charley-horse. I don't know who originated the name, but it is a dreaded ailment to any player. A muscle will contract much the same as it does in a cramp. But whereas a cramp will disappear in a few moments, a Charley-horse may remain for days. It is painful and cripples a player greatly. Rest and massage and just the right kind of exercise will eventually straighten out that muscle."

Ill health has wrecked many a player career. Perhaps the most tragic example of recent years was George Sisler's attack of influenza. This attack kept him out of the game for an entire season after he had just broken the modern batting record and had been voted the most valuable player in his League. Moreover, when he did return, the effects of this illness rested like a heavy blight on his record.

Many a team has also been thrown out of the running by sickness. To cite one of a vast number of possible examples, Jack Hendricks said, "You can't win a pennant with your men in the hospital. When the race was thirty days old I had just two men of my original line-up in uniform. What chance had the club in the face of such a handicap?"

Sickness, of course, is to a degree inevitable. A player, however, may insure reasonable good health by proper care of himself. As we have just noted, some players, and eminent veterans at that, scoff at certain training rules. But these men inherited an unusual equipment of physical strength and in spite of their seeming indiscretions, lead healthy lives of exercise in the open air. In the main, the player who observes the simple rules of health will unquestionably improve his batting and all-round playing ability.

When the Fans Razz

THE typical baseball crowd is a noisy crowd. They are forever shouting criticism or applause at the players. How does this vociferous comment effect the work of individual players?

Jake Daubert said, "Many people are curious to learn the effect of razzing from the stands. I suppose no two players react to this in just the same way. Some are nettled a good deal by remarks from the players. Others take it in good part. It is sometimes embarrassing to hear the bleachers whoop it up when you make a good play, and you wish they wouldn't make so much noise about it. The customary panning for an error is as needless as it is unpleasant. The unfortunate player who has made the error feels worse about it than anybody else."

Miller Huggins said, "I never object to criticism, feeling as I do that when I accept a position in the public eye I must also expect my share of knocks."

John Evers said, "I have played baseball when literally thousands of people were yelling at me until they were black in the face. I let them rave. I could yell as loud as any of them, but not as loud as all of them put together. They had the floor so I went about my business."

Hugh Jennings said, "As player and manager for many years, I have had my share of knocks. When I was winning, the public noticed it, spoke about it. When I was losing I learned to expect criticism. Some times, though, it seems a little severe, for the crowd not only forgets what happened last year, but even what happened last inning. This worries some ball players, but it never worried me. On the contrary, it's a sign of interest. If the crowd wasn't interested they wouldn't roast the player when he falls down on the job."

The foregoing are expressions of opinion from baseball men who accept criticism as inevitable. They take it as a part of the game. Most players, however, are not so stoical, but they cultivate a measure of indifference to criticism. For example, Ty Cobb said, "You sometimes hear a ball player say that he does not care a rap for public opinion. He is either intentionally faking or else he is fooling himself. I do not believe a player ever lived who was not influenced by the manner in which he was treated by the fans. It is human nature to give heed to what others say about you."

Bob Bescher said, "The bugs don't bother me much. I can stand about anything in the way of criticism from the bleachers. As a matter of fact the Big Leaguer does not hear much of what is said to him anyway when his mind is intent on the game. But what I do hear seldom gets my goat. About the only thing I object to is a rooter with a high, squeaky voice that stands out above the roar of the stands. When such a bug, with such a voice does his stuff, he gets on my nerves a bit, but it's not bad."

Rhody Wallace said, "I used to worry some, but I guess it's a safe bet a man can get used to any kind of a job if he makes up his mind to. I soon got so I didn't hear the crowd as anything more than a distant, hazy murmur."

Friendly rooting helps a player forget much critical comment from the stands. Larry Lajoie, in his declining years, said, "I should worry when I still have one friend with me in the crowd. What friend? Who else but Mrs. Lajoie? I suppose she has busted a new pair of gloves, but she can use up a new pair every day if she wants to. She still thinks I am a great ball player if nobody else does."

Occasionally players deny emphatically that they pay any attention whatever to the comments of the bugs. Ed Walsh said, "When I am in the game I never think of anything else. Hooting or joshing is all one to me for I seldom even hear it."

The veteran schools himself to accept criticism. But beyond a doubt it has been a destructive force in baseball. This is particularly true of the rookie. More than one promising career has been blighted at the very beginning by hostile demonstrations from the stands. Addie Joss said, "The fans can make or break a ball club. They can kill a young pitcher by yelling, 'Take him out.' The manager may win one ball game by listening to the clamour, but lose a lot of others by the breaking of a young fellow's nerve and confidence in himself."

Perhaps no player on record was ever subjected to the merciless panning that followed Fred Merkle for years after his historic failure to touch second base in a decisive ball game. Once, in despondency, he said to McGraw, "Listen to them hoot. You're making a mistake to keep me here. They don't want me." But

McGraw replied, "I wish I had more players like you. Don't pay any attention to those weathercocks. They'll be cheering you the next time you make a good play."

Most rookies tremble in their shoes at the derisive comments of a big city crowd. Guy Morton said, "I have been troubled with what you can call 'stage fright.' It's quite a proposition to put a young fellow, fresh from the Bushes, up there before all those people, facing Big League pitchers and knowing that his job and his prospects are in the balance. It's asking a good deal to expect him to keep a cool head and a steady hand."

Babe Ruth, when he was still something of a novice in the Big Leagues, said, "I shall never forget how Ping Bodie was booed by the fans all around the American League circuit. Bodie was always a natural hitter, but just because he struck out several times and was a little awkward in his way, the fans started to boo him every time he came to bat. This handicapped Bodie. He got excited and wanted to drive the ball out of the park. It made him over-anxious to aim at balls which were not even near the plate. His batting fell off so that he was finally released."

Walter Lutzke said, "I have learned one thing. A player must get accustomed to the razzing of the fans. It's discouraging at times to have your best work passed over in silence while a slip on your part calls forth floods of abuse from the crowd. Sometimes it seems to me that my playing career has been one long razz. When I was at Kansas City the crowd rode me so much my wife urged me to quit the game. I doubt if mere criticism from the fans has driven many players out of baseball. But it has made a lot of them miserable. A good many players say they don't mind criticism, but nobody is compelled to believe this."

The criticism which hurts the most is the razzing of the home crowd. John Bassler said, "In general the player doesn't mind hoots and jeers when he is on the road. The crowds are naturally pulling for the home team and against him. But when he comes home it's different. There he expects support and if he gets criticism instead, it hurts. But after all, a ball player good enough to stick in the Majors must be able to do his stuff regardless of conditions."

Some players condone even the criticism of the home crowd, but they resent personal abuse. Hank Gowdy said, "The Giants don't object to the booing of the fans. They get booed now even at home. They've grown accustomed to the sound. It's not inharmonious when properly done. But some verbal attacks from the fans are inexcusable."

Cactus Cravath, one of the most peaceable of players, once related the following experience. He said, "One day I had just struck out in the pinch. There was a certain bug who had been riding me pretty hard all through the game. As I went out to the field, after the side was retired, I heard him cut lose with a line of conversation that I wasn't disposed to stand for from any one. So I went over the fence and singled him out and said, 'What are you bawling me out for? Did I ever do you an injury? I am out here trying to earn a living and the least you can do is give me a chance. Where do you work anyway?' He didn't say anything for a minute. I guess he thought I was coming over the fence to attack him. Finally he gave me his address. 'Well,' said I, 'suppose I came down tomorrow morning to your office and started to bawl you out the way you have me. What would you think? You would bust me in the nose, if you had backbone enough. And you would be right. That's what I would do to you if you were a man and fair enough to meet me face to face.' I didn't hear any more from him for the rest of the afternoon."

Ty Cobb once created a mild riot by vaulting the fence and pummeling a spectator who had ridden him too hard. Cobb was bitterly condemned for this, but John Evers considered the act excusable. He said, "My sympathies are all with Cobb. The player hears a lot of remarks that are all well enough, but why should he be expected to stand for personal insults? One season I was sued for twenty-five thousand dollars because I answered a rough neck in the grandstands. He bawled me out first and I answered him back and he was going to sue me. Can you beat that? If I sued everybody who ever bawled me out and got a nickle from each one, I would be a millionaire."

Sometimes undeserved criticism acts as a powerful stimulus on a player. For example, Irish Meusel said, "I believe the roasting that the crowd gives us actually helps the Giants to win ball games. It's a kind of backhanded favor, but they thrive on it. You know that criticism acts as a spur on the game, nervy type of athlete."

I once met Old Hank Gowdy emerging from the player's bench as the crowd started razzing the Giants. "So they are giving us the Sea Lion, are they?" said Hank. "Well, let them exercise their lungs. A lot of damage that does us. A ball player with any guts thrives on abuse. It's a better tonic than applause."

Players may thrive on abuse, but they don't like it. On the contrary they generally seek to win the commendation of the crowd. For example, Ty Cobb said, "I have always been ambitious to please the fans, I believe this has helped me greatly. I would not give a snap of my fingers for a ball player who failed to try his hardest at all times. But you can take it from me, it is easier to try when you know the spectators appreciate what you are doing."

John Evers once told me an experience which impressed him deeply. He said, "Brooklyn has been one place where the crowd always panned me to a turn. They've yelled 'Rowdy' at me more times than there are slivers in the bleacher seats. So when I sauntered out on the field the other day, after a pretty long lay off from my bum arm, I expected the same old chorus. Instead of that the crowd gave me a hand. At first I thought it was a new way of kidding they had invented for me. But they seemed sincere. It gave me a peculiar feeling, one that I am not used to."

Helpful applause undoubtedly has spurred many an individual and many a ball club to success. George Stallings, in attempting to explain the remarkable reversal of form which carried the Boston Braves from tailenders to World's Champions in a single season, said, "When we returned from a most disastrous road trip, it looked as though we were permanently anchored in last place. The boys were very much down in the mouth and talked, among themselves, about sneaking into town the back way. They counted on a cool reception. But to our astonishment, when we went to the park, there were over five thousand hustling fans there to welcome us home. It put new life into the boys to feel that they were playing before a loyal crowd like that. When we did start to win, with our pitchers in good shape, we took a lot of close games that we were losing earlier in the season. Once started, with the old jinx shaken off and the crowd with them, the boys gained confidence which grew stronger day by day until that whirlwind finish at the season's close when they had the pennant already in hand and felt that nothing could stop them."

Some players have felt their lack of personal appeal to the public. Otto Miller said, "Somehow I never seem to get the crowd with me. This is doubtless my fault, or rather my failing. During the winter when I have leisure and get to thinking over the past season's work, I often make the resolution that next year I will show more pep and ginger and play to the grandstands. But I never do. So I suppose it isn't in me."

Sometimes a red letter event will bring a player an outpouring of temporary fame that is pleasant while it lasts. During the World's Series which he starred with two home runs, Casey Stengel said, "I have received over two hundred letters so far from the bugs. A few are from friends or from people I know casually. But most of them are from people I never heard of. They wish me well and it's rather pleasant to feel that so many people are interested in you enough to write about it. But if we don't win the Series my correspondence is due for a sudden drop." Casey well understood that the spotlight seeks the winner.

Always the player can feel that far away in the obscure hamlet that he came from there are people who are watching his record with friendly interest. And this in itself is a comforting thought. Rollie Zeider, when a member of the team that played the Red Sox for the World's Championship, mentioned a queer quirk of this native town rooting when he said, "Will the people back home stand behind me and the Cubs, or will they root for Everett Scott and the Red Sox? We both come from the same town. A fellow ought to be able to feel that he has his home town behind him, but I'm not so sure."

Criticism from the stands in the heat of action is one thing. Criticism to a player's manager or employer is much less palatable. Ed Walsh said, "It's not pleasant to hear a bug ask the owner of your club why he keeps that Big Stiff, referring to yourself, in a uniform? But the wise player merely grits his teeth and works all the harder."

Doubtless the criticism of other players causes more friction on the ball field than the abuse of the bleachers. John Evers said, "Other ball players have ridden me until I was stiff in the joints. But that's all in the day's work. If they could ride me any harder than I could ride them, that was my misfortune. When I am playing a game, I allow my opponent the same cards I use myself."

The joshing of the fans has come to be an expression of the American sentiment. To those who criticize it most it is a rather harmless method of letting off steam. Baseball, however, is not entirely an American game. For example, Ira Thomas reminds us, "Every nationality has its own method of accepting defeat or victory. The Cuban for the most part is courteous, after the old Spanish custom. There are some points in which he is far superior to the typical American crowd, although he is fully as emotional. For one thing, a Cuban can not stand a shut out. He would rather face defeat by the score of 20 to 1 than 1 to 0."

Herbert Hunter, the Apostle of baseball in Japan said, "In Nippon our game has reached a stage where even solemn old Buddhists, clinging to the traditions of centuries long dead, will toss their tassled silken caps in the air and plead with some Japanese 'Babe' Ruth to 'paste that pill.' "

Doubtless much of the almost meaningless chatter from the stands is in the way of well meant though futile advice. As Arthur Fletcher said, "The fans are a queer lot, but they all know how to manage a ball club. They even write me letters about it. One especially industrious bug wrote me a letter giving a series of different line-ups that I should use for every day of the week against all kinds of pitching. The other day I sent a runner home from third on a play which turned out badly. He was caught at the plate. As I came into the bench, feeling none too happy over the turn of events, four loud-voiced men with fog-horn voices who occupied a box, yelled at me in chorus, 'Why did you send him home?' I took off my hat and smiled more affably than I felt and said to them, 'Gentlemen, I should have been only too happy to accommodate you, but you should have spoken a little sooner.' Second guessing is a habit with the fans. It's so easy to tell what should have been done after you have gone and done it."

No doubt William Killifer was right when he said, "Baseball is a business that is everybody's business. There are generally at least a thousand grandstand managers at every game. Where a play goes wrong, the manager is sure to hear about it. But that's baseball. If these things didn't interest the public it might be better or it might be worse, but it wouldn't be baseball."

How Press Notices Influence a Player's Work

"A BALL player has two kinds of reputation," said John Evers. "One is the kind that is based entirely upon ability, the other the kind the newspapers give him."

Most players are wise enough to recognize the fact that their own success and their value to their club depend, to some extent, upon the publicity they obtain. Muddy Ruel said, "A ball player works for his club in two distinct ways; for his work on the field and his power as a drawing card. Baseball has become a show business. Some are inclined to criticize this as a defect. I can not agree with them. All successful business has a strong element of 'show.' Hence, a ball player can be of value to his club through his drawing power as a star."

Many a player believes that his comparative obscurity is due to the fact that he never appealed to the press. George Whiteman, star of the World's Series of 1918, was a veteran rookie from the Minors whose career in the Big circuits was brief. In his hour of greatest triumph he said, "I have been good enough to play in the Majors for some years, but I never seemed to get the publicity that some of the fellows get. If people don't know about you, it is a cinch they won't exert themselves to get you on their ball club. Some fellows are lucky. The writers seem to come around looking them up. But they never came to me, so I went plodding along year after year, hoping that something would turn up."

Undoubtedly the power of the press has a tremendous influence in baseball. It is not always used wisely. George Stallings said, "The unfortunate thing is that the papers either overdo a thing or they neglect it. A player gets less credit than he deserves or he gets more than he deserves. There seems to be no halfway proposition of giving a man just what belongs to him."

Upon the same theme Clarke Griffith said: "Today a miracle man and tomorrow a has-been is the fashion in baseball. You can live on your reputation just about fifteen minutes. If you can't deliver and keep on delivering, it is curtains for you. There was Connie Mack. For years he was rated as the greatest manager in the game. Now he is leading his fifth club to a snug hole in the cellar. If you stood out in the middle of the street and started yelling about Mack as the greatest manager in the game right now, all the attention you would attract would be a patrol wagon or the ambulance. But if Mack was a great manager six years ago, he still is."

Under the favorable light of publicity player reputations sometimes grow like mushrooms, and unlike mushrooms, they last. For example, Ray Fisher said, "Look at Home Run Baker. How did he get that title? By heavy slugging for many years? No indeed. He's a hard hitter, but he won that title by his work in one World's Series. And that title has stuck to him ever since, although more than one player has beaten his record of home runs in a season."

Some players go to the extreme length of asserting that stars are made by the newspapers. Dick Rudolph said, "Star players are made by the press. The writers take paper records and play them up until they fasten a reputation to a man that he often doesn't deserve. The public sees through the eyes of the press. Once established, a great reputation is likely to last for years, while the honest merits of some player who perhaps never gets into the papers at all are wholly ignored."

Hero worship by the public sometimes becomes burdensome. Babe Ruth once said, "It's not pleasant to be pointed out by people as you pass along the street. And a lot of the notice you get becomes a burden. Players, however, learn to take such things as part of the game. They have sense enough to know that part of their success as ball players at least depends on the way they appeal to the fans."

Not a few players strive to get press notices. Cactus Cravath said, "No one can honestly claim that I have sought publicity or tried to get favors from anybody. But there are ball players who do and I suppose they are the wise ones. Newspaper notices that the player gets are what count."

Dutch Reuther once philosophized as follows, "I suppose I would have been better off if I used more diplomacy. But I like to meet a man on the level and this scheming around to make a favorable impresssion was never in my line. I always wanted to break into the Majors as well as the next fellow. But I didn't want to get there bad enough to lollypop around the newspaper men or the scouts."

Even the owners find publicity a difficult problem. William Baker, President of the Philadelphia National Club, once said, "The magnate who wins the favor of the newspaper boys is pretty sure to win the favor of the public. For he can count on them to praise his virtues and condone his faults. And the public, believing much of what it reads, forms its opinion of the owner in consequence. Not all owners, however, are diplomatic in their treatment of the press. They may intend to be, but they lack the diplomatic touch. Perhaps they do something unconsciously to offend a prominent writer. When the tide of unpopularity sets in it is surprising how rapid it flows. Men in the street who couldn't, to save their lives, point to any tangible defect in an owner, are ready to throw a brick. It's an odd illustration of mob prejudice."

Jake Fournier's experience was so enlightening on the natural errors which a young player may make in regard to the power of the press, that it deserves quoting rather fully. Said Fournier, "When I went to Chicago, years ago, like most young fellows, I didn't appreciate the power of the press. Newspaper writers seemed rather queer to me. They made a lot of mistakes that looked ridiculous to us ball players. I don't know that I had anything against newspaper men. I certainly didn't realize what they could do for me or to me. In an argument with a newspaper man a player is nowhere. When he talks he can make himself heard to a few people who may or may not be interested in what he says. When a newspaper man talks, he can make himself heard to many thousands. If the player has a good year, the newspaper man can almost ignore that good year. If the player has a bad year he can pan him unmercifully and there is nothing really the player can do about it. I had some disagreements with the newspaper writers in Chicago, but they didn't worry me. I said to myself, 'Those fellows can pan me if they want to, but what will that get them? I am good enough to stick in this League and I am going to stick.' But when I came to, I found myself in Los Angeles. It was a good experience, though it didn't seem so at the time. It taught me that I could butt my head against the stone wall of publicity if I wished, but all it would get me was a sore head. The newspaper men could do me a lot of good. Why antagonize them? The more I thought

198

about this the more of a dumb bell I seemed to myself. Since that little episode the newspaper men are my friends. What I am in baseball I owe mostly to them. If I get good money, it is by virtue of the fact that the newspaper men have given me a good reputation. After all, what does it involve on my part? Just a little tact, just a little willingness to see the other fellow's point. Here is my advice to all ball players. Keep in with the newspaper men. If you think they don't always give you what you deserve, there's nothing gained by whining or kicking. Think of the times they gave you more than you deserved. Without the press baseball itself would never have developed. So where does the individual ball player get off resisting this great force? Does a ball player want to be a star? Who makes stars? Ability, yes, but more than ability, publicity. In the last analysis it is the newspapers that make stars."

No doubt Fournier's experience and his advice should prove valuable to many a young player. Not a few prominent baseball men, however, while they avoid antagonizing the press, are not above criticizing its inaccuracy. Miller Huggins said, "I do not object to the knocks which a manager is bound to get from the press. The writers, as I have met them, are conscientious and loyal to their work. And their duty demands that they record the game as they see it. Far from being offended at criticism I take unusual pains to analyze criticism to determine, if I can, how far it is acccurate and trustworthy. The critics invariably have the advantage of the second guess. I often wonder whether they keep as close tabs on plays they criticize as the managers do."

Ivan Olson said, "Some time ago there was a certain writer who gave me a great panning in his paper. I went to this fellow direct and asked him what he meant. After some conversation he admitted he might have gone a little too far. 'That's well enough,' I told him, 'but your admission is about like confessing we got the wrong guy after we hanged him. What you write the public reads. It will take me a long time, a month of good playing at least, to live down the reputation you have given me.' Publicity is a great thing, but it is much easier to say a thing in print than to unsay it afterwards."

Lee Fohl said, "Baseball owes a big debt to the sport writer. We are told that the writers have made the game. That may be going too far in strict accuracy. But if they haven't made it, they have at least made it great. I do not blame the writer for panning when it is deserved. A bone head play is worth a knock anytime. But it sometimes seems to me that newspaper men lose the proper perspective between good work and mistakes. If they gave the same respect to good plays they do to poor ones, surely not 10% of their columns would be occupied by knocks. A newspaper man is supposed to be a critic and criticism, as I find it, seems to be about nine-tenths pure fault finding. Take the usual written account of the game. If the home team lost, as it is bound to do some of the time, you can gamble that fully one-half the column write-up is devoted to denouncing errors, mental and otherwise, of the fielders, batters, pitchers, manager all combined. A little criticism is generally left over for the owner and a good deal for the umpire."

John Evers, always expressive, once grew critical. He said, "I have come in after a hard day's work and read some press account of what I have done that was all wrong and chewed it over for an hour or more before I could get it out of my mind. I don't know why a player should pay attention to such things, but he does. And my hide is not very thin, either."

George Foster, once pitcher with the Red Sox, had become bitter over the failure of the press to recognize his work. He said, "I don't mind what these fellows do now. They don't know any better."

Veterans often grow sensitive to newspaper predictions that they are nearly through. Casey Stengel said, "A lot of the newspaper boys have been kind enough to print nice things about me. But I don't altogether appreciate this talk about creaking joints and the rest of it. I am really not old enough yet to go with crutches and I have done fairly good work this season, if I do say it myself."

Sometimes erroneous newspaper accounts linger with a player's reputation long after they have been proven false. There was "Death Valley" Jim Scott for example. He said, "I was born at Deadwood, South Dakota, and have lived most of my life in Wyoming. I have never been in 'Death Valley' in my life. Some reporter must have come to me when I first joined the White Sox with a Nick Carter in his pocket and his head full of 'Death Valley' literature. He sized me up as a raw boned mountaineer and hung that 'Death Valley' monicker on me and the name has stuck ever since."

Ball players often resent the fact that newspaper writers burlesque or exaggerate certain qualities of theirs. Benny Kauff once felt aggrieved on this score. He said, "The newspaper men in New York are inclined to josh a fellow a little more than seems necessary. I have tried to treat everybody fairly. And while there is probably no ill feeling on their part, they have made me out a sort of swell headed gink."

Friendly publicity can be as dangerous as blighting criticism particularly where it is overdone. Carl Lundgren said, "Fame spoils many players until they learn that they must deliver and keep on delivering or lose their fame."

Hans Wagner said, "It takes a young fellow's nerve to be given too much publicity. A player would stand a better chance if no one ever heard of him until he put on his uniform. Then, if he had the goods they would know it instead of beginning to look for it before he started. A fellow with a big reputation must start hitting .300 right away or they think he is a frost."

Jack Bentley once characterized his own career with the pessimistic statement, "I began too early at the top."

Marty O'Toole, whose melancholy experience still lingers in the baseball memory, echoed this thought when he said, "There are times when success is the worst thing that can happen to a player. The fellow who gets a great flood of publicity when he enters the Majors must make good from the start or be branded as a failure. There are literally thousands of people who are looking for the first sign of weakness in a high priced rookie and are only too ready to begin the lemon chorus. Any kind of reputation, to be lasting, must be earned. It was no fault of mine that I entered the Majors loaded down with a reputation that Christy Mathewson would have staggered under."

Rube Marquard had the same unfortunate experience, but he was lucky enough to live it down eventually. He said, "I found myself the property of the New York Giants at the record price of eleven thousand dollars. This seemed a fine climax to a good season's work, but instead it proved the beginning of two years of bitter disappointment. The papers gave me a great send-off.

This was a fine boost for a newcomer, but they entirely overdid it. They set a standard for me that I could not live up to. I shall never forget my first game in Big League company. It is still so vivid in my memory that I can not look back upon it with any degree of comfort. We were playing Cincinnati. The people turned out in great crowds to see the new phenom. The papers said there were thirty thousand people present, but when I took my place on the slab I could see at least double that number. I was only eighteen at the time and anxious to make good, but I grew nervous and became extremely wild. When I determined to put them over the plate I had to depend upon my fast ball and these balls started coming back at me like rifle shots. I blew up completely. It wasn't a game, it was a slaughter. It was my only contest of the season, but it was enough. I was so badly rattled I didn't get over it all winter. I lost confidence in myself completely and those calls, 'take him out,' 'eleven thousand dollar lemon' and so on, they ring in my ears yet."

Some prominent baseball men claim to ignore newspaper comment. John McGraw once said, "I pay no attention to what the newspapers say. I have my own methods and I follow them. I have been managing the Giants for nineteen years and I think I understand the job better than any irresponsible second guesser who may happen to take a fling at me."

Some times a baseball man will ridicule publicity. Fred Mitchell once said, "The American League is superior to the National in just one important respect. They are the best press agents in the United States. Every time you pick up a paper in the summer months to find out who is trying to overthrow the government of Mexico, you see instead, in two inch type that stares at you, how Babe Ruth made another home run. You read further down the column and discover that he eats only five prunes for breakfast where it was commonly supposed that he had seven. You also learn about his taste in underclothes and how much his wife spends for her hats. I suppose this is what they call inside baseball. And if you don't hear about Babe Ruth you do hear about Ty Cobb or Tris Speaker or George Sisler or Walter Johnson. The Old National League can play the American on the field, but not in the newspapers."

Some baseball men frankly dislike publicity. George Stovall said, "I never wanted publicity. I don't like it. Let my work talk for me. If my work won't talk, there's nothing anybody can say that will talk. And if my work does talk, it isn't necessary for any one to say anything about it."

Doubtless Rogers Hornsby's attitude is the best, from the player's viewpoint. He said, "While the season is on I seldom read the newspaper accounts of the game. There is no advantage in doing this. On the contrary, to my way of thinking, there is a distinct disadvantage. The particular kind of baseball I am trying to play is not guided by the press or criticism of any writer. Neither am I trying to reconcile the standards I have set up for myself with the opinions of others."

In the last analysis, Old Sam Crawford's words ring true. "Whatever the newspapers say, or whatever the records say, the ball player is his own best judge. He knows whether he has done his work well. That knowledge is his greatest satisfaction and it is something that no other person can take away from him."

You Can't Beat the Official Scorer

THE batter may outguess the pitcher, outwit the opposing fielders, win the hair line approval of the umpire, but in the last analysis the obscure and often unknown official in the stands, the Scorer, determines whether his effort shall go as a hit or an error.

Donie Bush once said, "There never was and never will be any perfect system of scoring hits or errors. I am not blaming the scorers personally. No doubt they use their best judgment. Somebody has to decide just what you will call a certain play and that's their job."

Ty Cobb said, "There is always a lot of trouble over scoring. I don't suppose any player ever agreed with the scorers about the hits he has made."

In general a player nurses the grudge that he has been robbed of a hit here and there by the incompetency or the bias of some scorer. For example, Ivan Olson said, "They claim that I am inconsistent, but I think I am one of the most consistent players in baseball. I always hit about the same average. But the official scorers can't see it so. I generally get robbed of ten or a dozen hits every season and I generally have about the same number of errors tacked to my list that I don't deserve. It's tough to have the reputation of being erratic, for once that reputation is fastened on you the scorers will see that you live up to it."

Sometimes the official scorer's opinion is costly in that it robs a player of a record performance. There was Howard Ehmke's almost no-hit game against the Yankees marred by a scratch single by the first man up. Howard Shanks, who handled that scratch single said, "It was an error and no hit. I knew it was an error when I made it and felt disgusted to pull such a play at the beginning of a game. It's a crime to rob a man of a no-hit game on a break like that."

Dick Kerr once said, "I object to the official scoring. They gave Felsch an error on a long fly that was plainly lost in the sun. Such a break hurts two players and does no one any good. It robs the batter of a hit that he deserves and penalizes the fielder for an error that he didn't make. The only man it could possibly help is the pitcher, and it doesn't help him unless he is working for a no-hit game for the results to him are the same no matter what you call the play. He gets credit if he wins and is penalized if he loses. And all he has in mind is winning the ball game."

Sometimes a player admits the official scorer gave him the best of it. But he generally feels that he is discriminated against in the long run. Joe Jackson once said, "This year I have just one hit that didn't belong to me. The official scorer blundered in my favor. But to offset that, I will guarantee that he has robbed me of a dozen."

Rumors have occasionally flitted about the circuit that certain star batters were given all the breaks by home town scorers. George Sisler said, "There appeared in print a widely published statement to the effect that St. Louis scorers favored me on infield hits. I never attempted to deny this statement, although I am sure it is wholly unfounded. But I did attempt to combat that statement by allowing no further grounds for such suspicion. All my efforts were directed toward hitting clean, fair hits that could not possibly be called anything else."

Even when administered ably and accurately, official scoring is not wholly fair, as Edd Roush pointed out. "The records don't give an even break to the outfielders. Not more than once or twice a season will I dop a fly ball. Errors I get are on ground balls or throws to the catcher or the infield. Many, if not most of the errors charged against an outfielder, are not really errors at all, although they may look so from the Press Box. The outfield is much rougher than the infield."

Bob Meusel emphasized one undeserved handicap for the outfielders. "This," said Meusel, "is where the official scorer charges an error for a throw which bounds away from a catcher or an infielder. So long as the throw is accurately directed, no human skill can prevent its bounding from one side or the other. And yet scorers call this play an error because they haven't ingenuity enough to call it anything else. It is not an error in any true sense of the word, for an error is a play that the player should have made but failed to make."

Many a batter who has hit for .299 can not but feel that had the scorer given him his due somewhere down the line, an extra hit should have been added to his list that would have brought his record above the coveted .300 mark. Perhaps the most famous of such dissentions centered about Ty Cobb's last appearance as a .400 hitter. President Ban Johnson over ruled the official scorer at a certain contest and took the word of other competent scorers who disagreed with him, to give Cobb the one hit necessary to raise his average to the .400 mark.

In general, however, a batter must accept with what grace he can, the decision of the official scorer. Unjust as those decisions sometimes are, there seems no help for it. Furthermore, scoring, accurately done, is no sinecure. As John Evers said, "I think it takes a special knack to keep score. I am no good at it myself. The system isn't very logical. The work is left to newspapermen, many of whom do not continue in office long enough to grow familiar with their job. But they're the best we have and no doubt they do their best. So what more can you say?"

Ball Players' Superstitions

"IF I were superstitious," I would say the Yankees have a jinx on us," remarked Ed Barrow pessimistically when he was manager of the Boston Red Sox. The jinx is a frequently discussed though vaguely understood element in baseball that looms rather prominently in most activities on the diamond.

Many examples might be cited. A few will serve. George Stallings, though well educated and intelligent, was profoundly superstitious. His pet aversion was litter of any kind in front of the bench, not because such litter was unsightly, but because it was unlucky. Even birds which some times lighted on the ground in that vicinity, roused his ire. Ball players with a certain light-hearted malice, would drive him almost to the verge of apoplexy by strewing bits of paper around in front of the bench.

John Evers was perhaps the shrewdest of observers among old-time ball players. And John was unblushingly superstitious. One day having little to do, he walked all the way from the hotel to the ball park. The team won. So John felt obliged to walk to the park the next day and the next until defeat finally relieved him of this responsibility.

Many a player mannerism which has become famous, had its roots in some vague substratum of superstition. Here are a few of endless such mannerisms. Ty Cobb always swung three bats. Chief Bender never threw to anyone but Ira Thomas when warming up. Rube Oldring always wanted the Athletic mascot in a certain position when he went to bat. Russell Ford always adjusted his cap before pitching a ball. Jack Coombs was wont to juggle the ball a moment after receiving it from the catcher. Bill Donovan disliked to strike out the first batter up, he believed it a forerunner of bad luck.

Eddie Collins, college graduate and one of the brightest players in the history of the game, thus explained ball players' superstitions. He said, "When you mention a player's superstition, you tread on his sore toe. Superstition is a thing which nobody likes to discuss rationally because there is nothing rational about it. And yet, when you reach bed rock, I believe the vast majority of people have some obscure superstition somewhere in their makeup. Ball players are probably more superstitious than the average body of young men. But there is a reason. A ball player knows that, other things being equal, a strong club will defeat a weak one. But when you have said other things being equal you have said a mouthful. The ball player has seen too many games decided by some freak play not to have a profound respect for the element of luck in the game. Most players will admit that you must get the breaks to win. Now in plain English the breaks constitute that unknown element in every game which a player recognizes clearly enough but can not guard against. Hence, he develops a curious but quite inevitable trend of superstition. For, after all, superstition is only an attempt to provide for something that can not be foreseen. Ball players usually respect one another's superstitions, even when they appear most foolish. They recognize the fact that the other fellow is merely trying to keep or change his luck. And you will find the player much more willing to discuss the other fellow's superstitions than he is to discourse about his own. I believe I can truthfully say that I am no more superstitious than others. One form of superstition is a certain fixed habit that lingers on year after year without rhyme or reason. Another is caused by curious coincidences that seem to have no logical reason. For example, while I have no fear of Friday, the thirteenth, I recognize that July first is a tough day for the Collins family. I have suffered just three considerable accidents in baseball and every one of them occurred on July first. You won't find me slacking on that day, but you may be certain of one thing. I will be well aware what day of the month it is and heartily glad when I can cross that day off the calendar. A ball player may be superstitious, but queer things happen sometimes to make him so."

The objects of a ball player's superstitions are legion. The winning streak of "Dazzy" Vance which went fifteen full games, became hopelessly intertwined with the fate of "Dazzy's" undershirt. This shirt could not be washed as long as "Dazzy" remained victorious. Finally the inevitable happened and "Dazzy" expatiated upon the result. He said, "Well, the old shirt wore out at last. When my winning streak was stopped, they tried to wash it, but it wouldn't hold together. Now I am in the process of developing a new shirt. By the looks of the sleeves, it's pretty well developed but it hasn't proved a winner yet. Baseball is a curious game," continued "Dazzy," "and there is a lot of inside stuff to it. For example, when

I pitch, I always chew tobacco. I have two kinds of tobacco, Pitching tobacco and Hitting tobacco. My Hitting tobacco isn't so successful for me. It works best for the other fellow. One day in Boston, Fournier was in a slump, so I put some tobacco juice on his bat and told him he would come through all right. He made two singles and a home run. When we returned to Brooklyn, he came to me again and asked for some more of the 'Hitting' tobacco. I told him I was all out. I had nothing left but 'Home Run' tobacco. So he asked for some of that. I gave him some and sure enough, he made only one hit but it was a homer. I am not broadcasting what brand I use. Let the other players investigate and find out for themselves."

Hugh Jennings grew reminiscent one day on the subject of players' superstitions. He said, "My pet stunt used to be to jump across the base paths whenever I sauntered out of my accustomed place at short. I seldom missed this ceremony. Why did I do it? How do I know? Why does a ball player do all kinds of queer stunts? It's in the blood, I guess. I have watched the antics of batters at the plate for a good many years and some of the things they do are a revelation of human nature. A lot of them have more elaborate ceremonies than others, but almost all of them have some favorite contortions they feel called upon to go thrugh before they swing at the ball. I remember "Socks" Seybold when he was in his prime. He was naturally a good hitter and dearly loved his hits. But every time he went to the plate he felt obliged to go through a whole rigamarole of stunts which would take him a full minute or more to perform. If he omitted any detail of this ceremony he felt that he would pop up or strike out."

Ty Cobb in a half serious, half humorous vein, revealed his own mental reactions toward the players' superstitions. He said, "I pick up a hairpin once in a while for luck. You know, a hairpin means a base hit. One day I found three on the way to the club house. Sure enough, I made three hits that day. You know, we are not really superstitious. We merely do things once in a while because they seem the proper things to do under the circumstances. For example, there was that dog that followed me to he club house one day in Detroit. He was a homeless, friendly sort of a mutt and I 'couldn't seem to shake him. So I invited him into the clubhouse. He came willingly enough, wagging his tail and making friends with all the ball players. We left him in the clubhouse, went out and won the game. In fact, we had great luck that series, so we decided to show some appreciation of the mutt. We christened him 'Victory.' When we went to Washington, 'Victory' was so much a part of our schedule that we took him out on the bench, but things didn't work so well. We lost that game and couldn't understand it. The fellows talked it over and decided the charm didn't work when 'Victory' was on the bench. He was of more use to us in the clubhouse. The next day we left him in the clubhouse and sure enough, we won. He was in the clubhouse when we played the Athletics and we took the series handily. Then we returned to Detroit. This last road trip the trainer forgot and left 'Victory' behind. I knew nothing about it and was ready to fire the trainer when I heard it. The boys feels pretty much upset about it. True, 'Victory' was better in the clubhouse than on the field. But Detroit is a long way off. Whether he can make his influence felt at such a distance remains to be seen. This absent treatment all the way from Detroit is too uncertain. So you see from all this that ball players are not really superstitious. They simply have curious ideas about some things."

Habit undoubtedly plays a big part in superstition. For example, Tris Speaker said, "It has always been a habit of mine to pull grass in the outfield. I do not chew tobacco like many ball players. And as an outfielder likes to keep his jaws working on something, I take out the surplus energy on the grass. It is a habit, nothing more. But it is a habit I developed a way back in Texas in my semi-pro days and I guess it will stick with me always.

"Another habit of mine that people have talked about is drawing a line beside the batter's box with my bat every time I face the pitcher. People have called this a superstition, but I wouldn't say so. In the Minor Leagues they don't have the batter's box as clearly defined as they do in the Big circuits. When I was playing in the Sticks I used to draw a line with my bat where the outline of my box should be so that I could tell how much room I had to move around in. It got to be a habit with me and has followed me into the Big Leagues. It's a harmless fancy that doesn't hurt anybody."

Eddie Collins used to perform an even more curious rite that was a superstitious habit. He said, "I chew gum. When I go to bat I take the gum out of my mouth and put it on the button of my cap. If the pitcher gets two strikes on me, I take the gum off the button and put it back in my mouth. Why do I do this? It's not exactly a superstition. It's a sort of rite. If I didn't do it the spectators would be disappointed."

Superstition undoubtedly affects the work of many batters to some degree. Ray Schalk defends superstition. "Why do batters hitch their belts and wiggle their bats? Because it is natural to them. So long as these things don't interfere with their work, they are wise to stick to them. If they deliberately try to change, they have that on their minds and can't think so clearly of the work in hand. It requires all the batter's attention to study the pitcher and watch the ball. He can't be bothered with attempting to decide whether he will stand in a certain position or swing in a certain way. What he does he must do instinctively. His conscious effort must all be directed to the task in hand."

Ty Cobb echoed much the same opinion when he said, "I am not overly superstitions. Of course, if I have had a particularly good day at bat, I am apt to follow the same general routine the next day. I suppose everyone has a lingering remnant of superstition somewhere in his cranium. He realizes that it is foolish, but there is this much reason behind it. If you have fool ideas that litter up your mind, it is best to defer to them so that you may face the problem in hand with absolute concentration."

Batters sometimes attempt to overcome superstition. For example, Frank Snyder said, "I can't explain my poor average last year except on the grounds of superstition. Ball players are superstitious as a class, but I had a bad case. I got so that I couldn't hit. Now I am naturally a good batter and this season I concluded that there wasn't much to this superstitious stuff and cut out a good deal of my former worries and I have been going much better since I got rid of that surplus baggage."

Occasionally players deny that they are superstitious in the slightest regree. Ed Walsh said, "I have no superstitious fancies about anything. I was one of thirteen children and don't know that I have encountered hard luck because of that fact. And I'm not blaming any tough breaks that I may meet on some fool idea or other, because there is no sense to it."

No doubt the ideal mental attitude of the superstitious batter can be summed up in the brief statement of William Killifer when he said, "I am something of a fatalist. I have an idea that if a thing is going to happen, it is going to happen. That is all there is about it."

Sentiment in Baseball

"There is no sentiment in baseball," said Joe Tinker. "Personal friendship weighs very little with the manager and he should never give way to such sentiment." No doubt Tinker was correct in stating the attitude of the manager.

Fred Mitchell echoed the same thought on a wider plane when he said, "Any time you think you are going to have something handed to you in baseball, you want to pinch yourself to see if you are awake."

And yet, this rarity does happen. More than one rookie owes his start in the Big Leagues to a strain of sentiment in the opposing pitcher. Said Ivy Wingo, "Grover Alexander really started me on my Big League career by showing a little consideration which cost him nothing but was important to me. One day we played Philadelphia a double header. Alec pitched the first game and soon had a big lead. Our regular catcher was working, and as he would have to serve in the second game anyway, the manager thought it a good opportunity for me. The game was hopelessly lost so what I did or failed to do would make little difference. Alec knew I was a young rookie trying to make good, so when I faced him at bat, he laid the ball right over the center of the plate. I promptly hit it for two bases. The next time up he did the same thing and I responded with another two-bagger. Bresnahan, our manager, figured he couldn't very well take out a catcher who was hitting like that, so he left me in the second game. And I played pretty regularly from that time on. Alexander could, had he wished, have struck me out both times I faced him and he told me so afterwards. But he had the game won and figured I was only a rookie, so he let me hit to give me a bit of encouragement."

Such sentiment, however, sometimes reacts like a boomerang. Alexander said, "The first time I faced Rogers Hornsby I thought to myself I had never seen a batter who looked less formidable. I really pitied him. So I laid one over the plate for him and he came through with a safe smash. Since that time I haven't been able to get him out. He's hit me continuously, hit everything I had and seems to thrive on my pitching."

Jake Daubert once related an incident of the season when he won the National League batting championship. "Rube Marquard was pitching against us and he told me beforehand that he would give me a certain kind of a ball, so I knew what was coming. But do you think I could hit it safe? I couldn't to save my life. Whether it was this unexpected generosity on his part that upset me, I don't know, but I couldn't hit that ball on the nose."

There is a kind of sentiment in simple justice. George Moriarty said, "The umpire must be free from sentiment. That is one thing he must banish utterly. Absolute impartiality is rightly expected from him. He must be cold as ice, but he must be just."

Sentiment which displays itself in charitable impulses is rather common in baseball. As John McGraw said, "Baseball is not a parlor sport nor one that you can handle with kid gloves. It is rather a rough and forceful sport for men with backbone who can stand a few knocks. It has no place for the weakling but it has a certain consideration for the fellow who has been in hard luck and needs a helping hand. Since I have been with the Giants the Club has spent in charitable acts, most of which never got into the papers, a sum that many people would consider a comfortable fortune. No detailed account has ever been kept, to my knowledge, but to give some idea I will state that one hundred thousand dollars would by no means cover the amount. To be sure the Giants are a rich and powerful club, better able to help where help is needed, than many other clubs. Neither do I claim that the club has done more than it should have done. My only point in mentioning the matter at all is to spike the ridiculous rumor that baseball has no place for sentiment. Sentiment, however," added McGraw, "has no proper place in managing a ball club. I have allowed a good many players to go in my time and regretted the step, but the needs of the moment made it necessary."

Doubtless a manager must take such action, but a club owner not infrequently retains a man for whose services he has no real need. Charles Ebbets said, "A baseball magnate is not commonly accused of too much sentiment. And yet there is one item of expense in almost every World's Series which is purely a matter of sentiment. A winning ball club dislikes to lay off any of its players, even though useless, but carries such players on its roster rather than deprive them of the opportunity of playing on a pennant-winning club. To be sure this expense is not a heavy item, as items go, but it counts up nevertheless."

Baseball usually displays a kindly feeling to old time players who are in straightened circumstances, or to players who have met with serious injury. In spite of large sums of money spent in this manner, not a few prominent baseball men believe that still more should be done. Ty Cobb said, "What to do with permanently injured ball players is a big problem. There is a general opinion that something should be done with them. Baseball men are pretty generous. But something beyond mere charity is needed, some permanent provision for unfortunate cases that is fair and just and businesslike."

Yes, as McGraw says, "Baseball is a rough and forceful sport, but there's a lot of sentiment in the old game if a person knows where to look for it."

The Perfect Hitter

Has the perfect hitter ever existed? No, and he never will exist. For the near-perfect hitter is, after all, human and the inevitable limitations in mind and physical equipment make 100% perfection a goal which can never be attained.

There are, however, some hitters who so far excel even the higher grades of excellence, that they are properly known as super stars. Fellow ball players appreciate the superlative abilities of these super stars even more, perhaps, than the baseball public, with all its natural proclivities for hero worship.

John Evers said, "I have seen a lot of baseball in my time and some people might suppose that I would tire of it all. But I would pay my little dollar any afternoon to see Ty Cobb play. There's only one Cobb. There never was anybody like him and there never will be, in my opinion. That's what I think of his ability."

Eddie Collins, himself acknowledged by all the experts as one of the greatest players who ever lived, said, "I have never seen and never expect to see such truly wonderful playing as Ty Cobb has shown against us. I frankly admit that I have never expected and never expect to be as good as Cobb. The utmost that lies within the reach of any other player is to be considered second best."

Bob Bescher said, "Cobb is the greatest player in baseball. I have heard that he is swell headed. I do not believe this, but if he were, I should not blame him. I would be swell headed myself if I were as good a player as he."

Joe Jackson said, "In the years that I played in the Minors, I never saw another batter who I thought was a better man than I was. And in my years of experience with the Majors, I have met just one man who I was willing to acknowledge as a superior. That man was Ty Cobb. And I won't admit that even he had a better batting eye, but he could beat me out by a thousand and one little tricks."

Ty's admirers, while in the majority, are by no means unanimous. Ed Reulbach said, "I have seen Ty bat and fully appreciate his wonderful versatility. I have long been familiar with Hans Wagner's style. He gets his shoulders behind his swing more than Lajoie does and hits the ball harder. But from what I have seen of Lajoie, I would call him the greatest natural hitter I have ever met. He couldn't have a superior for in timing and in distance he was absolutely perfect."

Walter Johnson said, "I have always thought that Lajoie was the greatest natural hitter I ever saw. But Joe Jackson was just about in his class. Surely he was one of the greatest batters who ever lived. I do not rate Ty Cobb with those fellows. He would beat them by use of his amazing speed, his ability to bunt, to place his hits and all round effectiveness. But as a natural hitter, he wasn't in their class."

Naturally Hans Wagner has his supporters. Barney Dreyfuss said, "Wagner was one of those great natural ball players who happen once in a lifetime. He could play any position and play it well. He could cover first or third better than any other man we had on the squad and of course, neither corner of the diamond was his regular position. But he was so great a player that he could fill in anywhere."

Lefty Leifield said, "Hans Wagner was the grandest player that I ever looked at. He could hit anything, field anything and steal bases on any catcher or pitcher in the business. And he never made a mistake."

How about Babe Ruth? George Dauss said, "I consider Babe the most dangerous batter in baseball, but not the best. There's a distinction in this that most people fail to get. In Babe's case batting is half brute strength. He has a good eye, but can be fooled badly on a ball."

Walter Johnson said, "Babe Ruth uses his great muscular strength much the same as Ty Cobb used speed. It helps his batting and makes him the most dangerous hitter I ever saw. But he's not the best hitter I have seen. Babe can look worse in one game than Lajoie would look in a whole season."

Some of the old timers hark still further back for celebrities. Hugh Jennings said, "I consider Ed Delehanty one of the most wonderful hitters who ever handled a bat. But he was a great player in every way."

John Evers said, "In the years when the Cobb machine was going at its best, I do not think any player in the game, with the exception of Ty Cobb, did more brilliant work for his team than Frank Chance. He was a great batter, a great fielder and a great base runner."

Rogers Hornsby had his supporters. Grover Alexander said, "Hornsby is the perfect hitter. He can hit anything and hit it hard. There's none of this bunting, rapping out little grounders and that kind of stuff about Hornsby. He hits curves, slow balls, fast balls, any old kind of balls for good, solid smashes. He's the most dangerous batter I ever faced."

Zack Wheat said, "There have been a lot of nice hitters, but there has been only one Rogers Hornsby. He has kept me out of first place twice. But that's merely because he is a better hitter than I am. I have seen quite a bit of Babe Ruth in exhibition games in the spring. He can slam the baseball harder than any one I ever saw, but the person who tries to compare him with Hornsby as a real hitter is wasting his time. I don't think there is any comparison. Babe stands up there and swings a big bat and hits a lot of long drives. But he strikes out a lot and he misses the ball by the length of your arm. Hornsby strikes out seldom. Almost invariably he fouls the ball when he doesn't drive it out. And he's better in the pinch than at any other time. I do not believe his equal as a real hitter has ever lived."

The opinion of Ty Cobb, the master hitter, is most valuable. He said, "The greatest natural hitter I ever saw was Rogers Hornsby. Hornsby has the best stance at the plate of any of them. His position is as near perfect as I have ever seen. I would call it bomb-proof. He stands well back from the plate and steps into the ball. You can't fool him on a thing."

Miller Huggins said, "There is such a thing as compensation in the world. It's hardly fair to expect a ball player to be great in every way. If he is talented above the majority, you can not expect his mental attainments to match his physical gifts. Still really great players, the leading half dozen, all possess this prime essential of intelligence with their speed, fielding, ability and ability to hit."

"Hitting," as Harry Hooper remarked, "is a thing which always makes a good appearance. It shows on the surface. A good batter is known to be such. Doubles and triples make a big noise. The great hitter will always be popular. But," added Harry, "he isn't necessarily a great ball player, and a great ball player isn't necessarily a great hitter."

In short, baseball has its limitations. As Earl Neale said, "In football one man can, if he is good enough, completely dominate a game and win out single handed. In baseball, with the possible exception of the pitcher, he can hardly do this."

In brief, the perfect hitter does not exist. But the Delehantys and the Lajoies and the Wagners and the Cobbs and the Ruths and the Hornsbys all furnish by their stellar work a model for other batters to match, if they can.

The Importance of Batting

"Batting is the keystone of baseball," said John M Ward. This apt figure of speech is not only striking, but accurate. If baseball may be likened to an arch resting upon the firm foundation of pitching, supported upon the twin columns of fielding and base running, the apex of the structure, the culmination, the most conspicuous part, is batting.

John McGraw summed up batting's rank in the general scheme of things in the terse sentence, "Hitting in a team ranks next to pitching." All baseball experts are agreed on this point.

The aims of the team and the individual, however are necessarily different. The pitcher may, with his single arm, more than balance his eight associates on the club. But those eight associates have their place and among the qualifications which fit them for their respective positions batting ranks easily first.

Tris Speaker said, "The most important thing an outfielder can do is hit." Thus easily did he dispose of three of those eight other positions on the diamond.

Long George Kelly, doubtless one of the greatest first basemen who ever lived, commented, rather sadly, be it said, upon those talents which fit a man for playing first. Said Kelly, "A first haseman has a lot of work to do around the bag, and it's important work. But after all, the public seems to think very little of all this so long as he can hammer the ball. A first baseman may or may not be a good fielder and thrower, but he must hit."

Kelly's statement is but the echo of all the first baseman who have gone before him.

While it is true that the other three infield positions offer a wider latitude, hitting never for a moment loses its preeminent importance.

"You can have a shortstop on your ball club," said Hugh Jennings when he was manager of Detroit, "who is a weak hitter, provided he can field well enough. But you can't afford to have more than one weak hitter on your infield under any circumstances."

"Hitting," said Walter Schmidt, "is not the most important thing a catcher does. But it is the thing which the public sees." Other famous catchers agree that even behind the bat hitting is essential.

Pitchers who can not hit will be forgiven, or as Christy Mathewson said, "A pitcher is not a ball player, therefore, not a batter." But even pitchers find a vast advantage in being able to meet the ball effectively. This point was well illustrated by Wilbur Cooper.

"I believe," said he. "that hitting and fielding have won at least seven or eight games for me that I would otherwise have lost."

Not a little of Babe Ruth's brilliant pitching record was due to his phenomenal hitting. He won many of his own games with his bat.

There is a difference between importance and popularity. Bating is important, but it is even more popular with players and public.

The players are of one mind on this point. Nap Lajoie remarked years ago, "The player likes his hits. That means any player." Jake Daubert once said, "A ball player would rather be a good batter than anything else." Doubtless he meant to except pitchers, but we have known not a few pitchers who took more satisfaction from making a brace of healthy wallops in a game than they did from pitching their team to a victory.

What do managers think? Zack Wheat sagely hazarded a guess. "Fielding is good and so is base running, but the manager will overlook a lot of faults in the player who bats for .375." Zack said a mouthful when he made that statement.

Most managers have in their line-ups some fellow who is not a good fielder, not a good ball player, but he can hit. Sometimes they use him only as a pinch hitter and utility man. But if he can hit well enough, they'll find a place for him somewhere where his general lack of ability will be least conspicuous in order to secure the aid of his potent bat. Babe Ruth, for example, was a very indifferent outfielder when Ed Barrow first placed him there. But he stuck because of his terrific hitting.

Hans Wagner, just before he said good-bye to the National League circuit, remarked, "As I look back over the years I have spent in baseball—it's a long time now—I am convinced more than ever of the importance of batting. It's the hit that counts. You can't score many runs without the old bingle. And the man who can rap them out will always be in demand."

Jimmy Johnston once said, "Batting is the first thing a player thinks about when he crawls out of bed, and it's the last thing on his mind when the lights go out."

Ty Cobb would go even a step further, "The good player who is bound to be a success in life eats and sleeps baseball." And baseball, according to Ty, is written with a Big "B" that stands for batting.

INDEX

to F. C. Lane,
***Batting: One Thousand Expert Opinions
On Every Conceivable Angle of Battling Science***
(New York: *The Baseball Magazine*, 1925)

Prepared by Leverett T. Smith, Jr.

F. C. Lane's *Batting* is a tapestry of quotation, culled
from his many interviews as editor of *The Baseball
Magazine* between 1911 and 1925. Not only players, but
managers, umpires, owners, and others are quoted on
the various aspects of batting. This index distinguishes
between mentions of an individual when he is being
quoted and when he is the subject of a quotation.

J

K

L

M

T

V

W

Y

Z